Genealogies of Emotions, Intimacies, and Desire is a lucid and comprehensive overview of recent attempts to write the history of these aspects of human existence that are often thought to be eternal. The theories Brooks is concerned with all agree that love and intimacy are different in different times and places, but they disagree about how and why. Brooks explains these theories and explores their differences. A useful text for postgraduate courses and for anyone seeking to understand these influential theories, *Genealogies of Emotions, Intimacies, and Desire* is the first study to bring these related theories together to be considered side-by-side.

David R. Shumway, Professor of English, and Literary and Cultural Studies, Carnegie Mellon University and author of *Modern Love: Romance, Intimacy, and the Marriage Crisis* (2003) and *Rock Star: The Making of Cultural Icons from Elvis to Springsteen* (2014)

This is a thought-provoking and enjoyable publication and Ann Brooks makes a valuable contribution to a feminist sociology of emotion, intimacy and desire. The book provides a scholarly, in-depth study of the field by drawing skilfully on Foucault's genealogy of sexuality, applying his methodology whilst engaging with other key feminist thinkers in the field such as Lauren Berlant, to explore shifting discourses and patterns of intimacy from the Greeks and Romans through to medieval society and then through to the cult of Romantic love and its commodification in the twentieth century and beyond. Brooks also discusses the shaping of sexuality and desire in relation to post-colonialism and contemporary constructions of sexuality within the late modern context, where discourses of reflexivity create new modes of intimacy that are mixed in a complicated way with hope and cynicism and the unsettling of old gendered positions. This book is a timely publication and recommended for students and researchers engaging with the sociology of emotions and intimacy.

Candida Yates, Professor of Culture and Communication, Bournemouth University and author of *The Play of Political Culture, Emotion and Identity* (Palgrave Macmillan, 2015)

Routledge Studies in Social and Political Thought

For a full list of titles in this series, please visit www.routledge.com

106 **Re-Grounding Cosmopolitanism**
Towards a Post-Foundational Cosmopolitanism
Edited by Tamara Caraus and Elena Paris

107 **Panarchy: Political Theories of Non-Territorial States**
Edited by Aviezer Tucker and Gian Piero de Bellis

108 **Gramsci's Critique of Civil Society**
Towards a New Concept of Hegemony
Marco Fonseca

109 **Deconstructing Happiness**
Critical Sociology and the Good Life
Jordan McKenzie

110 **Novels and the Sociology of the Contemporary**
Arpad Szakolczai

111 **Liberty, Toleration and Equality**
John Locke, Jonas Proast and the *Letters Concerning Toleration*
John William Tate

112 **Jürgen Habermas and the European Economic Crisis**
Cosmopolitanism Reconsidered
Edited by Gaspare M. Genna, Thomas O. Haakenson, and Ian W. Wilson

113 **Genealogies of Emotions, Intimacies, and Desire**
Theories of Changes in Emotional Regimes from Medieval Society to Late Modernity
Ann Brooks

Genealogies of Emotions, Intimacies, and Desire

Genealogies of Emotions, Intimacies and Desire excavates epistemologies which attempt to explain changes in emotional regimes from medieval society to late modernity. Key in this debate is the concept of intimacy. The book shows that different historical periods are characterised by emotional regimes where intimacy in the form of desire, sex, passion, and sex largely exist outside marriage, and that marriage and traditional normative values and structures are fundamentally incompatible with the expression of intimacy in the history of emotional regimes.

The book draws on the work of a number of theorists who assess change in emotional regimes by drawing on intimacy including Michel Foucault, Eva Illouz, Lauren Berlant, Anthony Giddens, Laura Ann Stoler, Anne McClintock, Niklas Luhmann and David Shumway. Some of the areas covered by the book include: Foucault, sex and sexuality; romantic and courtly love; intimacy in late modernity; Imperial power, gender and intimacy, intimacy and feminist interventions; and the commercialisation of intimacy.

This book will appeal to students and scholars in the social sciences and humanities, including sociology, gender studies, cultural studies, and literary studies.

Ann Brooks is Professor of Sociology at Bournemouth University, UK.

James Gillray: Fashionable Contrasts:—or—the Duchess's little shoe yielding to the magnitude of the Duke's foot. Originally published by Hannah Humphrey on January 24, 1792.

Genealogies of Emotions, Intimacies, and Desire

Theories of Changes in Emotional Regimes from Medieval Society to Late Modernity

Ann Brooks

LONDON AND NEW YORK

First published 2017 by Routledge

2 Park Square, Milton Park, Abingdon, Oxfordshire OX14 4RN
52 Vanderbilt Avenue, New York, NY 10017

Routledge is an imprint of the Taylor & Francis Group, an informa business

First issued in paperback 2018

Copyright © 2017 Taylor & Francis

The right of Ann Brooks to be identified as author of this work has been asserted by her in accordance with sections 77 and 78 of the Copyright, Designs and Patents Act 1988.

All rights reserved. No part of this book may be reprinted or reproduced or utilised in any form or by any electronic, mechanical, or other means, now known or hereafter invented, including photocopying and recording, or in any information storage or retrieval system, without permission in writing from the publishers.

Notice:
Product or corporate names may be trademarks or registered trademarks, and are used only for identification and explanation without intent to infringe.

Library of Congress Cataloging-in-Publication Data
Names: Brooks, Ann, 1952– author.
Title: Genealogies of emotions, intimacies, and desire : theories
    of changes in emotional regimes from medieval society to late
    modernity / Ann Brooks.
Description: New York : Routledge, 2016. | Series: Routledge studies
    in social and political thought
Identifiers: LCCN 2016009986 | ISBN 9781138821859 (hardback) |
    ISBN 9781315743073 (e-book)
Subjects: LCSH: Emotions—Social aspects. | Social change. |
    Culture—History.
Classification: LCC BF511 .B77 2016 | DDC 302/.1—dc23
LC record available at https://lccn.loc.gov/2016009986

ISBN: 978-1-138-82185-9 (hbk)
ISBN: 978-0-367-17828-4 (pbk)

Typeset in Times New Roman
by Apex CoVantage, LLC

Contents

Foreword DAVID KONSTAN		ix
Acknowledgements		xxiv
	Introduction: What's Love Got to Do with It?	1
1	Genealogies of Emotions, Intimacy and Desire: Theories of Changes in Emotional Regimes from Medieval Society to Late Modernity	15
2	Foucault's Genealogy of Sexuality: Foucault, Sex and Power	32
3	Narratives of Romantic Love	45
4	"Mapping Intimacy through Sex in Twentieth Century Colonial Cultures": The Work of Laura Ann Stoler and Anne McClintock	66
5	Love and Intimacy in Late Modernity: The Transformation of Intimacy	88
6	"The Intelligence of Emotions": Intimacy, Emotions and the "Turn to Affect"—Feminist Interventions	102
7	Intimacy, Emotions and the Public Sphere: From Sentimental Ideology to "The Queen of America"—The Public and the Private in the Work of Lauren Berlant	117

Conclusion 131
Author Biography 141
Index 143

Foreword

Foucault's History of Sexuality

The Production of Sexual Discourses in Classical Antiquity and Beyond[1]

In the first volume of the *History of Sexuality*, Foucault demonstrates the reciprocal production of sexual discourse and its object in the nineteenth century, with particular reference to children's masturbation:

> What this actually entailed, throughout the whole secular campaign that mobilized the adult world around the sex of children, was using these tenuous pleasures as a prop, constituting them as secrets (that is, forcing them into hiding so as to make possible their discovery), tracing them back to their source, tracking them from their origins to their effects, searching out everything that might cause them or simply enable them to exist. Wherever there was the chance they might appear, devices of surveillance were installed; traps were laid for compelling admissions; inexhaustible and corrective discourses were imposed; parents and teachers were alerted, and left with the suspicion that all children were guilty, and with the fear of being themselves at fault if their suspicions were not sufficiently strong; they were kept in readiness in the face of this recurrent danger; their conduct was prescribed and their pedagogy recodified; an entire medico-surgical regime took hold of the family milieu. The child's "vice" was not so much an enemy as a support; it may have been designated as the evil to be eliminated, but the extraordinary effort that went into the task that was bound to fail leads one to suspect that what was demanded of it was to persevere, to proliferate to the limits of the visible and the invisible, rather than to disappear for good.
>
> (Foucault 1978: 42)

The prose is ornate: clauses are elegantly balanced or grow to a crescendo, while themes are rhetorically reiterated in graceful variations. In its lushness, it creates an almost suffocating sense of the blanket of discourse that, according to Foucault, began to envelop sex and to smother people as sexual beings.

The account is as much mimetic as descriptive: we can feel the pressure of all those reports, consultations, warnings, admonitions that were internalised and rehearsed even in solitude. The flow of language is not halted by footnotes or references; we are expected to recognise the phenomenon described in our own beings and bodies, where it has been inscribed for two centuries. The very disproportion between the quantity of words so authoritatively pronounced, whether by doctors or by Foucault, and the occasional caress of a small child's wee parts, of which we are barely reminded by Foucault's chaste, almost medical reference to the "vice," invites us not so much to disinter the object buried under so much talk as to wonder if it is really there as something physical, hidden as it is under a cloud of words. Thus we are led to surmise that the thing itself is only the underside or complement of talk. Foucault has said nothing to prove that all that elaborate, ostensibly repressive scientific apparatus and verbosity were designed really to extend or augment the practice of infantile masturbation, and it is open to doubt whether they did so. It is *thoughts* of masturbation that are kept alive by such official speech. Foucault shows how it works by producing the same effect in us, his readers, and by much the same means. Hence, we suspect; and that suspicion is all that is required by his argument, for we, the readers, are his evidence. As Ladelle McWhorter has written in a moving account of her personal encounter with Foucault's work: "Reading Foucault's text was not a cognitive act so much as it was a re-cognitive act . . . It showed me precisely what I saw" (McWhorter 1999: 28).

Hayden White once claimed that "the authority of Foucault's discourse derives primarily from its style (rather than from its factual evidence or rigor of argument)." He suggested that it has no centre: "It is all surface—and intended to be so . . . And this is consistent with the larger purpose of a thinker who wishes to dissolve the distinction between surfaces and depths" (White 1987: 105–106, cited in Halperin 1995: 211, n.132; cf. Rouse 1994: 102–103). For Foucault, there is no place from which to speak outside the universe constituted by discourse.[2] Seen this way, what happened at the end of the eighteenth century in the domain of sexuality was not that certain practices changed and hence the way of talking about them. The new discourse *was* the change. In a sense, there was nothing for the technical nomenclature and clinical accounts of perversions to hide or repress. For Foucault, the practices owe their existence to the ways in which they are articulated.[3] This is why Foucault rejects what he calls "the repressive hypothesis": even as discourse and its opposite—determinate silences—censor and expurgate, they found the domain that is ostensibly concealed. Whatever the elisions, sex is continually being hammered home. Foucault's own insistent, almost incantatory lyricism in regard to the so-called repressed content of discourse, together with his calculated evasions and scientific formulations that mimic the patterns of our reigning clinical discourses, exhibit how the process works.

With the relentless concentration on sex in official and unofficial discourse, all sex, down to those diminutive caresses by tiny hands, acquired an extraordinary importance. Nothing was left vague or indefinite: with the will to classification that is part of the nature of scientific discourse, every variety of sex became a category in itself, and one's sexual practices, endlessly examined and exposed, became part of one's identity. What you did in the domain of sex was what you were. As Foucault writes: "the project of a science of the subject has gravitated, in ever narrowing circles, around the question of sex. Causality in the subject, the unconscious of the subject, the truth of the subject in the other who knows, the knowledge he holds unbeknown to him, all this found an opportunity to deploy itself in the discourse of sex. Not, however, by reason of some natural property inherent in sex itself, but by virtue of the tactics of power immanent in this discourse" (70).

Foucault's idea of power, as elaborated in the first volume of *The History of Sexuality*, was conceived of as specific to the new discourses that emerged in the nineteenth century, and was radically distinct from previous operations of domination. The new kind of power is omnipresent rather than focused: "it is produced from one moment to the next, at every point, or rather in every relation from one point to another. Power is everywhere; not because it embraces everything, but because it comes from everywhere" (93). When Foucault asserts that "discourse transmits and produces power," he means modern discourse, and power of this kind; this is the discourse that "reinforces" power, "but also undermines and exposes it" (101; cf. Halperin 1995: 41). The power that sustains sexuality, and is sustained by it, creates the conditions of possibility both of action and of resistance. The discourses of sex do not repress and control, any more than they liberate. "Sexuality must not be thought of as a kind of natural given which power tries to hold in check, or as an obscure domain which knowledge tries gradually to uncover" (105); it is rather the whole "surface network" that finds expression and indeed its essence in the discourses through which it circulates.

But if this is so, the question poses itself: what was the nature of sexuality before this construct, with its "few major strategies of knowledge and power" (106), came into being? People were not silent, of course, before they began to talk so much about sex. What did they say? Was there discourse, in Foucault's sense, and did it produce and transmit, but also undermine, a kind of power before the modern age? What was the object that it constituted and erased, if it was not sex? And where, if anywhere, was the site of the subject or the self?

These are the questions that remained when Foucault came to the end of his radical revaluation of the nature of both sexuality and power. Foucault's passing contrast between a modern European *scientia sexualis* and premodern *ars erotica* needed to be fleshed out into a full-blown analytics of the ancient construction of sex and self.

When Foucault undertook to examine the construction of sexuality and the self in the classical world several years later, he addressed himself to the same kinds of sources that had served him in his analysis of modern sexuality. That is, he looked to medical literature, advice on conduct and comportment, dream manuals—texts that encoded the expertise of the age, analogous to those that provided the venue for the interminable scientific discussions of sex in the nineteenth century.[4] Of course, it did not follow automatically from Foucault's analysis of modern sexuality that didactic literature was the locus in which the discourse of sexuality would be chiefly located in antiquity. Quite the contrary, the predominance and proliferation of these pseudo-scientific genres in the construction of sexuality, at a time when sex was banished or displaced, or at least denied recognition, at more informal levels, is precisely what made the discourse of the nineteenth century unique in history. Why assume that ancient Greek tracts offering advice on the body and on sex played a comparable role?

Many critics have, indeed, faulted Foucault precisely for limiting his inquiry to texts which, in their view, give a very partial and incorrect picture of sexual attitudes in Greece and Rome. How could he omit any reference to tragedy, comedy, lyric poetry, magical spells, and the like, which are full of material relating to love and sex, and give the lie to some of Foucault's most general claims (cf. Goldhill 1995: 44–45)? Of course, Foucault was not claiming to offer a complete account of ancient sexual behaviour. What people did, and how this was reflected in myths or imaginative literature, were not his primary concern. Such sources might tell us about sex, indeed, but not about sexuality, at least if sexuality is understood to be constituted by certain ostensibly repressive discourses that serve simultaneously to define and classify practices that determine one's sexual identity.[5] Sexuality in this sense requires regimentation and control; it defines a way to be that is to be both natural and difficult to attain, based on repression yet unconstrained, constitutive of identity by virtue of deviations that it itself encodes and categorises as such. If there were any place in classical literature where such a discourse might be located, it might well be in just those kinds of texts in which Foucault was looking for it. But why would Foucault assume that such a discourse existed at all in the ancient world, or that it had a hegemonic role in the construction of the self?

The answer is that he did not. What Foucault sought and discovered in the classical Greek medical, hortatory, and edifying literature was something very different from the minatory rules and regulations of nineteenth century discourse. Instead of the repressive apparatus of modern scientific or quasi-scientific prescriptive classifications, he found injunctions to self-mastery, to behaviour worthy of a free person and citizen, to a decent moderation in relation to self and others. In place of prohibitions, there were guidelines, in place of restrictions, suggestions and examples, in place of repression or the extermination of evil impulses, an ideal of proper management of the body and soul alike, respectful of all the human impulses provided only that they maintained their due place and observed due measure (cf. Nehamas 1998: 179). In all this, Foucault saw something that struck him as the very antithesis of the austere, uncompromising character of rule-bound, systematising, almost Linnaean morality that marked the modern era's approach to conduct, especially in the domain of sex.

The Greeks, as Foucault read them, put the emphasis rather on ways of using, exploiting, and managing the human pleasures—what Foucault called "usage," reflecting among other things the sense of the Greek term *khrêsis*. They were concerned with the tending and care of the self as a whole, which Foucault translated as "souci de soi" from the Greek *therapia heautou*. And Foucault interpreted this attention to the ways of handling, ministering to, or manipulating sexual pleasure and the configurations of the self as an encouragement to finding one's own personal signature in the world, of stylising one's manners and character not in accordance with commonplace models or the behaviour of the many, but in an individual way, as a sign of difference and even of superiority. Instead of imposing a crushing uniformity on conduct, ancient handbooks summoned their readers to devise a way of being that was their own, subject only to the constraint that the final product reveal the coherence of the self through its domination of properly subordinate elements, whether in the soul, in the household (i.e., women, children, slaves), or in the community as a whole, as evidenced in the adult male citizens' privilege of occupying political office. As Foucault put it in the conclusion to Volume Two: for the Greeks, "reflection on sexual behavior as a moral domain was not a means of internalizing, justifying, or formalizing general interdictions imposed on everyone; rather, it was a means of developing—for the smallest minority of the population, made up of free, adult males—an aesthetics of existence, the purposeful art of a freedom perceived as a power game" (252–253).

Finally, Foucault discovered in this kind of ethical stance and paradigm of moral activity a usable model for the present, particularly in regard to sexuality. For it seemed to Foucault that, for all the social limitations which, as he knew very well, inhered in ancient Greek and Roman societies and limited the models of free comportment that they projected to a small caste of wealthy males, these guides, with their emphasis on the stylisation of the self as opposed to its regimentation, spoke to a new ideal of self-fashioning that was emerging in our time, and in particular within the gay, lesbian and queer sub-cultures which served as the crucible of a whole array of new configurations and possibilities of the sexual self (cf. Nehamas 1998: 177; Spargo 1999: 23–26).

Not only was the kind of discourse Foucault was investigating in the second and third volumes of *The History of Sexuality* different from that explored in Volume One; the character of Foucault's own description changed as well. For example, in summarising the chapter on "The Moral Problematization of Pleasures," he writes:

> The foregoing is only a rough sketch for preliminary purposes; a few general traits that characterized the way in which, in classical Greek thought, sexual practice was conceptualized and made into an ethical domain. The elements of this domain—the "ethical substance"—were formed by the *aphrodisia*; that is, by acts intended by nature, associated by nature with an intense pleasure, and naturally motivated by a force that was always liable to excess and rebellion. The principle according to which this activity was

meant to be regulated, the "mode of subjection," was not defined by a universal legislation determining permitted and forbidden acts; but rather by a *savoir-faire*, an art that prescribed the modalities of a use that depended on different variables (need, time, status). The effort that the individual was urged to bring to bear on himself, the necessary ascesis, had the form of a battle to be fought, a victory to be won in establishing a dominion of self over self, modeled after domestic or political authority. Finally, the mode of being to which this self-mastery gave access was characterized as an active freedom, a freedom that was indissociable from a structural, instrumental, and ontological relation to truth.

(Foucault 1985: 91–92)

Gone is the florid, mesmerising quality of the first volume. The language here is simple and orderly, given to instruction, like the didactic tracts Foucault was following, rather than to casting a spell through the sheer authority of elegant reiteration. In a review of the French edition of the second volume of *The History of Sexuality*, David Halperin contrasted Volume One with Volume Two, which he described as "becomingly modest in its tone, cautious in its interpretations, conservative in its adherence to ancient literary sources, and tentative in its conclusions".[6] Once again, Foucault seems to have adjusted his style to the phenomenon being described.

But if Foucault was in fact investigating something different in the texts that constituted the ancient disciplines of the body and of sex, are the later volumes in fact continuous with Volume One? Ought one to include them under the rubric of "The History of Sexuality" at all, as opposed, perhaps, to the "Prehistory of Sexuality"?[7] Was Foucault's "focus on the history of ancient sex" simply "part of his interest in the history of ancient ethics," as Arnold Davidson suggests (Davidson 1994: 115; cf. Bernauer and Mahon 1994: 143)? Is sex merely an incidental motif in *The History of Sexuality*, and if so, does sexuality indeed have a history?[8]

I shall return to these questions below, but I should like first to inquire whether the differences that Foucault delineated between ancient ascetics and modern scientific discourses in regard to sex are in fact cogent. To some extent, Foucault's results may depend on the kinds of didactic texts he elected to examine. If he had consulted classical astrological handbooks, for example, he might have found that a complex classification of sexual orientations or behaviours was presumed to be natural or given at birth. Thus, Bernadette Brooten, in her book, *Love between Women*, argues that, in Ptolemy (second century A.D.), "a highly volatile planetary gender system accounts for highly diverse human sexual behavior".[9] So too, I wrote in connection with the astrologer Dorotheus, who lived in the first century A.D. and whose text survives in an Arabic translation of a Persian version of the Greek original: "On the surface of it . . . the idea that sexual preference is indicated by the stars at a person's nativity would seem to suggest that homoeroticism, and in particular the roles of catamite and tribad, are innate and inalterable" (cf. also Manilius 5.140–56 and Claudius Ptolemy 3.14.171–73; 4.5.188). I did, however, register a certain hesitation. For I noted that "the planets and constellations indicate not just sexual style but also such matters as wealth and poverty, number of children, success in marriage or business, health and sickness, slavery or freedom, one's profession, personal continence, traits of character—a whole range of consequences, most of which we would not necessarily classify as aspects of a person's identity or inborn characteristics that mark one's inner nature" (Konstan 1997; on Dorotheus, see also Brooten 1996: 119–123). The mere fact that a trait is inborn is not sufficient for it to enter into the construction of identity. Hair colour, after all, is innate as well. There has, I think, been some confusion between the idea that a characteristic is natural, as opposed to acquired, and the distinct notion that it defines a special type of person; the latter surely is always mediated by discourse.

In her examination of ancient Greek medical texts (143–173), Brooten affirms: "Contrary to the views of Foucault and others . . . some ancient writers saw particular same-sex acts as symptoms of a chronic disease that affected the entirety of one's identity" (143),[10] an observation that squares with the argument advanced by Amy Richlin and others that sexual roles were both enforced and constitutive of identity in classical antiquity.[11] The fact that the ancient "classification system differs from that developed in the nineteenth century," Brooten concludes (162), "does not mean that it is any less medical." Indeed, Brooten argues that ancient writers, whether Christian or pagan, were more punctilious than we ourselves are in classifying sexual types: "Whereas we often dualistically define sexual orientation as either homosexual or heterosexual, they saw a plethora of orientations" (3).[12]

Now, the very fact of their multiplicity should alert us to the possibility that such "orientations" may have functioned very differently from the way they do today. What of a person, for example, who enjoys being penetrated by adult males but is given to playing an active sexual role in respect to boys or women? This is a type not easily assimilated either to the modern model of homosexual versus heterosexual or to the alternative dichotomy between active and passive dispositions that is now commonly taken to characterise the classical paradigm of sexuality. Craig Williams, in his fine book, *Roman Homosexuality* (Williams 1999), allows that the figure of the *cinaedus* or effeminate male "could in fact justifiably be said to be a species or a personage" (210), but he concludes that "the deviance of the *cinaedus* is ultimately a matter of gender identity rather than sexual identity, in the sense that his predilection for playing the receptive role in penetrative acts was not the single defining feature of his identity but rather a sign of a more fundamental transgression of gender categories" (210–211). But why limit so severely the category of the sexual? Was there a "transgression of gender categories" that did not ultimately come down to sexual practices?[13] And is not identity always overdetermined?

In fact, the primary site in which the discourse of sexuality circulated in antiquity may not have been advice literature at all. To be sure, writing had an important function in classical Greece, but we may inquire whether those genres that lent themselves to literary composition would have carried anything like the authority they do in modern society. The written materials that Foucault privileged ought to have roused his suspicions just because of their resemblance to modern sites of repressive discourse. In a largely oral culture, one might have been better advised to examine such forms as popular or symposiastic songs and lyrics, public drama, epic, celebratory occasional poetry like Pindar's odes—genres that circulated widely and carried enormous prestige. The kind of control exercised here was different from that implicit in modern medical and other technical discourses: it was not confined to credentialed experts (apart from poets) in quite the same way, or draped in the mantle of science with its enormous ideological stature. But it had huge authority, enjoyed wide popular diffusion, and was at least potentially the vehicle of a powerful discursive regime, and not simply a source of evidence for sexual behaviours. These forms of discursive production may well have regulated sexual roles more strictly than the explicitly didactic texts analysed by Foucault.[14]

Foucault understood perfectly well that sexual behaviour in classical Greece was oriented along an axis of active and passive, penetrator and penetrated, and that these roles were aligned in Greek ideology with social positions that were both hierarchical and exclusive: the active part pertained to adult male citizens, while women, children of both sexes, and slaves were classified as receptive both by nature and by custom. The asymmetrical character of Greek erotics thus subtended a sexual regime based on domination and subordination. Of course, a free adult male *could* be penetrated, and this introduced a zone of tension and instability in the ideological model. But the real point of anxiety centred on the possibility that such a subject might *desire* to assume the passive function: this was the class of ostensibly effete males variously labeled as *cinaedi*, catamites, pathics, and the like. A whole range of behaviours had been codified as unmasculine—ways of walking, particular gestures, hair styles, and the like—and were to be carefully avoided by real men.[15]

Because Foucault was concentrating on the ethical issue of self-mastery or *enkrateia* in the classical texts, he tended to treat domination and subordination in social relations as projections of the hierarchy within the self. Correspondingly, he saw this element of personal discipline (*askêsis*) as analogous more to government than to oppression. "Just as, within the house, it is the man who commands, and just as, within the city, it falls neither to slaves nor children nor women to exercise power, but to men and men only, so too must each one make his manly qualities prevail over himself" (Foucault 1984: 96; my transl.; cf. Foucault 1986: 82). Now, if self-mastery is a preeminently masculine virtue, then it follows that women are the more libidinous sex and less able to control their erotic impulses. Indeed, this image of women is pervasive in Greek literature, for example Aristophanic comedy, where they are also characterised as bibulous and mendacious. We have seen, however, that Greek popular ideology situated men as the unique subjects of erotic desire, whereas women were located in the position of objects. Men pursued, women were pursued in lyric poetry and love elegy: the masculine role in sex was analogised to that of a hunter or soldier.[16] When we take into account the polarisation of sexual identities on the basis of active versus passive functions, which is not of course strictly congruent with differences of gender, we encounter the paradoxical situation in which adult males are normatively cast as lovers, women and boys as beloveds, and yet the masculine ideal—at least according to the didactic literature that Foucault privileged in his investigation—is that of governing the passions, whereas women and effeminate men are paradigmatically lacking in temperance or self-control and hence imagined as supremely susceptible to lust and other appetites. Women and *cinaedi* are thus overdetermined as both erotically inert and aggressive.

I do not believe that we are obliged to resolve this inconsistency in the sexual imaginary of the Greeks, any more than in modern ideological constructions of sexuality.[17] As David Halperin elegantly argues in *Saint Foucault*, "homophobic discourse" is a "paradoxical combination of incoherence, propositional indeterminacy, and social efficacy" (Halperin 1995: 43). Halperin concludes: "If the term 'homosexuality' turns out . . . not to describe a single, stable *thing* but to operate as a placeholder for a set of mutually incompatible, logically contradictory predicates . . . that is because homosexuality and heterosexuality do not represent a true pair, two mutually referential contraries, but a hierarchical opposition in which heterosexuality defines itself implicitly by constituting itself as the negation of homosexuality" (44). Thus the homosexual can be labeled as both sick (and hence not morally culpable) and blameworthy, in spite of the incompatibility of these descriptions in modern ethical thought (46). So too, women could be seen in ancient Greece as simultaneously passive, and therefore subject to male authority, and erotically undisciplined, hence in need of male control. This contradictory determination of women permits, in turn, the overdetermined constitution of masculine identity as the negation of the female. As that which dominates women, the male occupies the place of that which governs them, that is, of *erôs* itself.

Foucault failed fully to explore this paradoxical construction of sex in the classical imaginary in part, I think, because his attention was directed not to the nature of *erôs* so much as to *aphrodisia*, that is, the sexual act. In Volume One of *The History of Sexuality*, Foucault addressed himself to the way in which modern discourses of the body minutely classified not just acts but also forms of desire. The modern regime of confession, for example, compels one to reveal "one's crimes, one's sins, one's thoughts and desires, one's illnesses and troubles" (59)—not just what you do, but what you want to do. When he turned to the classical world, however, Foucault looked not so much to desire as to pleasure: *L'usage des plaisirs* was the title he chose for Volume Two. The term *aphrodisia*, like pleasure but unlike *erôs*, is neutral in regard to active and passive functions. Thus, the elaboration of an ethical ideal of self-fashioning based on the management of pleasure could sidestep the complex determination of erotic roles predicated on the dynamics of desire.[18] When Foucault moved from the analysis of sexuality to "the history of ancient ethics," as Arnold Davidson put it, he really did change the subject.

I have been suggesting that attention both to a broader range of classical didactic literature and to other discursive sites such as popular song might soften the contrast Foucault drew between the modern construction of sexuality and the ancient therapy of the self. But we may also observe that the stylisation of behaviour as an ethical practice, which Foucault discovered in his classical sources and sought to recuperate as an ideal of modern life, had a marked place in nineteenth century thought as well—nowhere more so, perhaps, than in the writings of Henry David Thoreau. Thoreau was by no means alone, however, among his contemporaries in this regard. Longfellow, in his Harvard lectures on Goethe, had claimed: "His model was the perfect man, as man; living, moving, laboring upon earth in the sweat of his brow."[19] So too, "Frederic Hedge wrote an essay on self-culture. Horace Greeley had a talk he called 'Self-culture'; so did William Ellery Channing," in which he argued that "self-culture is possible because we have the power of 'acting on, determining, and forming ourselves.'" Emerson gave a whole series of lectures on the subject, under such titles as "Self-knowledge and Self-mastery" in November 1828, "Self-culture" in September 1830, and "Self-improvement" in February 1832, this last repeated 14 times in the next four years.[20] The transcendentalists were influenced, to be sure, by the German idea of *Bildung* and by John Stuart Mill's program of "the culture of the inward man," but, as Richardson notes, the "essentially individualistic inwardness of personal culture may owe something to the eighteenth-century revival of Stoic thought."

I do not mean to assimilate the transcendentalists' vision of autonomy and self-mastery to that of the classical thinkers. Nevertheless, Alexander Nehamas' claim that "Foucault belongs to the individualist strain of the tradition of philosophy as the art of living" is, if not uncontroversial, as Nehamas allows, nevertheless not implausible either (Nehamas 1998: 169). In explaining the shift in focus in Foucault's last writings, it has become commonplace to advert to Foucault's experience of California.[21] It is true, as David Halperin reminds us, that Foucault explicitly distanced himself from the shallow "Californian cult of the self" ("On the Genealogy of Ethics": 362 cited in Halperin 1995: 74). But the American engagement with the care of the self, for all its narcissistic aspects, has its roots in a deep individualist strain.[22] Henry Abelove had reason to conclude, in a brilliant article, that Thoreau's vision of America has found a contemporary expression in the idea of a queer nation (Abelove 1993: 17–27).

Foucault's shift of emphasis from sexuality to ethics, in the interval between the publication of the first volume of *The History of Sexuality* and the subsequent two, may have been motivated, then, by a change in his own interests and hence the kinds of texts that summoned his attention (cf. Gutting 1994b: 5–6). For it has proved possible to identify counter-strains to the discourses that Foucault isolated in both epochs that connect, as it were, on the diagonal. But this does not mean that there is a methodological gap or *coupure* between Volume One of *The History of Sexuality* and Volumes Two and Three. The universal control exercised by the surveillance techniques of modern science in the domain of sexuality, as elsewhere, which Foucault conceptualised with increasing rigor beginning with *Discipline and Punish*, permits only indirect forms of resistance, as opposed to revolutionary liberation: one cannot emancipate that which is itself constructed by the very procedures of regimentation and enforcement that ostensibly repress it. One must respond rather with irony, be creative, provocative, on the move, with a view to opening up possibilities only dimly envisaged rather than programmatically articulated. It is hopeless to challenge the dominant discourse with an alternative theory, because this discourse is fundamentally incoherent and thus impervious to rational argument. The mobile, inventive stylisation of the self that Foucault found in ancient didactic texts—and which he could have discovered also in the American tradition of self-culture—is just the tactic to employ against the regulatory discourses that constitute the modern sexual self. *The History of Sexuality* has its unity just in the twin conception of dispersed power, as defined in Volume One, and the ethic of self-fashioning that constitutes its dialectical other (cf. Halperin 1995: 111).

Questions remain, and invite further research. Whether classical Greek ethics really did constitute a non-prescriptive summons to self-fashioning, as Foucault conceived it, is a topic in need of fresh analysis. Certainly, it was less trammeled by anxious prohibitions than early Christian morality, which sought to mortify sexual desire, or the puritanical streak in the Victorian and American traditions. Not everyone will agree that the stylisation of life that Foucault appreciated in classical texts constitutes either a necessary or an adequate response to the nature of power in the modern world.[23] Reviewing a book on Foucault and the classics, Kristina Milnor writes: "I do not think that feminists have done justice to Foucault until we acknowledge that, fundamentally, his work is not about sex"—or, she adds, about "prison, or medicine, or madness. It is about power and the mechanisms of social systems" (Milnor 2000: 305). This is true enough—but *The History of Sexuality* is also about identity. In the modern epoch, identity has been constructed under a regime of surveillance that has been obsessively concentrated upon sex. It may be that Foucault's fixation on the autonomous stylisation of the self in classical texts Greece led him to understate the ways in which, there too, the sexual self was fixed, essentialised, and rendered a site for the construction of identity, even if this identity took different forms, under the pressure of different kinds of discourse. But Foucault saw more clearly than anyone the ways in which the classical discourse of sexuality differed from the regimes that succeeded it. It is thus entirely appropriate that the book before you, which traces transformations in the way desire, sex, and intimacy were conceived and experienced from the Middle Ages down to today, should begin with a chapter on Foucault. By way of a preface to this excellent study by Ann Brooks, and at her generous invitation, I have tried to indicate why Foucault found it necessary to turn to classical antiquity in order to understand fully the new regimes of sexuality, power, and identity that arose in Western Europe, and so to set the stage for the long history that followed.

David Konstan

Notes

1. This preface is a version, lightly revised, of "The Prehistory of Sexuality: Foucault's Route to Classical Antiquity" published in *Intertexts* 6 (2002) 8–21; I am grateful to the editor and publisher of the journal for permission to reproduce it here.
2. Cf. Smart (1983: 96), criticising attempts by Marxist writers (e.g., Lecourt 1975) to reduce Foucault to "a theorist of the superstructure."
3. Cf. Nehamas (1998: 175): "Instead of being repressed, sexuality was to a great extent *created* in the nineteenth century".
4. On the emergence of scientific discourses as forms of cultural discipline under the Roman Empire, see Wallace-Hadrill (1997).
5. If we agree with Foucault, moreover, that "'sex' is historically subordinate to sexuality" (Foucault 1978: 157), then such sources, taken by themselves, do not even tell us about sex.
6. Cf. Black (1998: 42–43); Halperin (1986: 277). Halperin later (1995: 5) retracted his relatively harsh characterisation of Volume One.
7. Norris (1994: 159), following Boyne (1990: 144), affirms that a shift from Nietzschean suspicion to a positive ethics in Foucault's epistemological stance "can be located with a fair degree of precision as occurring between Volume One of *The History of Sexuality*" and the following volumes.
8. Cf. Black (1998: 45): "If sexuality was a specifically modern phenomenon limited to the past century and a half, how was Foucault's shift, in the second and subsequent volumes of the history, to ancient Greco-Roman and early Christian culture to be considered part of the project? Wasn't Foucault actually writing a *pre*history of sexuality?"
9. Brooten (1996: 128); on astrological handbooks in general, see 115–41.
10. Brooten concentrates her discussion chiefly on Soranus.
11. See Richlin (1993); also the summary of the debate between Foucauldians and feminist scholars (with ample bibliography) in Skinner (1996).
12. Aristides Quintilianus *On Music* (perhaps third century A.D.), distinguishing masculine and feminine elements of style, begins by explaining how the soul seeks out a gendered body: the soul "not only desires body, but a body of a particular kind. She loves either male or female, sometimes one or the other by itself, sometimes a weird and extraordinary mixture of the two. And if souls fail to find a body such as they want naturally, they bring about changes by their own activities and assimilate the body to themselves. Then feminine looks bloom on men, so that their life is seen to be feminine too, and masculine looks are seen on women, whereby we can infer a similarity of character also. There are beardless men and bearded women, males with languishing eyes and women with militant gaze. In each case, one can detect a character corresponding to the outward form" (trans. D.A. Russell in Russell and Winterbottom 1972: 553–554).
13. McNay (1992: 77–79), following Daraki (1986), charges Foucault with privileging the opposition between active and passive sexual roles at the expense of gender: "the idea of passivity cannot be totally separated from that of femininity because both occupy a similar position in a series of structurally analogous binaries" (78).
14. The authority of poetry, and its status as a rival to philosophical discourse, are among the reasons for Plato's hostility to it; cf. Asmis (1992: 338–342); Ferrari (1989: 92–95).
15. On the category of "real men," see Williams (1999: 163–165).
16. On the equation between hunting and sexuality in early Greek thought, see Barringer (forthcoming); the sources are chiefly pictorial, but confirmed by textual evidence.
17. Cf. Fox (1998: 19): "an ethics of mastery occupies a particular discursive position, and is far from being a clear reflection of contemporary Athenian practice".

18. Paul Allen Miller points out to me that the shift from desire (or *erôs*) to *aphrodisia* was among other things Foucault's "way of sidestepping psychoanalysis"; see also Black (1998: 44–47).
19. Richardson (1986: 55); the following quotations are taken from the section entitled "Self-Culture" in Richardson's biography of Thoreau, to which I am much indebted.
20. The relation between the transcendentalists' ethic and Foucault's deserves further study; Hans (1995) is hostile to Foucault and of little value.
21. Nehamas (1998: 176) remarks that "out of the sometimes silly, often valuable, and to him always fascinating self-absorption of his California friends, colleagues, and students, Foucault formulated his deepest and most important idea, the care of the self".
22. Contrast Halperin (1995: 71): "Modern systems of morality, by contrast [with the Greek], have tended to allocate little or no role in ethical practice to comparable techniques of self-fashioning".
23. Compare Barthes (1975: 55): "Bataille does not counter modesty with sexual freedom but . . . with *laughter*" (ellipsis in original).

Bibliography

Abelove, Henry. 1993. "From Thoreau to Queer Politics" *The Yale Journal of Criticism* 6(2): 17–27.
Asmis, Elizabeth. 1992. "Plato on Poetic Creativity." In Richard Kraut (ed.), *The Cambridge Companion to Plato*. Cambridge: Cambridge University Press, 338–364.
Barringer, Judith. 2002. *Manhood, Myth, and Valor: The Hunt in Ancient Greece* Baltimore: The Johns Hopkins University Press.
Barthes, Roland. 1975/1973. *The Pleasure of the Text*. Trans. Richard Miller. New York: Hill and Wang.
Bernauer, James W. and Michael Mahon. 1994. "The Ethics of Michel Foucault." In Gary Gutting (ed.), *The Cambridge Companion to Foucaul*, 141–158.
Black, Joel. 1998. "Taking the Sex Out of Sexuality: Foucault's Failed History." In David H.J. Larmour, Paul Allen Miller and Charles Platter (eds), *Rethinking Sexuality: Foucault and Classical Antiquity*. Princeton, NJ: Princeton University Press, 42–60.
Boyne, Roy. 1990. *Foucault and Derrida: The Other Side of Reason*. London: Unwin Hyman.
Brooten, Bernadette J. 1996. *Love Between Women: Early Christian Responses to Female Homoeroticism*. Chicago: The University of Chicago Press.
Daraki, Maria. 1986. "Foucault's Journey to Greece" *Telos* 67: 87–110.
Davidson, Arnold I. 1994. "Ethics as Ascetics: Foucault, the History of Ethics, and Ancient Thought." In Gary Gutting (ed.), *The Cambridge Companion to Foucault*. Cambridge: Cambridge University Press, 115–140.
Ferrari, G.R.F. 1989. "Plato and Poetry." In George A. Kennedy (ed.), *The Cambridge History of Literary Criticism. Vol. 1: Classical Criticism*. Cambridge: Cambridge University Press, 92–148.
Foucault, Michel. 1978/1976. *The History of Sexuality, Volume 1: An Introduction* Trans. Robert Hurley. New York: Random House.
Foucault, Michel. 1984. *L'usage des plaisirs: Histoire de la sexualité 2*. Paris: Gallimard.
Foucault, Michel. 1985/1984. *The Use of Pleasure: Volume 2 of the History of Sexuality* Trans. Robert Hurley. New York: Pantheon Books.
Foucault, Michel. 1989. "Interview: Sex, Power, and the Politics of Identity." In Silvère Lotringer (ed.), *Foucault Live: Collected Interviews 1961–1984*. New York: Semiotext(e), 382–390.

Fox, Matthew. 1998. "The Constrained Man." In Lin Foxhall and John Salmon (eds), *Thinking Men: Masculinity and Its Self-Representation in the Classical Tradition*. London: Routledge, 6–22.

Goldhill, Simon. 1995. *Foucault's Virginity: Ancient Erotic Fiction and the History of Sexuality*. Cambridge: Cambridge University Press.

Gutting, Gary (ed.). 1994a. *The Cambridge Companion to Foucault*. Cambridge: Cambridge University Press.

Gutting, Gary. 1994b. "Introduction. Michel Foucault: A User's Manual." In Gary Gutting (ed.), *The Cambridge Companion to Foucault*. Cambridge: Cambridge University Press, 1–27.

Halperin, David. 1986. "Sexual Ethics and Technologies of the Self in Classical Greece. Review of Foucault 1984" *American Journal of Philology* 107: 274–286.

Halperin, David M. 1995. *Saint Foucault: Towards a Gay Hagiography*. New York: Oxford University Press.

Hans, James S. 1995. *The Site of Our Lives: The Self and the Subject from Emerson to Foucault*. Albany: State University of New York Press.

Konstan, David. 1997. "Conventional Values of the Hellenistic Greeks: The Evidence from Astrology." In Per Bilde, Troels Engberg-Pedersen, Lise Hannestad and Jan Zahle (eds), *Conventional Values in the Hellenstic World*. Aarhus: Aarhus University Press (Studies in Hellenistic Civilization 8), 159–176.

Larmour, David H.J., Paul Allen Miller, and Charles Platter (eds). 1998. *Rethinking Sexuality: Foucault and Classical Antiquity*. Princeton, NJ: Princeton University Press.

Lecourt, D. 1975. *Marxism and Epistemology: Bachelard, Canguilhem and Foucault*. London: New Left Books.

McNay, Lois. 1992. *Foucault and Feminism*. Boston: Northeastern University Press.

McWhorter, Ladelle. 1999. *Bodies and Pleasures: Foucault and the Politics of Sexual Normalization*. Bloomington: Indiana University Press.

Milnor, Kristina. 2000. "Review of Larmour, Miller, and Platter, 1998" *Classical World* 93: 304–305.

Nehamas, Alexander. 1998. *The Art of Living: Socratic Reflections from Plato to Foucault*. Berkeley: University of California Press.

Norris, Christopher. 1994. "'What is Enlightenment?' Kant According to Foucault." In Gary Gutting (ed.), *The Cambridge Companion to Foucault*. Cambridge: Cambridge University Press, 159–196.

Richardson, R. 1986. *Henry Thoreau: A Life of the Mind*. Berkeley: University of California Press.

Richlin, Amy. 1993. "Not Before Homosexuality: The Materiality of the Cinaedus and the Roman Law Against Love Between Men" *Journal of the History of Sexuality* 3: 523–573.

Rouse, Joseph. 1994. "Power/Knowledge." In Gary Gutting (ed.), *The Cambridge Companion to Foucault*. Cambridge: Cambridge University Press, 92–114.

Russell, D.A. and Michael Winterbottom (eds). 1972. *Ancient Literary Criticism: The Principal Texts in New Translations*. Oxford: Oxford University Press.

Skinner, Marilyn B. 1996. "Zeus and Leda: The Sexuality Wars in Contemporary Classical Scholarship" *Thamyris* 3(1): 103–123; also available through "Diotima" at http://www.uky.edu/ ArtsSciences/Classics/skinzeus.html

Smart, Barry. 1983. *Foucault, Marxism and Critique*. London: Routledge and Kegan Paul.

Spargo, Tamsin. 1999. *Foucault and Queer Theory*. Cambridge: Icon Books.

Wallace-Hadrill, Andrew. 1997. "*Mutatio morum*: The Idea of a Cultural Revolution" In Thomas Habinek and Alessandro Schiesaro (eds), *The Roman Cultural Revolution*. Cambridge: Cambridge University Press, 3–22.

White, Hayden. 1987. "Foucault's Discourse: The Historiography of Anti-Humanism." In *The Content of the Form: Narrative Discourse and Historical Representation*. Baltimore: The Johns Hopkins University Press, 104–141.

Williams, Craig. 1999. *Roman Homosexuality: Ideologies of Masculinity in Classical Antiquity*. New York: Oxford University Press.

Acknowledgements

I would like to acknowledge the support of a number of individuals and organisations in supporting the development of this project. My deepest thanks to David Konstan at New York University for contributing the Foreword which provides an immensely powerful introduction to the book. I also thank Professor Konstan for the range of interesting discussions which this collaboration generated. My thanks also to Bournemouth University for supporting a number of conference presentations which facilitated work on the project. I wish to acknowledge my on-going collaboration as an International Investigator with the Australia Research Council (ARC) funded Centre of Excellence for the History of Emotions 2011–17 which has supported my research in many ways. The project was initiated while I was a Visiting Scholar in the Department of Sociology at the University of California, Berkeley from 2011 to 2012 and the library at UC Berkeley provided invaluable resources for planning this book. To my friends and colleagues John Scott, David Lemmings, Lionel Wee, Bryan Turner, Candida Yates, Barry Richards for their continual enthusiasm and great support of my work. Max Novick at Routledge New York has been a superb editor over two books and has never faltered in his support for my ideas. My thanks to the entire UK team at Routledge for their support on all aspects of production and marketing. Finally to the Russell-Cotes Gallery in Bournemouth for providing a wonderful environment to think and write.

Professor Ann Brooks
August 2016

Introduction
What's Love Got to Do with It?

The history of love and intimacy shows a fascinating interweaving of social, economic and cultural influences and explanations. The focus of this book is on the historical emergence of romantic love and intimacy in the West. And as Shumway (2003: 11) shows: "'Romantic love' in this sense is best understood as a culturally specific discourse. . . ." which is most clearly defined in the history of Western culture.

In fact the traditional meaning of love does not relate directly to passion or intimacy:

> The traditional meaning of *love* is not romance but social solidarity; it corresponds to the capacity for bonding rather than the capacity for infatuation. For most of Western history, as Luhmann argues, 'What was considered important is not living out one's own passions, but rather a voluntarily (and not compulsorily or slavishly) developed solidarity within a given order'.
>
> (Luhman 1986: 130; Shumway 2003: 12)

Romance as a historical and cultural discourse has political and economic dimensions. In medieval society, romance emerged as an alternative discourse to conventional marriage which was officially sanctioned by the aristocracy. It offered a discourse which provided a cultural alternative and offered "shifts in manners and morals in the courts of feudal Europe" (Shumway 2003: 13). It is argued by a number of writers that this was also marked by the idealisation of love. Shumway argues that part of this was the role that women played in idealising love. Previously women had been seen as a corrupting influence, but they came to be idealised within the discourse of romance and at the same time love was also idealised.

The emergence of the discourse of romance as a "counter-discourse" established the separation of love and marriage. As Duby (1988: 145) wrote: "Whether love and marriage were compatible was the great question that agitated the courts of Champagne and Ille-de-France." The relationship between love and marriage was captured in Capellanus's (1941) twelfth century treatise on courtly love, *The Art of Courtly Love*, where he states: "Everybody knows that love can have no place between husband and wife" (Capellanus 1941: 100).

The history of love and intimacy has been documented in a number of significant texts including Denis de Rougemont's (1956) *Love in the Western World*, Niklas Luhmann's (1986) *Love as Passion: The Codification of Intimacy* and Anthony Giddens's (1992) *The Transformation of Intimacy* among others which bring together historical and sociological perspectives and indicate the historical shifts in the development of love and intimacy.

Love, Intimacy and the Rise of the Bourgeoisie

Class, gender and sexuality are all important points of intersection in the historical development of love and intimacy. Shumway (2003: 7) shows that:

> Historians have long connected the rise of companionate marriage and the later association of romantic love and marriage to the rise of the bourgeoisie. The aristocrats needed marriages of alliance to preserve their power and wealth, and the working class typically married for the economic advantage that extra hands brought to the household . . . It is rather the new middle-classes—the petit bourgeoisie and the professional managerial class—who are positioned economically and educationally to develop new patterns of love and intimacy. The expansion of the professional managerial class throughout most of the twentieth century is one of the conditions that enabled the discourse of intimacy to develop.

The relationship between sexuality, love and intimacy provides an important dimension of this book and is explored through Michel Foucault's (1978) *The History of Sexuality, Volume 1: An Introduction* (see below and Chapter 2). Many of the debates were established before same-sex marriage was legalised so some of the commentary regarding marriage and sexuality has been superceded. Giddens (1998: 145) argues that because previously gays could not marry, they: "have therefore been forced to pioneer the more open and negotiated relationships which subsequently have permeated the heterosexual population." These debates are explored in the chapters of this book.

Historians are themselves divided about the relationship between love, intimacy and marriage. Lawrence Stone (1977, 1988) argues that in the sixteenth and seventeenth centuries:

> . . . for all classes who possessed property, that is the top two-thirds economically, marriage before the seventeenth century was arranged by the parents, and the motives were the economic and political benefit of the kin group, not the emotional satisfaction of the individual.
>
> (Stone 1988: 20)

He also notes elsewhere (Stone 1977) that marriage before 1660 lacked even affection but he notes that: "diaries, letters, ballads, and church court cases" (Stone 1977: 99–105) prove otherwise.

It is more generally recognised that in the seventeenth century a new type of marriage emerged in England which Stone calls "the companionate marriage". However unlike the twentieth century version of this (see Giddens 1992) this was not one based on romance "but was based mainly on temperamental compatibility with the aim of lasting companionship" (Stone 1977: 392).

However while Britain was languishing in "the companionate marriage," the French were developing a more passionate environment for relationships. Luhmann (1986: 130) states that the French aristocracy developed a social code for what was in effect adulterous love which he calls somewhat appropriately "*amour passion*." He maintains that manuals printed during the time gave instructions on seduction. Shumway indicates that there was a reaction to this as expressed in different cultural forms from the late eighteenth century including Mozart's opera *Don Giovanni* and Laclos's novel *Les Liaisons Dangereuses*. This presents the seducer as an evil person and an exploiter of women.

As indicated earlier it was the extension of individualization alongside the rise of capitalism which allowed the bourgeoisie to influence the direction which love and intimacy took in Britain. However, as Shumway (2003: 19) shows, the nineteenth century provided a wide range of responses to the relationship between love, intimacy and marriage and he claims that the relationship was more clearly defined in America than elsewhere. Cancian (1987: 17) comments that in the early nineteenth century:

> marital intimacy, in the modern sense of emotional expression and verbal disclosure of personal experience was probably rare. Instead husband and wife were likely to share a more formal and wordless kind of love, based on duty, working together, mutual help and sex.

This book excavates epistemologies which attempt to explain changes in emotional regimes from medieval society to late modernity. In particular the book explores the role of intimacy as a driver of emotions and takes Stoler's (1997, 2002) concepts of "the personal and political in emotional regimes," and "mapping intimacy through sex" as significant in this debate. Methodologically this book is guided by the idea of a "historical epistemology of concept formation" (Somers 2008) which involves a systematic study of key conceptual frameworks developed by theorists in understanding the relationship between emotional styles and historical change. Key in this debate is the concept of intimacy. The book draws on the work of a number of theorists in assessing changes in emotional regimes, drawing on intimacy including: Berlant (1997, 2000), Foucault (1978), Giddens (1992), Illouz (1997, 2012), McClintock (1995, 1997), Stoler (1997, 2002, 2006) and a range of contemporary feminist and social theorists. More specifically the book considers the concept of "genealogy" as a methodological strategy and focuses on the relevance of genealogy as a methodology in assessing historical change. Finally it draws on interdisciplinary perspectives from sociology, history, cultural theory, feminism and anthropology.

In using genealogy as the framework of analysis, the author is guided by the work of Foucault (1978) and Somers (2008), but the source of this model is ultimately Foucault who viewed genealogy as "anti-science". In the volumes of his book and particularly in *Volume 1* of *The History of Sexuality*, Foucault adopted two strategies of argumentation which are pertinent to the arguments of this book: firstly he hoped to make us aware of the historically unique character of modern sexual culture; and secondly he offered an alternative perspective on the history of sexuality. Through detailed examples from the Middle Ages onwards, Foucault showed how sex was the focus of much that influenced historical change. Foucault offered historically rich, empirically dense social analyses. The model and mode of analysis adopted by Foucault is examined in this book as a core concept in understanding models of change in emotional regimes. The book explores changes in emotional regimes and includes an understanding of intimacy, sexuality and desire as fundamentally embedded in discourses of emotion. Stoler (2002: 9) comments: ". . . the notion of the 'intimate' is a descriptive marker of the familiar and the essential, and of relations grounded in sex". The main claim which underpins the book as a whole is that intimacy is incompatible with traditional normative structures such as marriage and the family within heterosexual, patriarchal structures, such as marriage, and in homophobic cultures. The book shows how intimacy has largely existed outside conventional bourgeois structures of marriage and the family and thus that intimacy and marriage are fundamentally incompatible in drawing on different historical emotional regimes.

Aims and Objectives

The key emphasis of this book is to show that different historical periods are characterised by emotional regimes where intimacy in the form of desire, sex, passion, and sexuality largely exist outside marriage, and that marriage and traditional normative values and structures are fundamentally incompatible with the expression of intimacy in the history of emotional regimes. Reddy (2001) shows how the management of emotions in communities reflects relationships of power and politics, and he maintains that social change occurs as individuals resist and challenge dominant emotional regimes that limit "emotional liberty".

In excavating epistemologies, the author examines bodies of knowledge or "epistemological frameworks" which include either single theoretical paradigms as in the case of Foucault's useage of "genealogy", or to a cluster of theories which form an epistemology, as in the useage of the framework of "reflexive modernization" which includes a range of theoretical paradigms offered by Beck and Beck-Gernsheim (1996), Giddens (1992) and Illouz (1997, 2012), all of whom address the issue of "detraditionalisation" of norms and values in late modernity. Another example is the useage of "affective frameworks" to cover a cluster of theories drawn from a range of feminist theorists: Berlant (1997, 2000), Hochschild (2003), Illouz (1997, 2012) and Swidler (2001), among many others, who attempt to explain "the emotionalisation of society" but using different points of emphasis (see Chapters 6 and 7).

The choice of the word "excavating" is an archeological metaphor which is appropriate given the value of Foucault's use of the framework in his book *The Archeology of Knowledge*. In this context I am excavating a range of epistemologies to assess their relevance in understanding intimacy (in its various forms of love, sex, desire, sexuality and passion) as shown in different historical periods. This includes sociological analysis of theories and thinkers who have contributed to theoretical debates and epistemological frameworks. For example Foucault's use of genealogy was designed as an epistemological and methodological framework to analyse sex and sexuality. I draw on this in the book to show how Foucault's analysis of sex and sexuality over different historical periods supports my main claim which underpins the book as a whole, which is that intimacy is incompatible with traditional normative structures such as marriage and the family which characterise traditional patriarchal structures and homophobic cultures.

Foucault's use of genealogy in his analysis of sexuality is just one example of an epistemological framework to explain the above. It offers an analysis of the intersection of sex and power as an expression of intimacy and as a driver of emotional change and as stated shows how intimacy operates outside traditional normative structures and values. Foucault highlights this in showing that sex, love, desire and passion exist outside marriage and also outside traditional heterosexual relations. Foucault is primarily focused on the issue of sex as an example of intimacy not emotions *per se* (see Foreword by David Konstan).

Foucault's model of genealogy is useful as a framework for understanding a range of epistemologies, in this case for understanding how intimacy acts as a driver for emotional and historical change. These epistemologies are then outlined in the chapters of the book as follows:

- Genealogy of sexuality (Foucault, sex and sexuality) (Chapter 2).
- Romantic love, courtly love and the bourgeois family (including Swidler—on bourgeois love and capitalism) (Chapter 3).
- Carnal knowledge and imperial power (power, sex and colonialism—Stoler) (Chapter 4).
- Post-colonial emotions and intimacy (intimacy, sexuality, nationalism and power—McClintock) (Chapter 4).
- "Reflexive modernization" intimacy and individualism (Giddens, Beck and Beck-Gernshiem, and Illouz) (Chapter 5).
- "Turn to affect" intimacy and feminism (Berlant, Illouz, Hochschild and feminist and social theorists) (Chapter 6 and 7).

The relationship between sex and power is an important dimension of the analysis of intimacy, emotions and social change and is a useful way to analyse theorists such as Foucault and Stoler. Stoler (1997, 2002) while influenced by Foucault, does offer a critique of Foucault which is developed in Chapter 4.

Imperial Power, Gender and Intimacy

Stoler as a historical anthropologist provides detailed empirical analysis of her work in colonial cultures. However fundamental to both Foucault and Stoler is the analysis of power and in particular the relationship between sex and power, Stoler is particularly influenced by Foucault's concept of "biopower". As I indicate in Chapter 1:

> There are interesting comparisons between the way Foucault and Stoler analyse the relationship between sex and power, and in their assessment of race and power. While recognising the contribution of Foucault's analysis and drawing on his genealogy of race, Stoler critiques "Foucault's history of the carnal" and while acknowledging the methodological insights offered by "Foucault's histories of racial discourse and biopower" (2002: 19) she seeks to link micro and macropolitics in colonial cultures by raising the question : ". . . how and why [do] microsites of familiar and intimate space figure so prominently in the macro-politics of imperial rule"
>
> (2002: 19)

Historians such as Margaret Hunt see Stoler as a theoretical "dissident" and much closer to Foucault than others. In this book I analyse Stoler's theoretical and empirical contribution and assess it across most of her major works. Her contribution to the relationship between intimacy, sex, power and colonial cultures is assessed for the significance of intimacy as a driver of emotional and historical change.

Romantic Love

A further important development of the relationship of intimacy, emotion and social change is captured in the development of discourses around romantic love. The issue of romantic love narratives and their relationships to broader patterns of social and emotional change is covered in Chapter 3. Romantic love narratives framed as courtly love were part of broader framework as noted in Chapter 3 which posed romantic/courtly love as initially thriving outside traditional marriage.

The character of romantic love framed as "courtly love" and desire were both "idealized and sacrilized" (Gross 2005: 303), but in all these romantic love narratives, romantic love was not understood as marital love, and did not thrive within marriage.

Perhaps of greater interest however is the attempt to recast these narratives of romantic love within the framing of the "bourgeois family" as can be seen from the work of Swidler (2001: 112) among others, she notes:

> ... the courtly ideal of love comes to us reshaped by the bourgeois culture of early English capitalism ... [this] took its quintessential form in the eighteenth-century English novel.... Both readers and writers were steeped in the individualism of the world's most capitalist and Protestant nation. Love became the focal myth of that individualism.

The theorisation of the relationship between the bourgeois family, romantic love and the onset of capitalism will be fully explored in the book and different theoretical frameworks considered.

Intimacy, Emotion and Nationalism

Another theme developed by the book is the relationship between intimacy, emotion and nationalism. Sara Ahmed (2004) in *The Cultural Politics of Emotion* focuses on the association of emotions with a conceptualisation of love for nation or community, emphasising the fluidity of emotions. This relationship is also reflected in one of the major theorists who provide a focus for this book, Anne McClintock, whose important sociological and cultural analysis of intimacy offers an original theoretical framing of the debates which might be seen as contributing to an epistemological analysis of intimacy. McClintock's work provides original analysis of the relationship between psychoanalysis, nationalism and intimacy as developed in Chapter 4.

Intimacy in Late Modernity

A further theme developed in the book is the changing nature of intimacy in late modernity which is paralleled by a growth in individualism and reflexivity. The emergence of the "reflexive modernization" thesis developed in the work of Beck and Beck-Gernsheim (1996) and Giddens (1992) has been an important theoretical intervention into traditional conceptions of intimacy and provided a backdrop for a huge number of social, cultural and feminist theorists. The intersection of late capitalism with relationships was framed within a model of "detraditionalisation" and theorists either supported or provided a critique of the model developed. These debates are explored in Chapter 6 through the work of a number of theorists including Hochschild (2003), Illouz (1997) and Jamieson (1998) and others who explore the changing pattern of intimacy in late modernity.

"The Intelligence of Emotions": Intimacy, Emotions and Feminist Interventions

Feminist and cultural theorists have provided a wide range of concepts and theories in understanding the changing nature of intimacy and this is captured in the concept of "the turn to affect". The theoretical contributions to this framework have been significant and wide-ranging and some of the theoretical interventions are captured here in the work of Lauren Berlant (Chapter 7) and Eva Illouz (Chapters 5 and 6) as well as in the work of a number of other feminist theorists.

The following chapters develop how the book explores the genealogical history of intimacy, emotion and desire:

> Chapter 1: Genealogies of Emotions, Intimacy and Desire. Theories of Changes in Emotional Regimes from Medieval Society to Late Modernity.
> Chapter 2: Foucault's Genealogy of Sexuality: Foucault, Sex and Power.
> Chapter 3: Narratives of Romantic Love.
> Chapter 4: "Mapping Intimacy through Sex in Twentieth Century Colonial Cultures": The Work of Laura Ann Stoler and Anne McClintock.
> Chapter 5: Love and Intimacy in Late Modernity: The Transformation of Intimacy.
> Chapter 6: "The Intelligence of Emotions": Intimacy, Emotions and the "Turn to Affect" —Feminist Interventions.
> Chapter 7: Intimacy, Emotions and the Public Sphere: From Sentimental Ideology to "The Queen of America" —The Public and the Private in the Work of Lauren Berlant.
> Conclusion.

Chapter Summary

Chapter 1: Genealogies of Emotions, Intimacy and Desire: Theories of Changes in Emotional Regimes from Medieval Society to Late Modernity

This chapter provides an overview of epistemologies which attempt to explain changes in emotional regimes from medieval society to late modernity. In particular the chapter explores the role of intimacy as a driver of emotions and takes Stoler's (1997, 2002) concepts of "the personal and political in emotional regimes" and "mapping intimacy through sex" as significant in this debate. The chapter considers key conceptual frameworks developed by theorists in understanding the relationship between emotional styles and historical change. The chapter explores changes in emotional regimes and includes an understanding of intimacy, sexuality and desire as fundamentally embedded in discourses of emotion. It investigates a range of epistemologies and theorists and explores their ideas in the context of different historical epochs.

Chapter 2: Foucault's Genealogy of Sexuality: Foucault, Sex and Power

Chapter 2 explores the work of Michel Foucault on "genealogy" and "sexuality". In using genealogy as the framework of analysis in this book, I am guided by the work of Foucault (1978) and Somers (2008), but the source of this model is ultimately Foucault who viewed genealogy as "anti-science". He rejected Enlightenment scientific culture and applied the model to the intersection of institutions and discourse in a number of his key studies, including *Madness and Civilization*, *The Archeology of Knowledge*, *Discipline and Punish* and the *History of Sexuality*. It is the latter book that provides the focus of interest for this book. In the volumes of *The History of Sexuality*, Foucault adopted two strategies of argumentation which are pertinent to this book: firstly he hoped to make us aware of the historically unique character of modern sexual culture; and secondly he offered an alternative perspective on the history of sexuality. Through detailed examples from the Middle Ages onwards, Foucault showed how sex was the focus of much that influenced historical change. Foucault offered historically rich, empirically dense social analyses. The model and mode of analysis adopted by Foucault is typical of the approach of most of the theorists examined in this book and using the model of changes in emotional regimes as the framework of analysis the book provides theoretical analysis and detailed historical examples.

Chapter 3: Narratives of Romantic Love:

Chapter 3 addresses the concept of romantic love and its manifestation in "courtly love". The history of romantic love is a fundamentally Western historical narrative and its roots can be found in European cultural history. Its origination is in Western cultural practices, typically the narratives of "courtly love" which was represented in verse in the eleventh and twelfth centuries. The use of the term "courtly love" can be traced to 1883 "when the French medievalist Gaston Paris [used it] . . . to characterize the passionate love uniting Lancelot and Guenievere in Chretien do Troyes's twelfth-century verse romance in Old French, *Lancelot ou le chevalier de la charrette*" (Burns 2001: 28 cited in Gross 2005: 303). This chapter explores narratives of romantic love, as captured in eleventh and twelfth century verse and in romantic tales as articulated in "courtly love". It also considers romantic love in the eighteenth and nineteenth centuries where there was an attempt to recast these narratives within the bourgeois family as "marital love".

Chapter 4: "Mapping Intimacy through Sex in Twentieth Century Colonial Cultures": The Work of Laura Ann Stoler and Anne McClintock

One of the foremost documenters of the relationship between intimacy, sex and colonial cultures is Laura Ann Stoler. Stoler (1997, 2002, 2006) has addressed issues of "the personal and political in emotional regimes" across a range of work.

Her work maps intimacy through sex in twentieth century colonial cultures and draws on gender, race and class in explaining the relationship between "carnal knowledge and imperial power". Stoler (2002: 14) comments on the relationship as follows: "[this perspective] takes up the intimate from yet another perspective: it treats sexual matters not as a metaphor for colonial inequities but as foundational to the material terms in which colonial projects were carried out." This chapter charts Stoler's work across a range of concepts and contributions to the epistemological framework around intimacy in the history of emotions.

In addition this chapter explores the work of Anne McClintock across a number of her key texts including *Imperial Leather* (1995) and *Dangerous Liaisons* (1997). McClintock's work provides an analysis of epistemologies of intimacy across discourses of race, gender and sexuality in colonial and post-colonial contexts. Her work brings together discourses of psychoanalysis, as well as feminism, nationalism and hybridity. Her work offers a range of conceptual frameworks for analysis of historical discourses around intimacy, power and desire.

Chapter 5: Love and Intimacy in Late Modernity: The Transformation of Intimacy

Late modernity—has witnessed an upsurge in epistemologies which attempt to explain how intimacy has changed in Western societies. Most have their etymology in sociological debate which maintain there has been a decoupling of intimacy and marriage/reproduction as traditionally understood. This chapter explores a range of theories incorporated within a broader epistemological framework, and while they have aspects in common, have taken different approaches: including "a liberalization of attitudes tied to globalization" (Giddens 1992); an emphasis on the individualised nature of intimacy (Beck and Beck-Gernsheim 1996); and how intimacy is structured by its encounters with late capitalism (Hochschild 2003, Illouz 1997, Kipnis 2003). The key concept all these theories have in common is an image of intimacy in late modernity which they call "detraditionalized", compared to 50 or 100 years ago. Changes in patterns of intimacy had occurred in urban centres in particular, concerning new images of love and eroticism, coming from philosophers, artists, writers and others from the middle of the nineteenth century, and had liberated intimacy from traditional frameworks making romantic love a more significant element of relationships (du Gay 1986, Laslett 1977, Shorter 1975). This chapter explores a wide range of debates which have characterised the epistemological frameworks defining intimacy identity and reflexivity in late modernity.

Chapter 6: "The Intelligence of Emotions": Intimacy, Emotions and the "Turn to Affect" —Feminist Interventions

The chapter looks at very recent interventions by a range of feminist and other contemporary theorists of "the turn to affect" in the humanities and social sciences. This major body of work explores a wide range of theories which can be captured in the epistemological shift in thinking around emotions, feelings and affect. These debates reflect the broader emphasis on the "emotionalisation of society" and how there is a "perceived growth in the range and intensity of emotions and emotional expressions in the public sphere" (Swan 2008). Affective frameworks have been shown (above) to be central in both feminist and post-colonial analyses as well as significant in issues of identity, nationhood and migration. This chapter reviews contemporary feminist theoretical debates and analyses how the "turn to affect" and the analysis of intimacy and emotions is defining a more dynamic set of relationships and discourses around emotions.

The intervention of feminist theory into narratives around the emotions has led to a deepening of the theoretical interest in emotion and affect which is now well established as "the affective turn". Cvetkovich (2003: 133) maintains that " 'the affective turn' . . . represents an intensification of interest in 'emotions, feelings and affect as objects of scholarly inquiry'." Greco and Stenner (2008: 5) indicate the importance in this development of a shift away from an emphasis on the superiority of " 'detached reason' and 'objective observation' to an emphasis on 'the emotional and the subjective'."

As shown below many feminist theorists have made political interventions into both theoretical and empirical methodological analysis. Arlie Hochschild (1983, 2003) has worked on addressing the intersection of the emotional and the structural. Drawing on rich streams of sociological theory such as interactionism and social constructionism, she has addressed this relationship over a range of work. Her work has contributed significantly to the social construction of emotions and explored the relationship of gendered, classed and sexualised relations of power in concepts such as "emotional labour" and "feeling rules" which have embedded the study of emotions into mainstream sociological theory. Hochschild's work across a wide range of areas also established the relationship between emotion, capitalism and neoliberalism, in particular her focus on the commercialisation of intimate life (Hochschild 2003), as well as encouraging the development of concepts such as "affective labour" as articulated further in the work of Adkins (2002), among others.

Eva Illouz's (1997, 2012) work is also concerned with how intimacy is structured by its relationship to late capitalism, in particular the relationship between romance and consumption. More recently, Illouz focuses on love in contemporary relationships and she investigates how it is shaped by the nature of relational and institutional arrangements and is critical of the cultural context of emotions in contemporary society.

Feminist theorists share with social theorists more broadly a focus on the ideologicalisation of intimacy in the course of the development of the twentieth and twenty-first centuries. What these theorists share is a focus on shifting values away from traditional conceptions of the bourgeois family. These theorists confirm patterns of detraditionalisation in late modernity and also confirm the central theme of this book which is a fundamental incompatibility between intimacy and traditional normative, heterosexual structures of marriage and the family.

Chapter 7: Intimacy, Emotions and the Public Sphere: From Sentimental Ideology to "The Queen of America" —The Public and the Private in the Work of Lauren Berlant

Chapter 6 focused on the shift in emphasis within feminist theorizing towards the "turn to affect", Chapter 7 reflects further on these debates. The shift among a range of feminist, cultural and social theorists has been to focus on "affect" and the work of contemporary theorists such as Sara Ahmed (2004), Laura Berlant (2000), Teresa Brennan (2004), Clough and Halley (2007), Gregg and Seigworth (2010) and Stoler (2006) among others, all focus on the development of theoretical perspectives on emotion and affect towards a deepening in understanding of these concepts. All have introduced a range of concepts and explored different empirical fields of research which have used frameworks drawing on affect and intimacy.

Chapter 7 focuses on one of the most groundbreaking and innovative theorists in the field—Lauren Berlant. Berlant's (1997, 2000, 2011) work on intimacy and affect focuses on the intrusion of the private into the public by showing how sexual practices which do not subscribe to a normative framework can be seen as a threat to established values, including traditional family values and heterosexuality. This chapter analyses Berlant's contribution to this area and to her work on the relationship between intimacy and therapy. Her work highlights how the concept of therapy has been taken to an extreme in U.S. society and shapes the relationship of emotion and the public sphere. Berlant (2010: 116), like other feminist theorists is interested in how emotion and affect can lead to transformation and change, although she is aware that changes on the personal level do not directly impact structural transformation.

Bibliography

Adkins, Lisa. 2002. *Revisions: Gender and Sexuality in Late Modernity*. Buckingham: Open University Press.
Ahmed, Sara. 2004. *The Cultural Politics of Emotion*. Edinburgh: The University of Edinburgh Press.
Beck, Ulrich and Elizabeth Beck-Gernsheim. 1996. *The Normal Chaos of Love*. Trans. M. Ritter and J. Weibel. Cambridge: Polity Press.
Berlant, Lauren. 1997. *The Queen of America Goes to Washington City: Essays on Sex and Citizenship*. Durham, NC: Duke University Press.
Berlant, Lauren (ed.). 2000. *Intimacy*. Chicago: University of Chicago Press.
Berlant, Lauren. 2010. "Cruel Optimism." In Melisssa Gregg and Greg Seigworth (eds), *The Affect Theory Reader*. Durham, NC: Duke University Press.
Berlant, Lauren. 2011. *Cruel Optimism*. Durham, NC: Duke University Press.
Brennan, Teresa. 2004. *The Transmission of Affect*. New York: University of Cornell Press.
Burns, E. Jane. 2001. "Courtly Love: Who Needs It? Recent Feminist Work in the Medieval French Tradition" *Signs* 27: 23–58.
Cancian, Francesca M. 1987. *Love in America: Gender and Self-Development*. New York: Cambridge University Press.

Capellanus, Andreus. 1941. *The Art of Courtly Love*. John Jay Parry (ed.). New York: Columbia University Press.
Clough, Patricia and Jean Halley. 2007. *The Affective Turn: Theorizing the Social*. Durham: Duke University Press.
Cvetkovich, Ann. 2003. *An Archive of Feeling: Trauma, Sexuality and Lesbian Public Cultures*. Durham, NC: Duke University Press.
De Rougemont, Denis. 1983/1956. *Love in the Western World*, rev. ed. Trans. Belgion Montgomery. Princeton, NJ: Princeton University Press.
Duby, George (ed.). 1988. *A History of Private Life, Vol. 2, Revelations of the Medieval World*. Trans. Arthur Goldhammer. Cambridge, MA: Harvard University Press.
Du Gay, Paul. 1986. *The Bourgeois Experience, Victoria to Freud, Volume 2: The Tender Passion*. New York: Oxford University Press.
Foucault, Michel. 1978. *The History of Sexuality, Volume 1: An Introduction*. New York: Vintage.
Giddens, Anthony. 1992. *The Transformation of Intimacy: Sexuality, Love and Eroticism in Modern Societies*. Stanford, CA: Stanford University Press.
Giddens, Anthony and Christopher Pierson. 1998. *Conversations with Anthony Giddens: Making Sense of Modernity*. Stanford, CA: Stanford University Press.
Greco, Monica and Paul Stenner (eds). 2008. *Emotions: A Social Science Reader*. London: Routledge.
Gregg, Melissa and Greg Seigworth. 2010. *The Affect Theory Reader*. Durham, NC: Duke University Press.
Gross, Neil. 2005. "The Detraditionalization of Intimacy Reconsidered" *Sociological Theory* 23(3): 286–311.
Hochschild, Arlie. R. 1983. *The Managed Heart: Commercialization of Human Feeling*. Berkeley: University of California Press.
Hochschild, Arlie, R. 2003. *The Commercialization of Intimate Life*. Berkeley: University of California Press.
Illouz, Eva. 1997. *Consuming the Romantic Utopia: Love and the Cultural Contradictions of Capitalism*. Cambridge: Cambridge University Press.
Illouz, Eva. 2012. *Why Love Hurts: A Sociological Explanation*. Cambridge: Polity.
Jamieson, Lynn.1998. *Intimacy, Personal Relationships in Modern Society*. Cambridge: Polity.
Kipnis, Laura. 2003. *Against Love: A Polemic*. New York: Pantheon.
Laslett, Peter. 1977. *Family Life and Illicit Love in Earlier Generations*. Cambridge: Cambridge University Press.
Luhmann, Niklas. 1986. *Love as Passion: The Codification of Intimacy*. Trans. Jeremy Gains and Doris. L. Jones. Cambridge, MA: Harvard University Press.
McClintock, Anne. 1995. *Imperial Leather: Race, Gender and Sexuality in the Colonial Contest*. New York and London: Routledge.
McClintock, Anne. 1997. "No Longer in a Future Heaven: Gender, Race and Nationalism." In A. McClintock, A. Mufti and E. Shohat (eds), *Dangerous Liaisons: Gender, Nation and Postcolonial Perspectives*. Minneapolis: University of Minnesota Press, 89–112.
Reddy, William. 2001. *The Navigation of Feeling: A Framework for the History of Emotions*. Cambridge: Cambridge University Press.
Shorter, Ella. 1975. *The Making of the Modern Family*. New York: Basic Books.
Shumway, David. R. 2003. *Modern Love: Romance, Intimacy and the Marriage Crisis*. New York and London: New York University Press.

Somers, Margaret. 2008. *Genealogies of Citizenship*. Cambridge: Cambridge University Press.
Stoler, Laura, A. 1997. "Making Empire Respectable: The Politics of Race and Sexual Morality in Twentieth Century Colonial Cultures." In A. McClintock, A. Mufti and E. Shohat (eds), *Dangerous Liaisons: Gender, Nation and Postcolonial Perspectives*. London and Minneapolis: University of Minnesota Press, 344–373.
Stoler, Laura Ann. 2002. *Carnal Knowledge and Imperial Power. Race and the Intimate in Colonial Rule*. Berkeley: University of California Press.
Stoler, Laura Ann. 2006. *Haunted by Empire: Geographies of Intimacy in North American History*. Durham, NC: Duke University Press.
Stone, Lawrence. 1977. *The Family, Sex and Marriage in England, 1500–1800*. New York: Harper and Row.
Stone, Lawrence. 1988. "Passionate Attachment in the West in Historical Perspective." In William Gaylin and Ethel Person (eds), *Passionate Attachments: Thinking about Love*. New York: Free Press.
Swan, Elizabeth. 2008. "You Make Me Feel Like a Woman: Therapeutic Cultures and the Contagion of Femininity" *Gender Work and Organization* 15(1): 88–107.
Swidler, Anne. 2001. *Talk of Love: How Culture Matters*. Chicago: The University of Chicago.

1 Genealogies of Emotions, Intimacy and Desire

Theories of Changes in Emotional Regimes from Medieval Society to Late Modernity

Introduction

This chapter investigates epistemologies which attempt to explain changes in emotional regimes from medieval society to late modernity. In particular, it explores the role of intimacy as a driver of emotions and involves a systematic study of key conceptual frameworks or epistemologies developed by theorists in understanding the relationship between emotional styles and historical change. Key in this debate is the concept of intimacy. The chapter considers the concept of "genealogy" and focuses on the relevance of genealogy as a methodology to assess historical change as used by Foucault. I use the concept of "genealogy" as a framework for assessing historical change through intimacy and sexuality as used by Michel Foucault (1978) in the volumes of his book, *The History of Sexuality, Volume 1: An Introduction*. The chapter explores changes in emotional regimes and includes an understanding of intimacy, sexuality and desire as fundamentally embedded in discourses of emotion. As Stoler (2002: 9) comments: ". . . the notion of the 'intimate' is a descriptive marker of the familiar and the essential and of relations grounded in sex." Beyond Foucault, the chapter examines intimacy as a "driver" of emotional change in different historical periods from medieval society to late modernity. The chapter also focuses on "courtly love" in the eleventh and twelfth centuries as well as intimacy within the bourgeois family of the eighteenth and nineteenth centuries. The relationship between intimacy and sex in the context of colonial cultures is also explored as well as changes in the nature of intimacy and the growth of reflexivity in late modernity. I show how different historical periods are characterised by emotional regimes where intimacy, sexuality and desire existed outside marriage and that marriage and intimacy are incompatible in the history of emotions.

1. Foucault's Genealogy of Sexuality

In this chapter, I consider the concept of "genealogy" as a methodology to assess historical change as used by Michel Foucault. Foucault viewed genealogy as "anti-science" and he called his alternative to a scientific vision of human studies, "genealogy". In doing so he rejected much of the Enlightenment historical vision, including: "the quest to liberate humanity through uncovering the laws of social order and change and the appeal to grand theory as providing a standpoint from which to prescribe a program of social reconstruction" (Seidman 1998: 233). Foucault maintained that it was the configuration of power and knowledge which had been submerged by the scientific emphasis on grand theory, drawn from the Enlightenment, which was the key dimension of genealogy. In the volumes of *The History of Sexuality, Volume 1: An Introduction*, Foucault adopted two strategies of argumentation which are pertinent to this book: firstly he hoped to make us aware of the nature of intimacy and the historically unique character of modern sexual culture; secondly he offered an alternative perspective on the history of sexuality.

The History of Sexuality, Volume 1: An Introduction, consists of critical historical studies and illustrates "Foucault's idea of genealogical social analysis by outlining the social context, purpose, logic, and political implications of this project" (Seidman 1998: 236). Through detailed examples from the Middle Ages onwards, Foucault showed how intimacy and sex were the focus of much that influenced historical change. Foucault offered historically rich, empirically dense social analyses and some of the examples are considered here. In pursuing this form of social analysis Foucault breaks with the pattern previously established in the social sciences of excavating so called "laws of social behaviour" and by explaining individual behaviour within these laws. This had been part of the evolution of theorising in the social science through the work of Marx, Habermas, and Durkheim among others. Historical detail in the work of these and other theorists was not significant in terms of the micro-politics of individual behaviour, but was incorporated into grand models of social change. Such grand schemes of social change provided a rhetoric for the growth of social movements but avoided any references to the complexity of history in the mapping of social change. This was of course necessary to provide a clear utopian vision. Foucault, by contrast: "intended genealogy to recover the knowledges and the lives of those who gave voice to them that have been excluded for the purposes of deploying them in current social struggles" (Seidman 1998: 235).

Foucault's purpose in the volumes of *The History of Sexuality, Volume 1: An Introduction*, was to undermine the presumption of the universality of the modern system of sexuality. He did this by examining the intimate culture of ancient Greek and by showing that "Greek city states represented a different universe of sexual meaning from modernity" (Seidman 1998: 235). Foucault showed that Greek culture was centred around "pleasures" which included not only sex, but eating, exercise and marriage. However, as Foucault shows, enjoying pleasures needed to be indulged in with moderation and was directly related to social status.

> For example, adult free men were expected to be active in sexual exchanges, while the subordinate social status of women, slaves, and boys

required them to be sexually passive. Disapproval was not attached to particular sex acts or to a particular gender preference but to individuals who were immoderate in their pleasures or abandoned their appropriate role.

(Seidman 1998: 238)

In addition to the relationship between sex and status, Foucault also showed that there were significant differences in the meaning of homosexuality between ancient Greek culture and modern culture. The man/boy love in ancient Greek culture was viewed as a natural part of a range of relationships of intimacy within Greek culture. Foucault maintained that the Greeks did not define sexual desires as naturally divided between the same and opposing sexes, for example, adult free men were routinely expected to have boy lovers and to be married. However, in ancient Greece, intimacy between men and boys was not an alternative to marriage and there was no stigma or deviance associated with love between men and boys. It was not a situation of homosexuality or heterosexuality, there was simply "pleasure", which could be defined in a wide range of arenas. However, there were regulations as only free adult males could take boys as their lovers, but could not take other free adult males as lovers.

Love within marriage could exist in ancient Greece, and Foucault described "the emergence of a new ideal of an equal, intimate and sexual conjugal bond" (Seidman 1998: 239), however marriage was primarily organised around social obligations concerned with the management of the household. "Ideal love" was the love experienced in the intimate relationships between free adult men and boys, outside of marriage. Thus intimacy and eroticism primarily existed outside marriage.

Foucault defined the shift in ancient Greece to a "marriage-centred culture" as marking the turning point in Western society, very much as later theorists defined changes in the nature of intimacy in late modernity (see below). Foucault claims that sex was emerging as a domain around which regulations and prohibitions were emerging. He shows that non-marital sex was becoming a source of suspicion and social deviance, which he lamented.

Foucault saw the modern regime of sexuality as an example of the disciplining of sexual subjects and positioning them as objects of social control. He maintained that social control was built into the very regime of sexuality and how the norm of a "healthy fulfilled sexual life" defined social identities. In other words: "Foucault described a system of social control that operates less by coercion and repression than by the very cultural meanings and self-identities that it produces" (Seidman 1998: 241–242).

Foucault was a critic of the regime of sexuality throughout his life and lived largely outside the conventional model of sexuality. He maintained that the dominant regime of sexuality restricted sexuality to narrowly defined sexual pleasures, which forced individuals into limited identities and created stigmatised deviant populations. In other words, the regime of sexuality for Foucault acts to marginalise homosexuality and has defined a hegemonic framework for sexuality and marriage. However, Foucault never developed fully his vision of an alternative intimate culture.

2. Narratives of Romantic Love

The notion of "ideal love" which appears in Foucault's analysis of ancient Greece is one which as stated existed outside of marriage. This can also be seen in the concept of romantic love and its manifestation in "courtly love". The history of romantic love is a fundamentally Western historical narrative and its roots can be found in European cultural history. Its origination is in Western cultural practices, typically the narratives of "courtly love" which was represented in verse in the eleventh and twelfth centuries (see Bloch 1992, Duby 1994). The use of the term "courtly love" can be traced to 1883 "when the French medievalist Gaston Paris [used it] . . . to characterize the passionate love uniting Lancelot and Guenievere in Chretien de Troyes's twelfth-century verse romance in Old French, *Lancelot ou le chevalier de la charrette*" (Burns 2001: 28 cited in Gross 2005: 303). Swidler (2001: 112) maintains that in courtly poetry, love became seen as an "ennobling passion" rather than a "dangerous appetite" familiar to Greeks and Romans. Love from this perspective was seen as transformative of the self, encouraging the creation of "virtuous" and "noble" characters.

Whether we can describe narratives of romantic love with their expression in "courtly love" as an epistemology is not clear. Even if we treat them collectively as a single genre form, narratives of romantic love, as captured in eleventh and twelfth century verse and in romantic tales as articulated in "courtly love", can we argue that they constitute an epistemology? Unlikely if we wish to subject an epistemology to some type of empirical testing be it theoretical or other. Romantic love has traditionally been understood as on the side of erotic rather than marital love, where knights and other noblemen proclaimed their love for married noblewomen who regularly became involved in erotic love and extra-marital affairs which were generally but not always consummated. Swidler (2001: 112) observes that in order to understand the inner dynamics of romantic love, it is useful to trace its origins in European cultural history. She argues that there is general agreement among scholars that courtly love poetry, which emerged in Europe at the end of the eleventh century, created a significant new vision of love, self and society, which remained the code of the European nobility for centuries. The character of romantic love framed as "courtly love" and desire were both "idealized and sacrilized" (Gross 2005: 303), but in all these romantic love narratives, romantic love was not understood as marital love, and did not thrive within marriage.

In the eighteenth and nineteenth centuries there was an attempt to recast these narratives within the bourgeois family as "marital love". However, romantic love was generally not seen as a respectable basis for marriage within bourgeois society. While there was some choice in terms of marital partners, marriage was a social and economic relationship. However in the eighteenth century a certain amount of sentimentality entered into definitions of love and marriage in the West and the "ideal marriage" came to be redefined as one where the bride and groom loved one another. Some have argued that this was purely a middle-class response to the aristocratic critique of the bourgeois marriage as "cold" and "emotionless" but others see it as a result of cultural change and the redefining of emotions. Regardless of the reasons, the bourgeois culture of English capitalism began to redefine the narrative. Thus, as Swidler (2001: 112) notes:

> ... the courtly ideal of love comes to us reshaped by the bourgeois culture of early English capitalism ... [this] took its quintessential form in the eighteenth-century English novel. The writers and publishers who created the novel form courted a newly literate, middle-class reading public and sold their wares in a new kind of cut-throat literary market. Both readers and writers were steeped in the individualism of the world's most capitalist and Protestant nation. Love became the focal myth of that individualism.

More generally, marriage was seen as the lynchpin linking broader questions of class, mobility and money to issues of intimacy and individualism, and could symbolise "the new middle-class concern with individual merit and achievement" (Swidler 1980: 123).

Thus romantic love was a cultural creation, a mythology, created by literary groups framed by cultural practices and adopted by the bourgeoise to apply to bourgeois marriage in order to establish itself as a counterpoint to the aristocracy as a status group, but it cannot be seen as fundamentally embedded as an epistemology which explains intimacy in anything but the most superficial way. Perhaps nothing articulates the redundancy of romantic love as having social and historical relevance other than as a mythology, more than an analysis of intimacy in colonial cultures.

3. "Mapping Intimacy through Sex in Twentieth Century Colonial Cultures"

One of the foremost documenters of the relationship between intimacy, sex and colonial cultures is Laura Ann Stoler. Stoler (1997, 2002, 2006) has addressed issues of "the personal and political in emotional regimes" across a range of work. Her work maps intimacy through sex in twentieth century colonial cultures and draws on gender, race and class in explaining the relationship between "carnal knowledge and imperial power". Stoler (2002: 14) comments on the relationship as follows: "[this perspective] takes up the intimate from yet another perspective: it treats sexual matters not as a metaphor for colonial inequities but as foundational to the material terms in which colonial projects were carried out."

Additionally it also focuses on: (i) "the relationship between power and sexuality, between colonial technologies of rule and the management of sex" (Stoler 2002: 18); (ii) regards the "domesticating strategies of empire and considers 'the affective' as a 'charged political domain'" (Stoler 2002: 18); and (iii) [leads] "to a broader etymology of the 'carnal' that includes the sensual and affective passion and compassion, and the unsanctioned and the flesh" (Stoler 2002: 18). There are interesting comparisons between the way Foucault and Stoler analyse the relationship between sex and power, and in their assessment of race and power (see Chapter 2). While recognising the contribution of Foucault's analysis and drawing on his genealogy of race, Stoler critiques "Foucault's history of the carnal" and while acknowledging the methodological insights offered by "Foucault's histories of racial discourse and biopower" (Stoler 2002: 19), she seeks to link micro- and macropolitics in colonial cultures by raising the question: ". . . how and why [do] microsites of familiar and intimate space figure so prominently in the macro-politics of imperial rule" (Stoler 2002: 19). While an extensive analysis of Foucault's concept of "biopolitics" is beyond the scope of this chapter and indeed this book, essentially the focus on the micro operation of power as outlined by Foucault, gives the ability to analyse the network of power relations operating through intimacy and to understand these within the context of a broader structural spectrum of power within colonial relations. In understanding relations of power expressed through intimacy, Foucault's concept of "biopower" is useful in understanding power at the level of the individual and of sex, much like the operation of repression was explored in the work of Norbert Elias and Freud. As Stoler (2006: 16) comments: "Because expressions of intimacy are so implicated in the exercise of power, they provide strategic nodes of comparison, unevenly laced with state effects." A broader analysis of Foucault is explored more fully in Chapter 2.

A number of key issues are raised by Stoler (1997, 2002) concerning the centrality of intimacy and sex in colonial cultures: (i) intimacy in colonial cultures revolved around the issue of European manhood and "a moral panic" concerning the need to define heterosexual normativity in carnal relations; (ii) that intimacy took the form of "forced and financed arrangements of domestic and sexual service by housekeepers kept as live-in lovers and live-in maids whose children were fathered by their European employers" (Stoler 2002: 2); (iii) that heterosexual unions based on concubinage and prostitution acted to offset homosexual carnal relations between men; (iv) that the public and private are inextricably intersecting discourses in mapping intimacy; and finally (v) that underpinning these debates are the "racial and sexual politics of empire" (Stoler 2002: 9).

On the issue of intimacy *vis-à-vis* sexual protocols in nineteenth century Europe, Hyam (1986) suggests that imperial expansion equated in metaphorical terms with the "export of male sexual energy". This follows Said's (1979) view of *Orientalism* where he maintained that sexual submission and possession of "Oriental" women by European men provided the discourse where Orientalism was described as "a male power fantasy" and "an exclusively male province" (Said 1979: 207). As Stoler (1997: 346) notes: "sexual domination has figured as a social metaphor of European supremacy". Ming (1983) has observed that concubinage in the Indies' between 1887–1920 covered a range of situations of cohabitation outside marriage between European men and Asian women and "served colonial interests in a number of ways. It permitted permanent settlement and rapid growth by a cheaper means than the importation of European women . . . Nearly half of the Indies' European male population in the 1880s were unmarried and living with Asian women" (cited in Stoler 2002: 48).

Concubinage covered a range of domestic and sexual services arrangements which European men expected of non-European women in colonial cultures, who were often exchanged among European men and passed on when men left. This has parallels with the situation of women slaves in the pre-Civil War southern states in the United States. Elsewhere Stoler (1997: 347) describes the "domestic politics of colonialism" where "the regulation of sexual relations was central to the development of particular kinds of colonial settlements and the allocation of economic activity within them . . .".

In discussing the management of domestic and sexual relations in colonised South-East Asia, Stoler (1997: 348) shows how concubinage could be distinguished from prostitution:

> Referred to as *nyai* in Java and Sumatra, *congai* in Indochina, and *petite epouse* throughout the French empire, the colonized woman living as a concubine to a European man formed the dominant domestic arrangement in colonial cultures through the early twentieth century. Unlike prostitution, which could and often did result in a population of syphilitic and therefore non-productive European men, concubinage was considered to have a stabilizing effect on political order and colonial health- a relationship that kept men in their barracks and bungalows and out of the brothels, and less inclined to peverse liasions with one another.

Pollman's (1986) research amplifies the nature of domestic and sexual service within concubinage. Pollman shows that these roles carried a range of meanings of a sexual and domestic nature. The exact nature of the relationship depended, says Pollman, on the character of the individuals and on the prosperity of the European man. The reality of concubinage as Pollman (1986: 100) notes, was that colonised women lived in "abjectly subordinate contexts of slave or 'coolie' and lived in separate quarters and had few legal rights; they could be dismissed at any time without reason or notice and were exchanged between different employers and most significantly, as stipulated in the Indies Civil Code of 1848, they could not exercise any rights over the children emerging from concubinage".

While concubinage provided stability in maintaining the emphasis on heterosexual normativity in relationships and discouraged promiscuity at least in theory, there were problems:

> Grossly uneven sex ratios on North Sumatran estates made for intense competition among male workers and their European supervisors, with *vrouwen peraka* (disputes over women) resulting in assaults on whites, new labor tensions, and dangerous incursions into the standards deemed essential for white prestige.
>
> (Stoler 1985a: 33)

While concubinage provided stability for heterosexual relationships and acted to stop the development of homosexual relationships, it is unclear whether the potential for homosexuality was between European and native men or between European men. However, the really significant intervention came from European-born women who entered colonial communities.

European women brought a combination of racism to the colonies in relation to their attitude towards native women and men, as well as acting as moral "gatekeepers" for relationships with European men. Stoler (2002: 71) comments that European women acted to safeguard European men from "cultural and sexual contamination," the emphasis of the "'petit bourgeois" European women was to encourage men to concentrate on "hard work and physical exercise rather than sexual release" (Stoler 2002: 71). She shows that discourses around the role of European women were contradictory, on the one hand they were insecure and jealous of the sexual liaisons of European men with native women but more likely, as Kennedy (1947: 164) notes: "it was . . . plain feminine scandalization at free and easy sex relations" that led to their response. More generally the arrival of European women redefined colonial culture and relationships in terms of race and class. As Stoler (1997: 351) observes : "the material culture of French settlements in Saigon, outposts in New Guinea, and estate complexes in Sumatra was retailored to accommodate the physical and moral requirements of a middle-class and respectable feminine contingent . . .".

The implications of these changes was the decline of concubinage, but as Stoler recognises, this was not the direct result of European women's opposition but was linked to broader changes in the realignment of colonial cultures. Stoler (2002: 68) claims that: "Concubinage became the source of individual breakdown, racial degeneration and political unrest". The fallout of concubinage was the children, and while some men legally acknowledged their children, many returned to Holland, Britain and France and gave no support to mother and children. Children born of these unions [of concubinage] . . . were . . . physically marked and morally marred with 'the defaults and mediocre qualities of their [native] mothers'" (Stoler 1997: 360).

While native men, were legally punished for alleged sexual assault, European women were frequently seen as provocative in this process and provoking those desires. There were political dimensions to the attitudes to native men as Stoler (1997: 353) notes that in the late 1920s, there were labour protests by Indonesian workers and "Sumatra's corporate elite expanded their vigilante organizations, intelligence networks, and demands for police protection to ensure their women were safe and their workers 'in hand'" (Stoler 1985b).

Beyond the implied racism associated with the sexuality of native women was the racism associated with the sexuality of colonised men who were seen as posing a sexual threat to European women. Strobel (1987: 379) maintains that European women needed protection because men of color had "primitive" sexual urges and "uncontrollable lust", aroused by the sight of white women.

In the end, intimacy, sex and desire within colonial cultures can be understood as an epistemology which "mapped intimacy through sex" and was underpinned by race, class and gender captured in the following comment by Stoler (2002: 78): "Sex in the colonies had to do with sexual access and reproduction, class distinctions and racial demarcation, nationalism and European identity in different measure and not all at the same time."

Foucault, Sex and Power

Foucault's work on the relationship between sexuality and power offers a number of possibilities in developing new genealogies of the colonial. In *The History of Sexuality, Volume 1: An Introduction* (1978: 3) Foucault claims that sexual discourse is not opposed to and subversive of power but a "dense transfer point of it. . .". As has been shown above, sexuality was the pivotal point of intimacy and power and defined colonial identities along racial, gendered and class lines. As has been shown colonial subjects were classified and categorised along lines of coloniser and colonised. The significant contribution of Foucault to the debate is that he wrote a history of Western desire and sexuality which rejected biological explanations for sexual drives and ties an analysis of sexuality to explanations which highlight imperial power through classification and categorisation of colonial subjects.

Additionally, Foucault's contribution in *The History of Sexuality, Volume 1: An Introduction* which addresses discourses of imperialism, has been in the main ignored, in particular his linking of the history of sexuality to the construction of race. This dimension of Foucault's work which addresses race is part of his wider conception of power as micro rather than being part of the state's macro-power. "In Foucault's genealogy, racial discourse was a part of the technologies of sex that arose in the eighteenth century to regulate sexual conduct and by which populations could be expanded and controlled" (Stoler 2002: 149).

As Foucault (1978: 47) comments of this regulation, it was a discourse which managed sex by lodging desire in the home, as he puts it, that "tiny sexually saturated, familial space". Sex in the colonial context is described by Sommer (1990: 87) as "unproductive eroticism" and as not only "immoral" but as "unpatriotic". While there are significant differences between Foucault's and Stoler's position on the significance of race as underpinning colonial genealogies, both agree that sexual cravings are a social construct, with Stoler (2002) contrasting native men of passion whose "carnal appetites" needed to be "policed" and bourgeois men of character who could indulge their sexual appetites but essentially retained their bourgeois sensibility and white women displaying no sexuality compared to colonised women who were seen to lead to degeneracy because of their sexuality (see Chapter 3).

4. Intimacy in Late Modernity: Reflexivity and Detraditionalisation

Late modernity—has witnessed an upsurge in epistemologies which attempt to explain how intimacy has changed in Western societies. Most have their etymology in sociological debate which maintain there has been a decoupling of intimacy and reproduction as traditionally understood. A range of theories can be incorporated within a broader epistemological framework, and while they have aspects in common, have taken different approaches: including: "a liberalization of attitudes" tied to globalisation (Giddens 1992); an emphasis on the individualised nature of intimacy (Beck and Beck-Gernsheim 1996); and how intimacy is structured by its encounters with late capitalism (Hochschild 2003, Illouz 1997, Kipnis 2003). The key concept all these perspectives have in common is an image of intimacy in late modernity which is "detraditionalized," compared to 50 or 100 years ago. Changes in patterns of intimacy occurred in urban centres in particular, concerning new images of love and eroticism, coming from philosophers, artists, writers and others from the middle of the nineteenth century and had liberated intimacy from traditional frameworks making romantic love a more significant element of relationships (du Gay 1986, Laslett 1977, Shorter 1975).

In discussing the "detraditional" we mean the abandonment of traditional patterns of intimacy including: lifelong heterosexual marriage as the primary framework for the establishment of relationships, and for the procreation and raising of children; male dominance within heterosexual households; and marriage as opposed to cohabitation. Sexual intimacy has been redefined in late modernity with relationships following different trends including: serial monogamy, cohabitation, non-marital child bearing (Amato and Booth 1997, Musick 2002), same-sex relationships and marriage (Seidman 2002). In addition, divorce rates have risen to 50 per cent in many countries (43 per cent for Canada, 46 per cent for the U.S. and Australia, 55 per cent for Sweden, 43 per cent for the UK and 16.5 per cent same sex marriages in Canada), and single parenthood, remarriage and "blended families" (Amato 2000) are now much more the norm. There are three broad theoretical areas within the wider epistemological framework as follows:

(i) Intimacy and Globalisation

One of the most influential theories to emerge which analysed changes in intimacy in late modernity was put forward by Anthony Giddens (1992) in his book *The Transformation of Intimacy: Sexuality, Love and Eroticism in Modern Societies* (1992) which provides the most comprehensive analysis of the relationship between traditional normative patterns, values and intimacy as he notes: " . . . the past is not preserved but continuously reconstructed on the basis of the present" (Giddens 1992: 291–292).

For Giddens "detraditionalization" does not mean a different epistemological emphasis, it is not simply about the influence of nineteenth and twentieth century socio-economic movements such as urbanisation, democratisation, industrialisation but involves a fundamental intervention of political, economic and cultural values into individual lives. Giddens draws on the growth of overarching structural frameworks such as the modern nation-state and the emergence of global capitalism to explain the significant qualitative shift in the coordination of societal activity.

In late modernity, Giddens sees tradition as being "swept away". In this phase globalisation, increasing prosperity resulting from capitalism, gives both societies and individuals the opportunity for increasing reflexivity, a process which Giddens calls "reflexive modernization". The release from traditionalism, Giddens states, gives individual actors the capacity to exercise creative intelligence and to rely less on traditional relationship patterns. A good example of this is the move globally to same-sex marriage and how this is now being recognised in legislation in countries such as the U.S., Canada, Ireland, UK, Australia and elsewhere. The underpinnings of this epistemology is that intimacy and sex—and how and where they operate—is framed by the idea of reflexivity which establishes new patterns of intimacy outside of traditional marriage.

Giddens (1992) describes late twentieth century processes of social change which involve a process of transformation in the nature of self-identity and intimacy. In drawing together identity and intimacy, Giddens shows how structural factors and individual responses are inextricably interconnected. Giddens makes the case for the transformation of relations of intimacy within traditional heterosexual relationships and maintains there is now greater equality within relationships. He outlines what he describes as a transformation in the basis of relationships and of intimacy, to what he describes as a concept of "a pure relationship" where sexuality and intimacy are tied together. Within the transformation process, Giddens raises the possibility of equality and intimacy in personal life as manifestations of the democratising of gender relationships.

The type of intimacy involved in the "pure relationship" necessarily requires equality between individuals in the relationship. "The pure relationship" which is a result of a relationship characterised by democratic principles is matched by a pattern of sexuality which Giddens calls "plastic sexuality", is a form of sexuality which is free from conventional definitions. For Giddens "a revolution in female sexual autonomy" is an aspect of this, with women finding sexual pleasure in ways which are not dictated by men, and in addition the growth of homosexuality is another area.

The causes of these changes in the nature of relationships and patterns of sexuality comes from the nature of social change itself in late modernity. These produce changes in individuals in terms of their processes of reflexivity cultivating changes in identity and impacting on their relationships. As Giddens notes, in the conditions of the late twentieth century, personal relationships are the key site in which women and men find "forms of self-exploration" (Giddens 1992: 144). Giddens does recognise that "the pure relationship" because of its intensity is characterised by internal tension. For Giddens this is seen as important in the openness and intimacy of this new set of relationships. Other social theorists, Beck and Beck-Gernsheim (1996) (see below) maintain that there is a breaking down of traditional family obligations and a more fluid set of bonds based on negotiation.

Giddens describes such changes as being relatively recent, with developments having their basis in social movements such as a "revolution in female sexual autonomy and in the flourishing of homosexuality" (Giddens 1992: 28). However, Jamieson (1998: 263) notes that research "on heterosexual couples routinely continues to find that men exercise more power than women in partnerships: for example, having more choice concerning opting in and out of domestic work and childcare." Jamieson also notes that research continues to find that couples who "collaboratively generate a sense of caring, intimate and equal relationships" (Jamieson 1998: 263), also exhibit inequalities in the way the relationships are played out. In addition, Jamieson also shows that research suggests that the ways in which couples generate a sense of themselves and their partners as mutually caring often reproduce gender inequality. As she notes: "The creativity and intimacy of couples is not yet typically harnessed to gender transformation" (Jamieson 1998: 263). As Jamieson notes many couples neutralise the process of gender inequality by deploying gender-neutral devices to maintain a sense of equality. The assumption here is that a good relationship will be both equal and intimate.

Jamieson points out that the relationship between equality and intimacy is more complex than that portrayed by Giddens, and that a more objective equality in relationships terms does not necessarily imply a movement towards a "pure relationship". Giddens indicates that the high rate of dissolution of relationships reflects the fragility of the "pure relationship" and how it needs constant working at in psychological terms. However, the fragile nature of the "pure relationship" within the heterosexual couple is the result of the very contradictory nature of the relationship between equality and intimacy. As Jamieson comments, the tension emerges from the cultural emphasis on intimacy and equality in relationships and the structural framework of gender inequality which makes the interrelationship of equality and intimacy within "the pure relationship"—as defined by Giddens—difficult to achieve.

(ii) Intimacy and Individualisation

In addition to Giddens, other theorists who contributed to this set of "epistemologies of detraditionalization" are Ulrich Beck and Elizabeth Beck-Gernsheim (1996) in their book *The Normal Chaos of Love*. They agree with Giddens on the issue of a "pure relationship" and "argue that the emphasis on flexibility ... and contingency in intimate relationships today reflects not the influence of globalization but the particular form that the process of individualization has taken in the late modern period" (Gross 2005: 290).

The reasoning behind this is as follows, Beck and Beck-Gernsheim maintain that the nature of individualisation in late modernity is different from individualisation in "classical versions of modernization theory" (Gross 2005: 290). In other words they distinguish between what Archer (2000) calls "personal identity" which she argues becomes more significant than "social identity", in an era where consumption and work assume a more significant aspect of identity and where there is a greater sense of social dislocation. Beck and Beck-Gernsheim maintain that as regards intimacy, the growth of individualization has resulted in the decline of traditional models of intimate relationships. As they comment "normal" biographies of love are being replaced by "do-it-yourself biographies".

(iii) Commercialisation of Intimacy

Other theorists understand intimacy in relation to aspects of late capitalism. Illouz (1997, 1999) develops the linkages between romance and consumption, while Hochschild (2003) criticises "the commercialization of intimate life". All these theorists see "the ideologicization of intimacy as progressively developing over the course of the twentieth century ... all regard pre-capitalist intimacy and family life as having given expression to important, traditional social values that have now been pushed aside" (Gross 2005: 291).

Intimacy and "Reflexive Modernization" Theories: Discussion

Giddens (1992) provides the most comprehensive analysis of the relationship between traditional normative patterns, values and intimacy as he notes: " ... the past is not preserved but continuously reconstructed on the basis of the present" (Giddens 1992: 291–292). For Giddens, "detraditionalization" does not just mean a different epistemological emphasis, it is not simply about the influence of nineteenth and twentieth century socio-economic movements such as urbanisation, democratisation, industrialisation but involves a fundamental intervention of political, economic and cultural values into individuals lives. Giddens draws on the growth of overarching structural frameworks such as the modern nation-state and the emergence of global capitalism to explain the significant qualitative increase and shift in the coordination of societal activity.

Giddens amplifies his discussion by distinguishing between two phases of modernisation and by implication of detraditionalisation. In what Giddens calls "early modernity", tradition is weakened but it still serves traditional patterns and values. He provides the following examples to highlight this phase: social control is maintained through "traditionalistic mechanisms of shaming; ... traditional gendered division of labour; and particularistic identities ..." (Gross 2005: 292N5).

In late modernity, the second phase, Giddens sees tradition as being "swept away". In this phase globalisation, increasing prosperity resulting from capitalism, gives both societies and individuals the opportunity for increasing reflexivity, a process which Giddens calls "reflexive modernization theory". The release from traditionalism, Giddens states, gives individual actors the capacity to exercise creative intelligence and to rely less on traditional relationship patterns. A good example of this is the move globally to same-sex marriage and how this is now being recognised in legislation in countries such as the U.S., Canada, Australia and elsewhere, but it is a movement demanded by the people. As stated the underpinnings of this epistemology is that intimacy and sex and how and where they operate, is framed by the idea of reflexivity which establishes new patterns of intimacy outside of traditional marriage.

Despite the seductive nature of this new epistemological framework in sociology, known as "reflexive modernization", there are of course critics. Jeffrey Alexander (1996) objects to the theory as he sees "action" (agency) as being insufficiently developed in the theory. Other theorists have shown that tradition still has relevance in understanding intimacy, Martha Nussbaum (2001) shows that the relationship between love and the sacred is an enduring narrative in both Western literary and philosophical traditions.

Cancian (1987) shows that love was: '"feminized" in the 19th century, in other words to love someone or to be in love came to mean participating in this elevated, sacrilized feminized sphere" (Gross 2005: 300). In this depiction of gendered roles, men are seen to separate sex and love while women connect them and sex is seen as the most meaningful way of giving and receiving love for many women. As Cancian (1987) observes the feminised perspective on love reinforces gendered power differentials by leading to a conception of women as needing love more than men do, which is based on the conception of women's emotional dependence on men. Gross maintains: "The consequence was the emergence of a distinction between two kinds of sexuality: marital sexuality, around which there hung a sacred aura, connected as it was to notions of womanly virtue, family and procreation, and that, for this reason was de-eroticized; and non-marital sexuality, which though highly charged erotically was seen as profane and taboo" (Gross 2005: 300).

The narratives of eighteenth and nineteenth century romantic love outlined earlier in this paper are quite different to those being discussed in contemporary theorising around intimacy. Theorists such as Giddens (1992), show that while narratives around love and romance are important to individuals they have become more "androgynous" (see Gross 2005). In other words it is about shared interests, lifestyles, tastes and aspirations, as well as erotic love. As theorists such as Swidler (2001) and Gross (2005) observe: "even when older narratives of romantic love are rewritten by contemporary Americans, these rewritings themselves are governed and informed by other meaning-constitutive traditions, such as that of expressive individualism, with its roots in, among other discourses, those of liberalism and Protestantism" (Gross 2005: 304).

An additional point to note here is that the conceptualisation of intimacy as reflected in the theories outlined is one which reflects Western hegemonic middle-class understandings of intimacy. There are of course no universal conceptualisations of intimacy and love, and intimacy can mean different things to different groups in the U.S. and other societies. Collins's (2004) *Black Sexual Politics: African-Americans, Gender and the New Racism* and Gonzalez-Lopez's (2005*) Erotic Journeys: Mexican Immigrants and Their Sex Lives*, highlight more diverse perspectives on intimacy within the context of the United States. While this diversification of intimacy, emotions and desire is beyond the scope of this chapter, it presents an under-researched area for those wishing to further extend this discussion.

Conclusion

This chapter has sought to understand and analyse epistemologies which attempt to explain changes in emotional regimes in different historical periods. In exploring these debates I draw on a range of epistemologies and theorists who have investigated the role of intimacy and sex in driving the history of emotions. Drawing on Foucault's concept of genealogy and his model of "biopower" I show how the micro operation of power gives greater emphasis to understanding the nature of intimacy and sex over different historical epochs. What emerges from this analysis is that over different historical epochs the operation of intimacy, eroticism and sex, function outside conventional structures such as marriage as shown in Foucault's analysis of ancient Greece in *The History of Sexuality, Volume 1: An Introduction*, in the context of romantic love captured in courtly love, in an analysis of intimacy and sex in twentieth century colonial cultures, and in late modernity through the process of "detraditionalization" and the growth of reflexivity. The following chapters explore these theoretical debates and many more in much more detail to understand emotions, intimacy and desire, historically and contemporaneously.

Bibliography

Alexander, Jeffrey. 1996. "Critical Reflections on 'Reflective Modernization'" *Theory, Culture and Society* 13: 133–138.
Amato, Paul R. 2000. "Diversity Within Single Parent Families." In D.H. Demo, K.R. Allen and M.A. Fine (eds), *Handbook of Family Diversity*. New York: Oxford University Press.
Amato, Paul R. and Alan Booth. 1997. *A Generation at Risk: Growing Up in an Era of Family Upheaval*. Cambridge, MA: Harvard University Press.
Archer, Margaret S. 2000. *Being Human: The Problem of Agency*. Cambridge: Cambridge University Press.

Beck, Ulrich and Elizabeth Beck-Gernsheim. 1996. *The Normal Chaos of Love.* Trans. M. Ritter and J. Wiebel. Cambridge: Polity Press.

Beck-Gernsheim, Elizabeth. 2002. *Reinventing the Family: In Search of New Lifestyles.* Trans. P. Camiller. Malden, MA: Polity Press.

Bloch, R. Howard. 1992. *Medieval Misogyny and the Invention of Western Romantic Love.* Chicago: University of Chicago Press.

Burns, E. Jane. 2001. "Courtly Love: Who Needs It? Recent Feminist Work in the Medieval French Tradition" *Signs* 27: 23–58.

Cancian, Frances M. 1987. *Love in America: Gender and Self-Development.* Cambridge: Cambridge University Press.

Collins, Patricia Hill. 2004. *Black Sexual Politics: African-Americans, Gender and the New Racism.* New York: Routledge.

Duby, Georges. 1994. *The Knight, the Lady and the Priest: The Making of Modern Marriage in Medieval France.* Trans. B. Bray. Chicago: The University of Chicago Press.

Du Gay, Paul. 1986. *The Bourgeois Experience, Victoria to Freud, Volume 2: The Tender Passion.* New York: Oxford University Press.

Elias, Norbert. 1994/1939. *The Civilizing Process: The History of Manners and State Formation and Civilization.* Oxford: Basil Blackwell.

Foucault, Michel. 1978. *The History of Sexuality, Volume 1: An Introduction.* New York: Vintage.

Giddens, Anthony. 1992. *The Transformation of Intimacy: Sexuality, Love and Eroticism in Modern Societies.* Stanford, CA: Stanford University Press.

Gonzalez-Lopez, Gloria. 2005. *Erotic Journey: Mexican Immigrants and Their Sex Lives.* Berkeley: University of California Press.

Gross, Neil. 2005. "The Detraditionalization of Intimacy Reconsidered" *Sociological Theory* 23(3): 286–311.

Hackstaff, Karla B. 1999. *Marriage in a Culture of Divorce.* Philadelphia, PA: Temple University Press.

Hochschild, Arlie R. 2003. *The Commercialization of Intimate Life.* Berkeley: University of California Press.

Hyam, Ronald. 1986. "Concubinage and the Colonial Service: The Crew Circular . . ." *Journal of Imperial and Commonwealth History* 14(3): 170–186.

Illouz, Eva. 1997. *Consuming the Romantic Utopia: Love and the Cultural Contradictions of Capitalism.* Berkeley: University of California Press.

Illouz, Eva. 1999. "The Lost Innocence of Love: Romance as a Postmodern Condition." In Mike Featherstone (ed.), *Love and Eroticism.* London: Sage, 161-186.

Jamieson, Lynn.1998. *Intimacy, Personal Relationships in Modern Society.* Cambridge: Polity

Kennedy, Raymond. 1947. *The Ageless Indies.* New York: John Day.

Kipnis, Laura. 2003. *Against Love: A Polemic.* New York: Pantheon.

Laslett, Peter. 1977. *Family Life and Illicit Love in Earlier Generations.* Cambridge: Cambridge University Press.

Ming, Hanneke. 1983. "Barracks—Concubinage in the Indies, 1887–1920" *Indonesia* 35: 65–93.

Musick, Kelley. 2002. "Planned and Unplanned Childbearing Among Unmarried Women" *Journal of Marriage and Family* 64: 915–929.

Nussbaum, Martha C. 2001. *Upheavals of Thought: The Intelligence of Emotions.* Cambridge: Cambridge University Press.

Pollman, Tessa. 1986. "Bruidstaantjes: De Koloniale Roman, de Njai en de Apartheid." In J.R. Reijs, E. Kloek, and V. Jansz (eds), *Vrouwen in de Nederlandse Kolonien.* Nijmegen: SUNY.
Rosenwein, Barbara H. 2006. *Emotional Communities in the Early Middle Ages.* Ithaca, NY: Cornell University Press.
Said, Edward W. 1979. *Orientalism.* New York: Vintage.
Seidman, Steven. 1998. *Contested Knowledges: Social Theory in the Postmodern Era* 2nd ed. Oxford, MA: Blackwell.
Seidman, Steven. 2002. *Beyond the Closet: The Transformation of Gay and Lesbian Life.* New York: Routledge.
Shohat, Ella (ed.). 1997. *Dangerous Liaisons: Gender, Nation and Postcolonial Perspectives.* London and Minneapolis: University of Minnesota Press.
Shorter, Ella. 1975. *The Making of the Modern Family.* New York: Basic Books.
Somers, Margaret. 2008. *Genealogies of Citizenship.* Cambridge: Cambridge University Press
Sommers, Doris. 1990. "Irresistible Romance: The Foundational Fictions of Latin America." In Homi K. Bhabha (ed.), *Nation and Narration.* Berkeley: University of California Press, 71–97.
Stoler, Laura Ann. 1985a. *Capitalism and Confrontation in Sumatra's Plantation Belt, 1870–1979.* New Haven: Yale University Press.
Stoler, Laura Ann. 1985b. "Perceptions of Protest" *American Ethnologist* 12(4): 642–658.
Stoler, Laura Ann. 1997. "Making Empire Respectable: The Politics of Race and Sexuality Morality in Twentieth-Century Colonial Cultures." In A. McClintock, A. Mufti and E. Shohat (eds), *Dangerous Liaisons: Gender, Nation and Postcolonial Perspectives.* London and Minneapolis: University of Minnesota Press, 344-373.
Stoler, Laura Ann. 2002. *Carnal Knowledge and Imperial Power: Race and the Intimate in Colonial Rule.* Berkeley: University of California Press.
Stoler, Laura Ann. 2006. *Haunted by Empire: Geographies of Intimacy in North American History.* Durham, NC and London: Duke University Press.
Strobel, Margaret. 1987. "Gender and Race in Nineteenth and Twentieth Century British Empire." In R. Bridenthal, C. Koonz and S. Stuard, eds. *Becoming Visible: Women in European History.* 2nd ed. Boston: Houghton Mifflin.
Swidler, Anne. 1980. "Love and Adulthood in America Culture." In N.J. Smelser and E.H. Erickson (eds), *Themes of Work and Love in Adulthood.* Cambridge, MA: Harvard University Press, 120–147.
Swidler, Anne. 2001. *Talk of Love: How Culture Matters.* Chicago: The University of Chicago Press.

2 Foucault's Genealogy of Sexuality
Foucault, Sex and Power

Introduction

This chapter explores Michel Foucault's *The History of Sexuality, Volume 1: An Introduction*, and examines the contextualisation of this book within the framework of wider debates including genealogy, as a methodological framework, power and sexuality. Foucault as indicated in the Introduction, rejected Enlightenment scientific culture and idea of grand theories to explain human behaviour and he drew on a model of "genealogy" as an alternative to the "grand narratives" of Enlightenment thinkers. As shown in the Introduction and Chapter 1 of this book, Foucault set about to explain the historically unique character of modern sexual culture, and in addition he offered an alternative perspective on sexuality. Within this chapter Foucault's analysis of sexuality is examined in the context of social and cultural theory and in particular feminist theory, which has been significantly influenced by Foucault's writings. However, this is not to argue that those who have drawn on Foucault's analysis of sexuality have been uncritical of his work. Notable in this has been Laura Ann Stoler (1995, 1997, 2002, 2006) who makes a substantial intervention into Foucault's theoretical analysis by drawing on the experience of sexuality in colonial cultures to highlight the significance of race in understanding the history of sexuality (see Chapters 1 and 4).

Foucault's Critique of Enlightenment Thinking

Foucault's work can be understood in the context of philosophical traditions of continental thought. This included the twentieth century critique of the Enlightenment paradigm of scientific knowledge and the lack of agency inherent in this epistemological framework. As Falzon et al. (2013: 209) comment: "This means reading Foucault in relation to the tradition of Hegel, Nietzsche, Heidegger, the Frankfurt School, Habermas, Lyotard and others, as well as the French philosophy of science."

As part of this tradition there is a rejection of grand narratives and as Seidman (1998: 249) notes:

> Lyotard and Foucault propose successor projects to scientific social theory e.g., local narratives and genealogy ... Foucault's outline of the rise of

a disciplinary order that creates new identities and institutes normalizing controls from surveillance to therapies compels us to shift our conceptual strategies in ways no less dramatic than the 'revolution' in human studies linked to classical sociology.

Foucault argued that Enlightenment discourses as in medical-scientific courses lead to the regulation of individuals and create individuals as sexual objects.

Seidman makes the important point that whereas Foucault did not make any attempt to propose a general theory of modernity in the same way as Habermas or Talcott Parsons, nevertheless through his studies of sexuality, prisons, madness and the human sciences he was able to offer what Seidman describes as: "a disciplinary social order" (1998: 245). He (Foucault) saw genealogy (see below) as a possible form of anti-disciplinary politics which could provide a framework for analysis for human studies more generally.

Foucault shared with postmodernists and poststructuralists, the rejection of foundational claims about the social world. Alcoff (2013) shows that Foucault challenged foundational claims in the study of sexuality but as Alcoff (2013: 208) notes: " Foucault's work on knowledge is primarily critical rather than normatively reconstructive." Beyond this, Alcoff (2013: 209) also notes:

> He challenged some of the foundational claims about the ahistorical nature of desire, the objective and unchanging status of sexual identities, and the apolitical nature of empirical inquiry into sexuality. And he did so on the basis of his critique of the ways in which such claims came about within regulatory institutions.

Foucault also showed that the relationship between power and knowledge could also be strengthened by the flows of pleasure, understood in a broad sense. In *The History of Sexuality, Volume 1: An Introduction*, Foucault shows that: "Pleasure helps to spread and augment the flows of power, while power anchors and institutionalizes pleasure, and all of these relations operate through knowledge (*HS1*: 45 and 48)" (Alcoff 2013: 215).

There was also a more personal dimension to Foucault's analysis of sexuality which was directly related to his own homosexuality. Seidman outlines how Foucault found French society while it tolerated homosexuality, expected it to be kept discrete and even a sophisticated culture like France did not expect personal identity to be defined in such terms. However, in travelling to America in the 1970s, Foucault encountered a more open and explicit sexual culture. Identity was framed in terms of sexual orientation and lesbian and gay communities flourished. Thus a clearly defined liberation movement had at its core "an affirmative homosexual identity" (Seidman 1998: 236). As Seidman shows, Foucault's thinking about the idea of the gay community in America was critical in his analysis of sexuality:

> He particularly admired the creation of new ways of experiencing the body as a medium of pleasure and the creation of new forms of group life.

Foucault was troubled though, by the anchoring of this culture in what he took to be a unitary notion of sexual and social identity. Didn't the affirmation of a lesbian or gay identity reinforce a culture that assigned individuals mutually exclusive social identities? . . . Foucault was suspicious of a sexual liberation movement that was wedded to a rhetoric of authenticity and self–realization. Does normalizing gay identities amount to sexual liberation or the consolidation of a society that defines and regulates individuals by assigning them a unitary sexual identity? He was uneasy with a gay movement that seemed bent on becoming a quasi-ethnic community.

(Seidman 1998: 237)

The focus of his work on how sexual identity could be framed led him to consider the issue of social constraints more fully and what alternative ways of thinking could be established for looking at desire, pleasures, the body and intimacies. His development of this alternative perspective in *The History of Sexuality, Volume 1: An Introduction*, is outlined below.

Foucault's Concept of Genealogy

Foucault developed his concept of genealogy in opposition to Enlightenment scientific culture and a positive and optimistic vision of social change. Seidman (1998: 235) outlines Foucault's conceptualisation of genealogy:

Foucault once refereed to genealogy as "anti-science". Genealogy relinquishes the search for objective knowledge, secure intellectual foundations, essences, deep unifying patterns of meaning, and grand theories that comprehend the origin and endpoint of history. Indeed, in opposition to the Enlightenment scientific culture, genealogy does not offer a positive agenda of social reconstruction; it lacks a social utopian vision.

Foucault's use of genealogy as an alternative to grand theory was more than just a theoretical framework, it was a means to recover knowledges of those who had been lost. Foucault focused on the intersection of institution and discourse in genealogical analysis. In doing so he combined power/knowledge configurations which he felt had been submerged, hidden or repressed by Enlightenment science. It was this which Seidman claims: "is the critical object of genealogy" (Seidman 1998: 236). Throughout his major works, his focus was on applying this perspective to the human sciences:

Foucault's major studies: *Madness and Civilization*, *The Archeology of Knowledge, Discipline and Punish*, and *The History of Sexuality* examined the human sciences, for example, psychiatry, criminology, penology, demography, sexology, economics, and sociology . . . Foucault investigated the *social effects* of these knowledges. He asserted that discourses that aim to reveal the truth of the abnormal personality or human sexuality or the criminal help to create and control the very objects they claim to know.

(Seidman 1998: 236)

In an earlier book, *Postfeminisms: Feminism, Cultural Theory and Cultural Forms* (Brooks 1997), I showed how a number of feminist theorists have engaged with Foucault's concept of genealogy. Genealogy and the genealogical method was, as I showed, Foucault's method of studying history through the analysis of discourse. McNeil (1993) maintains that the genealogical method was designed to explore not who had power but rather the patterns of the exercise of power through the interplay of discourses. The genealogical method enables Foucault to chart the discontinuities of history and the play of power relations in the production of knowledges. Fraser (1989) draws some interesting comparisons between Foucault's concept of genealogy and ideology. Fraser (1989: 19) claims that Foucault, in opposing genealogy to ideology claims that:

> ... genealogy does not concern itself with evaluating the contents of science or systems of knowledge or for that matter with systems of beliefs... Rather it is concerned with the processes, procedures and apparatuses whereby truth, knowledge, beliefs are produced, within what, Foucault calls 'the politics of the discursive regime'.

Lynch (2013) shows how *The History of Sexuality, Volume 1: An Introduction*, marked a turning point in Foucault's thought and establishes his position on power as central in his thinking: " ... it presents Foucault's mature articulations of disciplinary power while also opening up new analyses of biopower and, in a more radical turn, bringing certain ethical problems to the fore" (Lynch 2013: 154).

As Lynch goes on to show, Foucault in holding this position, is grounding sexuality in another crucial phenomenon—power relations:

> In order to define sexuality as an effect and correlate of power relations, Foucault has to recast our understanding of the basic modes of how power is exercised: power is not top-down, or principally a form of repression but emerges, from micro-interactions, and is profoundly productive, constitutive of our very identities.
>
> (Lynch 2013: 158)

This interpretation of power is central in understanding genealogy in Foucault's philosophy, as Fraser (1989) shows:

> Foucault's most valuable accomplishment consists of a rich empirical account of the early stages in the emergence of some distinctively modern

modalities of power. This account yields important insights into the nature of modern power, and these insights, in turn bear political significance.

(Fraser 1989: 17–18)

This shift in emphasis on power in Foucault's analysis was an important one in terms of the relationship between poststructuralist views of power and ideology as outlined above. Lynch (2013: 159) shows how the distinction works:

> [The] genealogical study of power relations and in particular the emergence of a modern form of power that he termed 'disciplinary power' out of an older model of 'sovereign power,' was the dominant *leitmotif* of Foucault's work throughout the mid-1970s, culminating in *Discipline and Punish* and *The History of Sexuality 1*.

Foucault continually revised his conception of power and introduced the term "biopower" to describe the revised model. This is outlined by Foucault in *The History of Sexuality, Volume 1: An Introduction*:

> [At] the end of the eighteenth century ... there emerged a [singular] completely new technology of sex. ... sex became a matter that required the social body as a whole [biopower], and virtually all its individuals [disciplinary power], to place themselves under surveillance [*HS1*: 116].
>
> (cited in Lynch 2013: 159/160) (Lynch's brackets)

Foucault locates sexuality as both a problem of power but also a problem of knowledge, or of truth. In *The History of Sexuality, Volume 1: An Introduction* he traces the historical apparatus established to maintain the close normative management of sex. As Lynch (2013: 167) shows: "beginning with the confessional in the Middle Ages and continuing through contemporary psycho-analytic practice—by means of a contrast between 'two great procedures for producing the truth of sex'(*HS1*: 57)".

In other words, Foucault traces the knowledge—power regimes that defined the normative construction of sexuality historically. The deployment of sexuality is through the role of the family which Foucault recognises as a "dense transfer point" for discourses that control sexuality.

The History of Sexuality, Volume 1: An Introduction

In the opening chapters of *Volume 1* of *The History of Sexuality*, Foucault provides a critique of the "repressive hypothesis" put forward by Freud arguing that it is incorrect to focus on psychological controls over the expression of sexual drives. Smith (1999: 81) maintains that: "In the first volume of his trilogy on sexuality, Foucault outlines the central place of sexuality in the controlling discourses of modern society. He emphasizes the capacity of these invasive discourses to shape, construct and distort human impulses and the sense of self."

Foucault set out in *The History of Sexuality, Volume 1: An Introduction*, to offer an alternative perspective on the history of sexuality. As Seidman (1998: 237) shows:

> He proposed a radical rethinking of the origins and meaning of the modern culture of sexuality for the purpose, ultimately of imagining an order of bodies and pleasure beyond "sexuality" . . . In volumes 2 and 3 of his *History of Sexuality*, Foucault intended to undermine the presumption of the universality of the modern system of sexuality.

This begins to be apparent in the first volume of *The History of Sexuality* where Foucault identifies a number of areas including: the pleasures surrounding the body particularly in relation to sex, diet and medical treatment; relations between spouses; and relations between adult males and young boys. Importantly Smith (1999: 81) provides a more specific historical reference point for the period to which Foucault's analysis applies:

> Foucault's account relates mainly to Greek and Roman society between the fourth century B.C. and the second century A.D., although he makes occasional references back to Homeric times and has substantial comments on the medieval and modern in European history.

He used Greek culture to highlight how it was a culture centred around "pleasures":

> He argued that ancient Greek culture was not organized around a regime of separate sexual desires and acts, some of which, being dangerous or unnatural, were to be prohibited. . . . The Greek city-states represented a different universe of sexual meaning from modernity.
>
> (Seidman 1998: 238)

Seidman outlines Foucault's view of Greek culture:

> Instead of a culture organized around "sexuality" (i.e. discrete desires, acts and identities) Greek culture was centred around "pleasures" and an ethic of self-mastery. Pleasures included not only or primarily sex but eating, exercise and marriage.
>
> (Seidman 1998: 237)

However, as Seidman shows, there was a close relationship between pleasures and social status:

> For example, adult free men were expected to be active in sexual exchanges, while the subordinate social status of women, slaves and boys required them to be sexually passive. Disapproval was not attached to particular sex acts or to a particular gender preference but to individuals who were immoderate in their pleasures or abandoned their appropriate roles.
>
> (Seidman 1998: 238)

Smith argues that Foucault understood the contrast between Greco-Roman context and his experience of contemporary life. He focused on the kinds of relationships in Greco-Roman society which did not assign morality and shame to homosexual relationships. This is outlined succinctly by Smith (1999: 83):

> The idea was to maximize pleasure within these limits. In other words, pleasure and control could be combined within the everyday social world by exercising good judgement in the light of relevant knowledge about the body, diet, medicine and so on. This made a fascinating contrast with the modern world, as understood by Foucault, for here in his view, both pleasure and insight could be gained by transgressing limits, by deliberately going beyond the frontiers that led to high, physical, psychological or social risk.

Foucault shows that control of one's passions was directly related to status and one's ability to be a public figure.

Perhaps the most apparent difference between Greek and modern culture was shown in the meaning of homosexuality:

> Foucault insisted that the man/boy love in Greek culture has little, if any resemblance to modern homosexuality . . . the Greeks did not view sexual desire as naturally divided between the same and opposite sexes. Adult free men were expected to have boy lovers and to be married. Man/boy love was not a life-long alternative to marriage, there was no separate deviant culture of homosexuals and there was no stigma attached to man/boy love.
>
> (Seidman 1998: 238)

"Pleasure" as far as Foucault was concerned had a wide-ranging application and love and sex was just one aspect of a range of pleasures and love between adult free males and boys was simply one element of pleasure. Foucault also distinguished between "ideal love" as expressed between men and boys and "love" in marriage which was more about social obligations and maintenance of a household.

However he saw the shift to a self and marriage-centred culture as a turning point in the evolution of Western society and non-marital sex was becoming a target for suspicion. Seidman points out that Foucault remained a critic of the modern regime of sexuality until his death: "Foucault's case against the regime was that it reduced sexuality to narrow sexual pleasures, rigidly forced individuals into restrictive, mutually exclusive identities, created stigmatized, deviant populations and facilitated an efficient system of social control" (Seidman 1998: 242).

However as Seidman shows, Foucault never clarified his vision of an alternative intimate culture:

Anti-Psychology, Anti-Freudianism

A further dimension of Foucault's work which provided an important shift in understanding sexuality and away from Freudianism and towards social constructionism, was his critique of the repressive hypothesis and of Freudianism more generally.

Grace (2013: 226) contextualises the relationship between Foucault and the Freudians:

> From the *History of Madness* to the three volumes of *The History of Sexuality*, Foucault consistently argued for the historical specificities of the two principal human objects of psychoanalysis–madness and sexuality. Foucault now stands starkly removed from Freudian thought which cannot countenance ethnographic or cultural versions of madness or sexuality. Even psychoanalysis as propagated by Jacques Lacan assumes that (sexual) desire transcends local and particular milieu and holds the key to all forms of identity, reason and unreason. This is unacceptable to Foucault.

As Grace goes on to outline, Foucault accepted and indeed "embraced" the use of the unconscious in the French intellectual tradition particularly associated with the work of Lacan and Levi-Straus but he totally rejected the Freudian conceptualisation of the unconscious.

Underpinning Foucault's rejection of Freudianism is his rejection of repression and psychoanalysis as an explanation for sexuality. Lynch (2013: 157) maintains that:

> Foucault thus directly challenges both psychoanalysis and a number of contemporary political theories. He discusses—and recasts the importance of—Sigmund Freud at several points. Another implicit, though unnamed, target of Foucault's criticism is critical theorist Herbert Marcuse's *Eros and Civilization*, which essentially puts forth this "repressive" hypothesis.

As Grace goes on to say the demand from Foucault is to go well beyond psychoanalysis in the area of both sexuality and desire. Psychoanalysis had assisted Foucault's thinking around desire and had led to his formulation of an alternative genealogy of the modern subject as Grace (2013: 240) shows:

> From this perspective, the critique of desire is really the climax of Foucault's efforts to develop an alternative Nietzschean genealogy of the modern subject as a historical and cultural reality. . . . By way of conclusion, we could say that Foucault's relationship to psychoanalysis is therefore complex for good reason: psychoanalysis had acted for him as an important support and counter-tradition through which his alternative analysis could unfold. Rejecting the uniform representation of power as it exists in Freudian discourse finally enables us to shift analysis away from the individual and his or her psychosexual development and turn the spotlight on the social networks . . .

Foucault's analysis of the repression of sexuality is linked with the significance of the Victorian bourgeois family. Foucault saw the bourgeois family as instrumental in the repression of sexuality: "Sexuality was carefully confined; it moved into the home. The conjugal family took custody of it and absorbed it into the serious function of reproduction (*HS1*: 3)" (cited in Deutscher 2012: 122). Within this model of repressed sexuality: "One single space of sexuality was acknowledged," which Foucault identified as: "the legitimate and the procreative couple (*HS1*: 3)" (cited in Deutscher 2012: 122).

Foucault is clear about the reasons behind the linking of sex with procreation, he saw it as an attempt to dismiss any form of sexuality that did not fall within the reproductive discourse: "to say no to unproductive activities, to banish casual pleasures, to reduce or exclude practices whose object was not procreation (*HS1*: 36)" (cited in Deutscher 2012: 122).

Part of this framework involved the nineteenth century obsession with degeneracy as captured by Foucault:

> The concern with genealogy becomes a preoccupation with heredity; but included in bourgeois marriages were not only economic imperatives and rules of social homogeneity, not only the promises of inheritance, but the menaces of heredity; families wore and concealed a sort of reversed and sombre escutcheon whose defamatory quarters were the diseases or defects of the group or relatives of the group . . .
> (*HS1*: 124–125) (cited in Deutscher 2012: 133)

Linked to this is the relationship between sexuality, race and colonialism which is discussed below.

Biopower, Sexuality and the Politics of Race

A final dimension of Foucault's work is the relationship between biopower, sexuality and race. In her book *Race and the Education of Desire*, Stoler (1995) provides a systematic analysis of *The History of Sexuality* in relation to a backdrop of colonialism. While Stoler's work draws heavily on Foucault's conceptual analysis (see Chapter 4), she also highlights some of its limitations. Stoler is of course far from the only scholar drawing on Foucault, others include Comaroff (1985), Dirks (1987) and Ong (1987).

As shown above, central in Foucault's *The History of Sexuality, Volume 1: An Introduction* is his rejection of and attack on repression as an explanation for sexuality. Foucault saw power as critical to understanding sexuality as Stoler (1995: 3) comments: "Sexuality was 'a result and an instrument of power's design,' a social construction of a historical moment (*HS*: 152)." Power is seen by Foucault as intrinsic to the operation of sexuality as Stoler (1995: 3) shows:

> For Foucault, sexuality is not opposed to and subversive of power. On the contrary, sexuality is a "dense transfer point" of power, charged with "instrumentality" (*HS*: 103). Thus "far from being repressed in [nineteenth century] society [sexuality] was constantly aroused (*HS*: 148)".

One of Foucault's central concepts is "biopower" which he defined as "a political technology that 'brought life and its mechanisms into the realm of explicit calculations and made knowledge/power an agent of transformation of human life' (*HS*: 143)" (Stoler 1995: 3). The linking factor of sex with that of race, within his analysis, was through "the technologies of sex" which played a critical role as Foucault showed: "sex occupied the discursive interface linking the life of the individual to the life of the species as a whole (*HS*: 146)" (Stoler 1995: 4).

Stoler shows how, drawing on this premise, she understands the operation of power in colonial cultures, as she indicates: "the discursive management of the sexual practices of colonizer and colonized was fundamental to the colonial order of things" (Stoler 1995: 4). Stoler builds on Foucault's critique of the bourgeois family and sexuality to understand the broader imperial landscape:

> I pursue here a critique of Foucault's chronologies . . . rather to argue that the discursive and practical field in which nineteenth-century bourgeois sexuality emerged was situated on an imperial landscape where the cultural accoutrements of bourgeois distinction were partially shaped through contrasts forged in the politics and language of race. I trace how certain colonial pre-figurings contest and force a reconceptualising of Foucault's sexual history of the Occident and, more generally, a rethinking of the historiographic conventions that have bracketed histories of "the West".
> (Stoler 1995: 5)

The History of Sexuality and Imperial Discourses

In drawing on Foucault's *The History of Sexuality*, Stoler is also critical of crucial social, political and cultural dimensions, which Foucault ignores. She argues that eighteenth and nineteenth century discourses on sexuality in Europe need to be understood beyond Europe, and she is critical of Foucault's failure in ignoring empire and "racialized bodies":

> Imperial discourses that divided colonizer from colonized, metropolitan observers from colonial agents, and bourgeois colonizers from their subaltern compatriots designated certain cultural competencies, sexual proclivities, psychological dispositions, and cultivated habits.
> (Stoler 1995: 8)

The crucial question for Stoler, largely ignored by Foucault is how the imperial world "re-defined" sexuality and relationships of intimacy as she observes:

> If this re-routing of the history of sexuality through the history of empire makes analytical sense, then we must ask whether the racial configurations of the imperial world, rather than being peripheral to the cultivation of the nineteenth century bourgeois self, were not constitutive of it.
> (Stoler 1995: 8)

Race was not a concept that Foucault engaged with and as Stoler comments: "Racisms are not what Foucault analysed; he looked rather to the ways in which prior technology of sexuality provided a cultural susceptibility and discursive field for them" (Stoler 1995: 22). Stoler (see also Deutscher 2012) recognises that the emergence of racism was implied by Foucault in his analysis of the "bourgeois" body in the eighteenth century. Stoler argues that *The History of Sexuality, Volume 1: An Introduction*, shows that a new field of discourse emerged which was associated with racism and degeneracy even if Foucault did not define it as such, it was concerned with: "... body hygiene, the art of longevity, ways of having healthy children and of keeping them alive as long as possible" [which] "... attests to the correlation of this concern with the body and sex to a type of 'racism'" (HS: 125) (cited in Stoler 1995: 29).

The relationship between biopower and race was not direct and as Stoler shows it is linked to what is defined as the two "poles" of biopower that emerged separately, centuries earlier: "One pole centers on the disciplining of the individual, on the 'anato-politics of the human body'; the second centers on a set of 'regulatory controls' over the life of the species in a 'biopolitics of the population'(*HS*: 139)" (Stoler 1995: 33).

Underpinning Foucault's analysis of biopower is his focus on the "normalization of power" which he subsequently changed to the power of normalization in other words it is about the regulation of both the body and the species.

Racial Politics of Colonialism

Stoler considers whether the racial politics of colonialism produced European bourgeois sexuality and defined it, or was it the "eroticization of the exotic play" that gave Dutch, French and British colonialists both moral authority and power over the colonised. Regardless of the explanation, Stoler (1995: 115) shows that the intersection of gender, race and sexuality was dominated by Europeans:

> Europeanness was not only class-specific but gender coded. A European man could live with or marry an Asian woman without necessarily losing rank but this was never true for a European woman who might make a similar choice to live or marry a non-European. Thus, in the legal debates on mixed marriages in 1887, a European woman who married a native man was dismissively accorded native legal status on the grounds that her very choice of sexual and conjugal partner showed that she had "already sunk so deep socially and morally that it does not result in ruin . . . [but rather] serves to consolidate her situation."

Conclusion

Stoler argues that Foucault undermined an analysis of race by "marginalizing the link between nationalism and desire in both his genealogy of racism and his history of sexuality" (Stoler 1995: 136). As she shows in adopting this position, Foucault ignores "a key discursive site" where subjected "native" and colonised subjects were located (Stoler 1995: 136). Stoler's review of *The History of Sexuality* adds another dimension to understanding sexuality and colonialism and introduces a conceptual framework for understanding intimacy and desire within the context of genealogies of racism which is developed further in Chapter 4.

Bibliography

Alcoff, Linda M. 2013. "Foucault's Normative Epistemology." In Christopher Falzon, Timothy O'Leary and Jane Sawicki (eds), *A Companion to Foucault*. Oxford: Blackwell, 208–225.

Brooks, Ann. 1997. *Postfeminisms: Feminism, Cultural Theory and Cultural Forms*. London and New York: Routledge.

Comaroff, Jean. 1985. *Body of Power, Spirit of Resistance: The Culture and History of a South African People*. Chicago: Chicago University Press.

Deutscher, Penelope. 2012. "Foucault's *History of Sexuality*, Volume 1: Re-Reading Its Reproduction" *Theory, Culture and Society* 29 (1): 119–137.

Dirks, Nicholas B. 1987. *The Hollow Crown*. Cambridge: Cambridge University Press.

Falzon, Christopher, Timothy O'Leary, and Jane Sawicki (eds). 2013. *A Companion to Foucault*. Oxford: Blackwell.

Foucault, Michel. 1978. *The History of Sexuality, Volume 1: An Introduction*. New York: Vintage.

Fraser, Nancy. 1989. "Foucault on Modern Power: Empirical Insights and Normative Confusions." In Nancy Fraser (ed.). *Unruly Practices: Power, Discourse and Gender in Contemporary Social Theory.* Minneapolis: University of Minnesota Press, 17–35.

Grace, Wendy. 2013. "Foucault and the Freudians." In Christopher Falzon, Timothy O'Leary and Jane Sawicki (eds), *A Companion to Foucault.* Oxford: Blackwell, 226–242.

Lynch, Richard. 2013. "Reading *The History of Sexuality, Volume 1.*" In Christopher Falzon, Timothy O'Leary and Jane Sawicki (eds), *A Companion to Foucault.* Oxford: Blackwell, 154–171.

McNeil, Maureen. 1993. "Dancing with Foucault: Feminism and Power-Knowledge." In Caroline Ramazanoglu (ed.), *Up Against Foucault: Explorations of Some Tensions Between Foucault and Feminism.* London and New York: Routledge, 147–179.

Ong, Aiwha. 1987. *Spirits of Resistance and Capitalist Discipline.* Binghampton: SUNY Press.

Seidman, Steven. 1998. *Contested Knowledge: Social Theory in the Postmodern Era* 2nd ed. Oxford, MA: Blackwell Publishers.

Smith, Dennis. 1999. "*The Civilizing Process* and the *History of Sexuality, Volume 1*: Comparing Norbert Elias and Michael Foucault" *Theory and Society* 28: 79–100.

Stoler, Laura Ann. 1985. *Capitalism and Confrontation in Sumatra's Plantation Belt, 1870–1987.* New Haven: Yale University Press.

Stoler, Laura Ann. 1995. *Race and the Education of Desire.* Durham, NC and London: Duke University Press.

Stoler, Laura Ann. 1997. "Making Empire Respectable: The Politics of Race and Sexuality Morality in Twentieth-Century Colonial Cultures." In A. McClintock, A. Mufti and E. Shohat (eds), *Dangerous Liaisons: Gender, Nation and Postcolonial Perspectives.* London and Minneapolis: University of Minnesota Press, 344–373.

Stoler, Laura Ann. 2002. *Carnal Knowledge and Imperial Power: Race and the Intimate in Colonial Rule.* Berkeley: University of California Press.

Stoler, Laura Ann. 2006. *Haunted by Empire: Geographies of Intimacy in North American History.* Durham, NC and London: Duke University Press.

3 Narratives of Romantic Love

> Modern Love was romantic love. The romantic movement privileged feeling over reason, and in reaction against 18th century 'sense' romantic love expressed 'sensibility' and stood for authenticity and the truth of feeling. This is of course the great paradox and irony of modernity: that as scientific advance, representing reason and rational thought, transformed the material world, it unleashed unprecedented unreason and violence. Romanticism was one expression of this, as it moved in the direction of this underlying irrationalism.
>
> (Wilson 1998: 112)

Introduction: Historical and Contemporary Narratives of Romantic Love

Romantic love is often defined by contemporary theorists as a product of Western cultural history. However Octavio Paz (1996) in his analysis of love and the erotic—*The Double Flame: Essays on Love and Eroticism* shows that it can be found in all societies and in different historical periods. While the performance of "a culture of love" emerged within court societies in the West, as Featherstone (1998: 2) notes, and became an expression of love as a "privileged body of knowledge and practice by a small group of men and women," it was not restricted to the West. Drawing on Paz, Featherstone (1998) shows that:

> ... this form of courtly love emerged not only in Europe but in the Islamic world, India and East Asia too. The Chinese novel *Dream of the Red Chamber* by Ts'ao Hsueh-ch'in and the Japanese novel *The Tale of Genji*, by Murasaki Shikubu both describe love affairs in the courtly aristocratic world (Paz 1996: 29ff). Both books point to the close relationship between a high courtly culture and a philosophy of love-something which is absent from many accounts of the history of love.

This is true of the work of Evans (1998) (see below) but Paz also sees it reflected in what he regards as one of the most significant books on the history of love, Denis de Rougemont's *Love in the Western World* (1983). Paz also maintains there are further distinctions between West and East in terms of how love developed. The distinction was based on the fact that in the East, love was framed within religious traditions whereas in the West it developed as part of a critical philosophy. In addition, as Featherstone (1998: 15–16) comments: "Western love was influenced by conceptions of love developed by the Persians and Arabs, which shared with Christianity and monotheistic religions the notion of the eternal soul and the person."

In fact there are a number of social and cultural trends which can be identified in the history of love which are only partially addressed by a number of influential theorists. These include: (i) "the role of cultural specialists who made and circulated representations of love" (Featherstone 1998: 2); (ii) the growth in the power of women; and (iii) the growth of the literature of love, which took different forms within different historical and philosophical contexts. The history of love is therefore a social and cultural movement both reflecting changing philosophies, and driving them.

While Evans (1998) focuses on the history of love in post-Enlightenment European culture, she makes an interesting point about the apparent gap in explaining the history of love between classical Greek society and the emergence of romantic love in the twelfth century. She draws out issues of sexuality and class in her analysis and argues that the history of love often overlaps with the history of sex and "begins with an account of homoerotic love in classical Greece. It is assumed that the starting point of Western civilization was a society in which males loved males and had sexual relations with women for purposes of procreation" (Evans 1998: 270). She goes on to show that there is little explanation of the history of love between that point and the emergence of romantic love in the twelfth century where the focus of love is largely heterosexual but which is supported by a literature of "energetic sexuality."

There is a vast literature on romantic love in the twelfth century. De Rougemont's (1983) *Love in the Western World* talks about the Provencal poets as being an influential and potentially subversive group in the emergence of romantic love in twelfth century French Provencal poetry. The evolution of this literary genre shows the shift in the class based history of romantic love. As Featherstone (1998: 2) explains:

> Important here was the transition from chivalrous poetry written by noblemen for aristocratic women of their own strata to romantic lyric poetry written and performed by non-aristocratic professional poets who wandered from castle to castle. The poetry was not constructed to be read, but to be heard, with poems accompanied by music performed in the castle of the great lord.

There were class and gender aspects to this emergence of lyric poetry. The poets were inferior in social rank to the ladies they performed for. The subject matter of the poems was heterosexual love and given the class background of the poets they "were spoken in the vernacular form and not Latin" (Featherstone 1998: 3). This was also to allow the ladies of the court to understand the lyrics. Paz (1996: 72) adds additional layers of understanding in appreciating these Provencal poets. He shows that the poetry was influenced by the poetry traditions of Muslim Spain: "not only in adopting popular Arabic-Andalusian forms, but also in their emphasis on the custom of the Arabemirs in declaring themselves the slaves of their beloveds." Paz also claims that the emergence of romantic love was accompanied by the rise in status of women and that by comparison with the pattern of arranged marriages, love relationships were daring.

However other theorists do not share Paz's optimism for the apparent rise in women's power. Eva Illouz (2012: 8) offers a scathing critique of women's position within this period of chivalry and romanticism. As she comments:

> The weakness of women was thus contained in a cultural system in which it was acknowledged and glorified because it transfigured male power and female frailty into lovable qualities, such as 'protectiveness' for the one, and 'softness' and gentleness for the other.

Illouz (see below and Chapters 5 and 6) across a range of work has been highly critical of the concept of women in romantic love:

> Women's social inferiority could thus be traded for man's absolute devotion in love, which in turn served as the very site of display and exercise for their masculinity, prowess, and honor. More: women's dispossession of economic and political rights was accompanied . . . by the reassurance that in love they were not only protected by men but also superior to them. It is therefore unsurprising that love has been historically so powerfully seductive to women; it promised them the moral status and dignity they were otherwise denied in society and it glorified their social fate: taking care of and loving others, as mothers, wives and lovers.
>
> (Illouz 2012: 8)

One of the key factors that Illouz develops in her analysis is how the increasing emphasis on the relationship between romance and consumption in late capitalism relegated women to those of social carers reliant and dependent on men. This is explored more fully in Chapters 5 and 6.

Niklas Luhmann (1986) also considers the significance of romantic love in the modern world but sees it as an important means of "symbolic exchange". His analysis shares much with that of Anthony Giddens (1992) in showing how love and intimacy changes in late modernity. Luhmann maintains that love gains in importance in the transition from feudal to capitalist society. He offers a linear and somewhat unsophisticated analysis of love from premodern societies to industrial society, maintaining that in premodern societies love was restricted to certain groups and was highly stratified in terms of who one could love. Luhmann contends that with the rise of industrial society that love became less stratified and more focused on passion.

The growth of a literature on love in the eighteenth and nineteenth centuries Luhmann claims: "became socially important by helping to provide 'codes' between men and women, especially in the increasingly urbanized world of strangers. In effect, the growing predominance of passionate love had the function of encouraging strangers to meet and converse" (Featherstone 1998: 5). As Featherstone (1998: 5–6) goes on to note: "A parallel market to the economic market, the market of free emotions started to develop. A market which saw the new ideology of love increasingly extend its scope across the social space to undermine the 'restrictive practices' of class, religion and ethnicity. The growing democratization of love in the 18th century also saw love as increasingly linked to sexuality and both becoming central to marriage."

Mark Poster (1988) presents an entirely withering assessment of Luhmann's contribution. Luhmann is a systems theorist and he sets out to show that codes governing love in modern society can be differentiated from other codes. He uses Western love codes from the second-half of the seventeenth century to the present as his case study, but his main focus is on the period 1650 to 1800. As Poster (1988: 1295) shows:

> At the empirical level Luhmann shows that a complex pattern pivoting on the term "passion" regulated the medium of love at the start of the period. This figure of love developed outside the institution of marriage and concerned affairs of single men with married women. Toward the end of the eighteenth century, a new encoding of love as intimacy emerged, shifting its locus to marriage itself. Luhmann is careful properly to delimit the social location of each of these discourses, the first to the aristocracy, the second to the upper classes more generally.

Poster is highly critical of the limitations of the analysis which lacks historical detail and depth. He highlights some of the problems in using sociological models to understand historical complexity. Zygmund Bauman (1988: 1242) is more sympathetic in his analysis of Luhmann's model in arguing that: "Luhmann's dissection of the way love performs these incredible feats is passionately empathetic. His detection of the historical development of the codification of love (through 'ideal,' 'paradox,' and 'functional,' or problem-oriented stages) is erudite, credible and convincing."

Courtly Love

In order to fully understand how romantic love operated, Swidler (2001) maintains it is useful to look at its origins and evolution in European cultural history. As shown earlier, the significance of courtly love poetry which emerged in Europe at the end of the eleventh century was an important intervention in establishing a new conceptualisation of self and a new vision of love. As indicated earlier the lyric poetry was sung by troubadors in the courts of feudal France. Central in the love poetry was the role of noble women and the lyrics told of knights who were "made virtuous by love and of heroic deeds performed in the service of noble ladies" (Swidler 2001: 112).

While much in the Western history of love told of the dangers of love, in courtly poetry, love was seen as ennobling, rather than the dangerous appetite familiar to Greeks and Romans. Love in courtly poetry espoused by a knight encouraged the performance of heroic deeds and led to the transformation of the self, establishing a noble character. Within the courtly tradition, love was a spontaneous passion: "love at first sight" for an "idealized lover." Not only did it encourage virtue but it also led to individuals defying social convention in pursuit of a "higher destiny".

One of the key social theorists who detailed the character of courtly love and court society was Norbert Elias (1983) in *The Court Society* as well as in *The Civilising Process* (1994 [1939]). Featherstone (1998: 3) provides an excellent contextualisation of court society as outlined by Elias:

> The movement towards the fully developed court society such as the Versailles of Louis XIV described by Norbert Elias (1983) in the "gilded cage" of court life with its elaborate ceremonies and rituals, cultivation of formal conversation and good manners, provided a closed world replete with artifice, spying and intense rivalries in which the yearning for romantic relationships with social inferiors became a strong counter-ideal. As Elias (1983: 214ff . . .) reminds us, the sociogenesis of the romantic sentiment can be found not only in the middle classes but in the court society, where aristocrats who were subjected to the incessant self-control and calculation of court life developed a nostalgia for the simple life, not only manifest in a longing for country life but in a longing for the more expressive and spontaneous relationships of romantic love with trusted social inferiors.

As Swidler shows courtly love remained the dominant code of the European nobility for centuries, but the courtly ideal of love was gradually reshaped by the bourgeois culture of early capitalism and was expressed in its quintessential form in the eighteenth century novel. As Swidler (2001: 113) observes:

> Love in the novel remains a drama about virtue. But rather than simply inspiring heroic deeds, love becomes a test of individual character. In bourgeois love stories, individuals still discover and defend their integrity. But rather than betrayal and death, the bourgeois love story ends with a marriage in which the autonomous individual finds his or her proper place in the social world.

Modernity and Bourgeois Romantic Love

The history of love in the post-Enlightenment period has not been an uncontested one. As Evans (1998: 270) comments: "what we often accept as a fixed point in our culture is, in fact, one which has had diverse meanings. In particular what we can observe from this history is that love and romantic love most specifically has often been regarded as lower-class, irrational and deeply suspect."

In this case love is seen as "feminizing" challenging masculinity and undermining the traditional power structure. At the same time, love has been linked with greater autonomy for women and increased rights, while also leading to the domestication of men. So love can be seen as both a support for the powerless and at the same time a vehicle of oppression. Evans (1998: 273) is critical of the value of love arguing that: "Far from giving individuals a guide to the expression and articulation of emotional feelings, romance distorts and limits the possibilities of human relationships."

Love in Popular and Literary Fiction

One of the key drivers of love was the growth of popular and literary fiction which was the result of the growth of the print media. The impact of romantic fiction was both powerful and at the same time devastating. The historian Lawrence Stone comments in this regard: " . . . the romantic novel of the late eighteenth century and early nineteenth centuries has much to answer for in the way of disastrous love affairs and of impudent and unhappy marriages" (Stone 1977: 191).

Illouz reflects on the fact that the growth of literary fiction through the print media led to a cultural *malaise* about the impact of such fiction in creating "a (false) sentiment of love" (Illouz 1998: 162). Illouz uses Flaubert's *Madame Bovary* as an example of this *malaise* and says that it went a step further as she shows:

> Flaubert's heroine irreversibly crossed the boundary between "life" and the "novel", between the sign and its referent and paid with her own life for the confusion between fiction and reality, thus radicalizing the cultural *malaise* about mass printed romantic fiction.
> (Illouz 1998: 162)

However as Illouz elegantly points out this was not a malaise regarding romantic fiction but a contradiction in the nature of love and the failure of the bourgeois family:

> . . . Madame Bovary's tragic confusion did not refer to a moral discourse privileging marriage and "true" love over the illusions produced by

pernicious fiction. In Flaubert's narrative the power of romantic fiction pointed to the contradictions of the 19th century petit-bourgeois family, and the increasing centrality of love in the "disenchanted" fabric of everyday life.

(Illouz 1998: 162)

The novel *Madame Bovary* epitomised the romantic narrative of "le grand amour" in which love in the form of the desirability of another person could act as a form of salvation or redemption of their existence. Illouz (1998: 176) shows how Madame Bovary is a watershed of two different narratives:

Thus Madame Bovary clings to the idea that her relationship with Rodolphe is no mere 'affair' but rather the prelude to the great narrative she strives and waits for. In this respect, Emma stands on the threshold between the (modern) Romantic sensibility in which lives are spent waiting for or consuming themselves in a life-long 'master' narrative of love and the postmodern one in which several affairs – self-contained and 'local' narratives of love-occur serially in the course of a life.

Regardless of the "dangers" of romantic love, Evans (1998: 271) argues that there is a strong case for supposing that romantic love was a "formative part of the gradual ideological emancipation of women and the public definition of a specifically feminine set of interests." Crucial in this was the exercise of choice in the selection of partners. This was a movement still entrenched in class politics and patterns of inheritance, but for those not constrained by inheritance there was a much greater freedom to select a partner. Thus as Evans (1998: 27) outlines: "Women-through the discourse of romantic love could exercise choice in who they would marry and construct male behaviour in ways likely to produce love in women. Gallant forms of address, tests of devotion, commitments to fidelity, care and attention were part of the normal, and expected, behaviour of the man in love."

This significant shift in emphasis of "men in love" was subsequently reflected in eighteenth century English novelists and portrayed the man in love as not driven by power, money or gambling and as Evans shows as one divorced from "inexpressive masculinity" and driven primarily by the desire to show that he was in love. Heroes as diverse as Fitzwilliam Darcy in Austen's *Pride and Prejudice*, Tom Jones in the novel of the same name and (in the nineteenth century) Tolstoy's Count Vronsky in *Anna Karenina* all became apparently destabilized by their love for women (Illouz 1998: 271).

However the glamour of these passionate romantic heroes was thrown into relief by the growth of a critical school which offered a significant critique of romantic love. As Evans notes *Cosi fan Tutti*[1] was completed in 1790 and combined with the novels of Jane Austen offered a scathing attack on romantic love and at the same time endorsed sexual equality.

Contested Narratives of Romantic Love

As previously indicated romantic love narratives are frequently characterised by contestation. As Evans (1998: 266) indicates "in terms of English post-Enlightenment fiction the most profound, and the most articulate, critic of romantic love is Jane Austen." For many, romantic love narratives elevated women's autonomy and capacity for citizenship, for writers such as Austen, the very opposite is the case. Her tone is mocking and contemptuous of both women and men who renounce rationality for romance. As Evans (1998: 266) shows in writing of Austen's work:

> In all her novels she consistently mocks, satirizes and writes with deep contempt of these characters seduced into marriage by the physical appearance or apparent good nature of a partner. Clever, thinking, apparently rational men such as Mr Bennet in *Pride and Prejudice* find themselves—because of the fancies of love—married to women they cannot love and barely respect.

Central to all Austen's work (which is explored more fully below) is the question of rational choice. She strongly maintains that only rational discourse can provide a basis for human relationships. As Evans (1998: 266) notes:

> Unhappy marriages and ill-matched partners then result from those courtships in which the appearance and expectation of love was allowed to take precedence over rational understanding. Austen is, as Alasdair MacIntyre (1994) has argued, the definitive moralist of the Enlightenment and her morality—and her moral sense—is at its most sure in setting out the conditions on which heterosexual marriage should be established.

Throughout Austen's work there is the tension between the senses and rational behaviour which is never fully resolved in her work. So how significant was Austen's call for rational choice as against the appeal of romantic love. Evans (1998: 268) has little doubt as she states:

> Modernity opted for love and romance; a combination most usually expressed in Western culture as romantic love. Within this expectation, it became part of the normative structure of society to assume that people would "fall in love" (and equally out of love), and that being "in love" would provide the necessary and absolute legitimation for the construction (or destruction) of relationships. "Love at first sight", "true love", "endless love": all these descriptions of the nature of love became part of everyday speech and everyday assumptions. Within a culture in which "all you need is love" defined the aspirations of many individuals, the voice of Jane Austen-and other Enlightenment sceptics about romantic love-became muted and obscured.

Love, Courtship and Character: The "Prejudices" of Jane Austen

The approach of cultural sociologists to the work of Jane Austen probably differs significantly in the approach taken to that of the social historian or literary critic. Cultural sociologists are less interested in historical archival data and more interested in what Illouz (2012: 22) calls: "cultural testimonies of the assumptions that organized the self, morality, and interpersonal relationships of early to mid-nineteenth-century England." So Austen's work is not so much interesting as a set of literary texts but more so as offering a set of conceptual frameworks with which to:

> ... offer a conscientious reflection on class regulated matrimony and on emotional individual choice, ... and because they offer a good point of entry to understand the cultural system within which early to mid-nineteenth century English romantic feeling was organized, that is, the rituals and social rules, and the institutions which constrained the expression and experiences of sentiments.
>
> (Illouz 2012: 22)

Some of the key conceptual frameworks drawn on by Illouz in her analysis of Austen include: "character", courtship, "calling", authenticity and beauty. I want to consider these concepts and how they contribute to a cultural analysis of the social and cultural milieu within which Austen was writing.

In her presentation of character, captured in the characters of Knightley, Wentworth and Anne Elliott and in the book Emma (1816), the form of love that emerges is not based on "love at first sight" but on "attachment and habit". Love here is gradual and based on familiarity and strong bonds with families. For the character of Knightley, Wentworth and Ann Elliott, love is not about a rupture between passion and moral duty as there is an integration of both. In other words as Illouz (2012: 25) comments, it is impossible to separate the moral and the emotional.

Thus character does not focus on "interiority" but acts as a "bridge between the self and the public world of values and norms" (Illouz 2012: 26). For both women and men: "In the context of love and courtship, character designates the fact that both lovers derive their personal sense of value directly from their capacity to enact moral codes and ideals, rather than from the value bestowed on their inner self by a suitor" (Illouz 2012: 26).

So the question raised by Illouz (2012: 27) is how are love and morality connected? She maintains that: "what we call a moral self and sentiments consist in a specific 'ecology and architecture of choice,'[2] in which there is a high degree of congruence between private and public choices..." (see Chapter 6).

So how did this process work in practice and how did it impact on the wider social network? This brings into play the second concept, that of courtship. Courtship as Illouz (2012: 28) shows operated in England and the United

States through "a process of verification of the claims and credentials of suitors." Because a wide range of individuals participated in the process of evaluating a suitor, the choice a woman made was an extension of her family and social network. Illouz (2012: 28) gives the example of Anne Elliot in Jane Austen's *Persuasion*:

> ... in *Persuasion*, Anne Elliot is heavily influenced by Lady Russell, who deems her first true (and only) love, Captain Wentworth, inappropriate. Our modern sensibility can only relate to the fact that her negative evaluation of Wentworth forced Anne to renounce the object of her love. But from another perspective, Lady Russell's mistake derived from the fact that Anne's self was tightly protected because it was embedded in kin relationships.

Austen does highlight the limitations of the process by showing the inability of the wider social milieu to distinguish social status from inner value, but the broader picture showed a model of courtship which was highly structured and ritualised, particularly among the propertied classes.

One of the ways in which the ritualised process of courtship received expression was in the concept of "calling". This was a significant part of the courtship practice and control of the process was in the woman's hands and the invitation "to call" had to come from the woman's home. As Illouz (2012: 29) observes, the ritual of "calling" extended into the pattern of courtship interaction: "once the courtship was conducted, it advanced by subtle gradations, with couples first speaking, then walking out together and finally keeping company once their mutual attraction had been confirmed."

Illouz argues that within this ritualised pattern of courtship, emotions followed actions and declarations. She calls this "*a regime of performativity of emotions*: that is, a regime in which emotions are induced by the ritualized actions and expressions of sentiments" (Illouz 2012: 30).

As Illouz shows, central to the performative regime of emotions is the social rule that actions converge with intensions. She cites an etiquette manual of 1897 which offered instructions on this:

> *A gentleman's conduct towards Ladies*. Gentlemen are at liberty to invite their lady friends to concerts, operas, balls etc., to call upon them at their homes, to ride and drive with them, and to make themselves agreeable to all young ladies to whom their company is acceptable. In fact, they are at liberty to accept invitations and give them *ad libitum*. As soon, however, as a young gentlemen neglects all others, to devote himself to a single lady, he gives that lady reason to suppose that he is particularly attracted to her, and may give her cause to believe that she is to become engaged to him, without telling her so. A gentlemen who does not contemplate matrimony should not pay too exclusive attention to any one lady.
>
> (Illouz 2012: 30)

Illouz maintains that what distinguished relationships in premodern courtships from contemporary relationships is the issue of "emotional authenticity". She maintains that authenticity implies a real emotional ontology beyond the specific expression of feeling and involves a scrutiny of one another's emotion (see also Chapters 5 and 6). It is very clear that the emphasis here is on performativity and not authenticity.

Courtship, was of course, also part of an economic operation and probably the most significant one in most women's lives. A woman's dowry determined her market value in the marriage stakes and upon marriage the woman's property went to her husband. Thus, the selection process, including status and ranking and the assessment through the social environment all played into the process of mate selection. Beauty also played a part but was not a significant driver of romantic love as we discover below. As Illouz (2012: 40) states: "It is these mechanisms, at once social and moral, private and public, that regulated the middle-and upper-middle class choice of mate well into the nineteenth century at least in the English-speaking world. What changed in modernity are precisely the conditions within which love choices are made."

Bohemian Love

Bohemian ideologies of love provide a unique and vibrant set of discourses within the narratives of romantic love. Whereas the growth of a romantic literary tradition had offered a contestational set of discourses around love and marriage, some highly critical of romantic love, none had challenged love and marriage to the point of rejecting it entirely. However, as Wilson (1998: 111) shows, bohemian love did just that: "One of its central components, however, was a rejection of bourgeois marriage and conventional family norms and the espousal of a view of eroticism as a source of inspiration... for works of art."

Just as the discourses of romantic love did not show a consensus, similarly with the discourses around bohemian love which reflected cultural and geographical characteristics. As shown by Wilson's (1998) analysis of the history of bohemian ideologies of love, one tradition can be traced back to the French literary culture of the 1830s, where early bohemian thinking flourished, although they did not use that term. Featherstone (1998: 11) provides a valuable overview:

> Here we think of the novels of Gautier and Balzac and the poetry of Baudelaire which explored love and death in relation to marginality, transgression and homosexuality.... The Bohemia that grew up in Paris had a characteristic flouting of conventional bourgeois morality, taste and sexual mores. Baudelaire saw a new more virile type of womanhood as emerging in the city: lesbians, woman labourers and prostitutes. The *flaneur* can be seen as a feminine form of impotent wandering, a form of perpetual deferral, rather than mastery which was part of a process of feminizing men.... In the second half of the 19th century, we find a more commercialized image of the Bohemian as some of the characteristic inversions

of Bohemia became transformed into operas: Puccini's *La Boheme* and Bizet's *Carmen* being notable examples.

Beyond the literary and artistic traditions of France as providing one example of bohemianism, German bohemian culture in the period before the First World War provided an interesting expression of bohemianism, in combining an intellectual elite, psychiatry and something of an "erotic revolution". The third element in discussing bohemianism is that of Greenwich Village in the United States at a slightly later period.

The Bohemian tradition had a number of characteristics and provided for the emergence of the *"transgressive femme fatale."* The *"transgressive femme fatale"* had a broad range in the literature and in real life extending from the figure of Carmen in Bizet's opera *Carmen* to the real life bohemian author George Sand, whose life matched her published work in its unconventionalism and in its gender politics.

The image of Carmen is located at the intersection of the subcultural heroine and standard bearer of women's rights and female equality. As Featherstone (1998: 11) comments:

> ... Indeed, in many ways the figure of Carmen represents a projection of Bohemian free love and individualistic values combined with an idealized romantic vision of gypsy life. What is interesting about the figure of Carmen is the way in which it has subsequently become a powerful cultural image and modern myth. Within consumer culture Carmen–inspired fashions reappear periodically along with the Carmen-look on covers of women's magazines. The Carmen image challenged the possessiveness and passivity associated with more traditional feminine ideals of love; instead Carmen stands for a more active and individualistic ideal of non-exclusive love.

The transgressions of the *femme fatale* were only one dimension of bohemian love, homoeroticism and homosexuality were also important transgressive dimensions of bohemian love. As Wilson (1998: 115) shows, bohemianism had an appeal for both men and women but for different reasons. For men it provided an opportunity for anti-bourgeois behaviour as well as homosexuality:

> The combination of aristocratic outlawry and underworld association marked the emergent bohemian out as quintessentially anti-bourgeois. To flout the conventions and restrictions surrounding sexual behaviour in 19th century society was one obvious form of rebellion. Nineteenth-century bohemian men consorted with prostitutes and lived openly with their mistresses, refusing the conformity of bourgeois marriage.

As Wilson observes the majority of bohemian artists were heterosexual but beyond the superficiality of unconventional relationships were the homoeroticism and bisexuality that were central to bohemian life.

One of the books which highlighted the gender ambiguity characteristic of bohemianism was Theophile Gautier's novel *Mademoiselle de Maupin* published in 1835. Wilson (1998: 113) provides an insightful summary:

> Set in the 17th century, *Mademoiselle de Maupin* tells the story of a triangular love affair. At a country chateau d'Albert and his mistress Rosette meet a mysterious young man, Theodore, to whom both are strangely drawn. Matters come to a head during some amateur theatricals in which Theodore plays a female role, when d'Albert realizes to his horror that he is falling in love with the person he believes to be a man in drag. But of course Theodore is a woman—Mademoiselle de Maupin-in disguise, and the double error of the plot, whereby d'Albert falls in love heterosexually but believes his love is homosexual, while Rosette, also enamoured of Theodore, believes she has fallen in love with a man, 'acts to place homosexual love, both masculine and feminine, at the centre of a tale in which no-one actually admits to it'(Benichou 1992: 525). The novel ends ambiguously after Theodore /Mademoiselle de Maupin has slept with both Rosette and d'Albert during the course of a single night before leaving both of them of them forever.

The disruption of gender boundaries is highlighted by Theodore's comments: "I was imperceptibly losing the idea of my sex, and I remembered only at long intervals, hardly at all, that I was a woman . . . In truth, neither of the two sexes are mine . . . I belong to a third sex apart, which has as yet no name" (Gautier 1966: 356). Ambiguities of gender was not a new element in literary traditions and for the bohemians, homoeroticism was seen as the most transgressive form of erotic love. This is clearly articulated by Gautier (1966: 266) in his novel in the way d'Albert expresses his lust for Theodore:

> . . . as compelling as the perfidious sphinx with the dubious smile and ambiguous voice, before whom I stood without daring to attempt an explanation of the enigma . . . to love, with a . . . monstrous, in admissible love . . . to feel oneself devoured by longings that even the most hardened libertines would regard as insane and inexcusable; what are the ordinary passions besides this?

One of the underlying issues emerging from, not just, gender ambiguity but homosexuality was the character of masculine identity in the urban society that was emerging. One of the foremost documenters of social change in an urban context was Charles Baudelaire.

Baudelaire and the Flaneur

Charles Baudelaire was a friend of Gautier. Wilson (1998: 16) describes him as the "perennial rebel and poseur, the ultimate anti-bourgeois and bohemian." She frames his penchant for dandyism[3] as linked to his relationship with his mother. Perhaps of greatest interest was his development of the concept of the *flaneur* in the context of Parisian streets. It was Walter Benjamin, who, drawing on the work of Baudelaire, made the figure of the *flaneur* an object of scholarly interest. Baudelaire describes the *flaneur* in his book *The Painter of Modern Life* (1964a [1863]) as follows:

> The lover of life makes the whole world his family, just like the lover of the fair sex who builds up his family from all the beautiful women that he has ever found, or that are or are not-to be found; or the lover of pictures who lives in a magical society of dreams painted on canvas. Thus the lover of universal dreams enters into the crowd as though it were an immense reservoir of electrical energy.

Wilson argues that the "society of the spectacle was feminizing men . . . the voyeuristic flaneur or bohemian became a kind of woman as he observed the urban world, a project brought out by Walter Benjamin (1985: 40; . . .)" (Wilson 1998: 115–116). Wilson also maintains that Baudelaire identified new, more active women, in the urban context including female labourers, prostitutes and lesbians.

However as Janet Wolff (1985) comments in her iconic article "The Invisible *Flaneuse*: Women and the Literature of Modernity": "The public sphere, then, despite the presence of some women in certain contained areas of it, was a masculine domain. And insofar as the experience of 'the modern' occurred mainly in the public sphere, it was primarily men's experience" (Wolff 1985: 37). Some of the key social commentators on modernity, Baudelaire (1964b [1863], 1965a, 1965b), Benjamin (1973) and Simmel (1950a, 1950b) while drawing to a limited extent on the experiences of women, largely wrote about modernity as a male experience. Perhaps Simmel more than any other social theorist of the time drew on women in both public and private spheres. As Wolff (1985: 41) shows: "Simmel paid much attention to the condition of women. He wrote essays on the position of women, the psychology of women, female culture, and the women's movement and social democracy . . .".

Baudelaire's essays and poems also include reference to the lives of women and he includes a number of female city-dwellers in his work, most prominent being: the prostitute, the widow, the old-lady, the lesbian, the murder victim and the passing unknown woman. However, Baudelaire was no friend of women or their position in society. As Wolff (1985: 42) shows:

> Indeed according to Benjamin, the lesbian was for Baudelaire the heroine of modernism; certainly it is known that he originally intended to give the title *Les Lesbiennes* to the poems which became *Les Fleurs du Mal* (Benjamin 1973: 90). Yet as Benjamin (1973: 923) also points out, in the major poem about lesbians of the series, *Delphine et Hippolyte*, Baudelaire

(1975: 224) concludes by condemning the women as "lamentable victims", bound for hell. The prostitute, the subject of the poem *Crepuscule du Soir* and also discussed in a section of *The Painter of Modern Life* (Baudelaire 1967: 185 . . .), elicits a similarly ambivalent attitude of admiration and disgust . . . More unequivocal is Baudelaire's (1975: 166, 1967: 63–65) sympathy for those marginal women, the old woman and the widow; the former he "watches tenderly from afar" like a father, the latter he observes with a sensitivity to her pride, pain and poverty. But none of these women meet the poet as his equal. They are subjects of his gaze, objects of his "botanising".

Wolff also shows that Baudelaire was in fact a misogynist and this is brought out clearly in his letters and prose. As she shows in citing a letter written to a woman he idolised and idealised: "I have hateful prejudices about women. In fact, *I have no faith*, you have a fine soul, but when all is said, it is the soul of a woman (Letter to Apollonie Sabatier . . . italics in original)" (Wolff 1985: 42). As Wolff (1985: 43) notes: "The classic misogynist duality, of woman as idealised-but-vapid/real-and-sensual-but-detested, which Baudelaire displays . . . is clearly related to the particular parade of women we observe in the literature of modernity."

The literature of modernity has largely ignored the lives of women or presented these lives as seen through the gaze of men. Bohemian women could be seen as an early manifestation of the women's movement and their main concern was to claim the same rights in relationships as men. An interesting example of the bohemian woman is George Sand. As Wolff (1985: 41) observes, citing George Sand:

> The dandy, the *flaneur*, the hero, the stranger—all figures invoked to epitomise the experience of modern life-are invariably male figures. In 1831, when George Sand wanted to experience Paris life and to learn about the ideas and arts of her time, she dressed as a boy, to give herself the freedom she knew women could not share:

> So I had made for myself a *redingote-guerite* in heavy gray cloth, pants and vest to match. With a gray hat and large woollen cravat. I was a perfect first year student. I can't express the pleasure my books gave me: I would gladly have slept with them, as my brother did in his young age, when he got his first pair. With those iron-shod heels, I was solid on the pavement. I flew from one end of Paris to the other. It seemed to me that I could go round the world. And then my clothes feard nothing. I ran out in every kind of weather. I came home at every sort of hour. I sat in the pit in the theatre. No one paid attention to me, and no one guessed at my disguise . . . No one knew me, no one looked at me, no one found fault with me; I was an atom lost in that immense crowd. (Quoted in Moers 1977: 12)

Sand's disguise made the life of the *flaneur* available to her for a short time. As Wolff indicates the role of the *flaneuse* was non-existant in modernity. So let's look more closely at the life and writings of George Sand to assess its contribution to Bohemian thinking.

George Sand

Born Amanline-Lucile Dupin in 1804 and with the adopted authorial name, George Sand, Sand lived and wrote the bohemian life. Her life was as controversial, for the time, as her novels which scandalised the reading public. Her many well publicised romantic affairs included with the composer Frederic Chopin and the writer Alfred de Musset. She left her husband and lived with her lover. She was also thought to have had lesbian relationships. As indicated she also dressed in men's clothing at times, as did many other women. She claimed the clothes were much tougher and less expensive than the clothes worn by noblewomen of the time. She also claimed that they gave her more freedom to circulate in Paris and allowed her access to venues that were often barred to women.

She was prolific as an author publishing a wide range of novels including: *La Petite Fadette* (1849), *Consuelo* (1842a), *Mauprat* (1837), *Indiana* (1832), *Lelia* (1833), *A Winter in Majorca (*1842b), *Valvedre* (1861), *Lucrezia Floriani* (1847), *The Miller of Angibault* (1845), *The Master Pipers* (1852). While it is not possible to consider all of Sand's novels here, it is fascinating to reflect on some of her main novels and what they convey about her life and her philosophy.

Sand's book *Indiana* published in 1832 outlines the story of a French gentlewoman, Indiana, who is trapped in a loveless marriage to an older and sick husband, Colonel Delmore and who searches for love and passion elsewhere. Sand uses *Indiana* to surface the difficulties that arise from marriages based on social and economic expectations, where women in the nineteenth century faced impossible choices in whether to accept and unhappy marriage or a life of social condemnation.

Her book *Lelia* appeared in 1833 and many regard this as her best novel. Sand was 29 years old when she wrote this novel and it stunned Victorians by arguing for the same standards of morality for men and women and Sand maintained that both prostitute and the married woman were slaves to male desire. She also questioned monogamy, fidelity and monastic celibacy.

Sand was also a political writer and she wrote many essays and other works setting out her socialist position. When the 1848 revolution in France began, Sand started her own newspaper which was published in a workers' cooperative. She wrote: "I cannot believe in any republic that starts a revolution by killing its own proletariat."

Sand's (1852b) book *The Master Pipers* combines the personal and the political. The novel is a love story set in the regions of Central France. In the relationships she outlines, Sand shows how women should be treated as equals in the marriage. This book was written in the aftermath of the failed revolution of 1848, and there is a clear political and social message in the novel which is only by combining what is best in the French peasantry with a code of non-violence is there any possibility of profound social change.

The novel which is most closely related to Sand's own life is *Lucrezia Floriani*, published in 1847. Henry James called this novel "splendid". The novel tells the story of Lucrezia Floriani, a 30-year-old actress and mother of four children, with three different fathers, who meets and falls in love with Prince Karol, a moody introspective aristocrat. The novel is a thinly disguised narrative of the relationship between Sand and Chopin. While Sand claimed she had not intended to ridicule Chopin, the book's publication and widespread readership exacerbated the collapse of her relationship with Chopin. In 1849 Chopin died in Paris, penniless and while his funeral was attended by Delacroix, Liszt, and Victor Hugo, George Sand did not attend.

Sand was clearly a radical thinker and self-obsessed individual but a perfect example of a bohemian in her commitment to a bohemian lifestyle and in her authorship of a large number of radical novels.

The German Bohemian Tradition

The bohemian tradition in Germany was on the face of it less glamorous than the French tradition and much more explicitly committed to the erotic. It was also much more closely tied to the psychiatric tradition. The central figure in this movement was Otto Gross who Wilson (1998: 118) sees at the centre of the "erotic revolution." Featherstone (1998: 11) claims that he was within the tradition of love and eroticism and "his advocacy and practice of an erotic and anarchistic lifestyle made Gross a precursor of Wilhelm Reich, R.D. Laing and others, who were to be taken up by the 1960s counterculture."

Gross had close links with psychiatry as he worked as an assistant in a psychiatric clinic in Munich. He developed theories of sexual repression and free love and Wilson (1998) maintains his involvements with women were scandalous and sinister. For example, Gross had a series of affairs with women but when the situation became complicated he left poison for the women to encourage them to commit suicide. As shown below some of the women Gross had affairs with, were associated with the sociologist, Max Weber's circle.

Gross was an unattractive figure in his life and philosophy but his role in highlighting aspects of psychoanalysis is worth consideration. Wilson (1998: 120) outlines his role:

> [Gross] tried to adapt psychoanalysis to a radical world-view. His work had begun to diverge from Freud in 1908 or 1909, when, anticipating Wilhelm Reich, he redefined the sexual drive as a benign force which is distorted by social institutions. The logical conclusion of this position was that to act on all one's sexual desires was to diminish repression and was in itself liberating.

Perhaps more interesting was the influence of psychoanalysis itself after it crossed the Atlantic and the impact it had on the American bohemian community and the growth of centres of bohemian culture such as Greenwich Village to highlight the intersection of the "erotic revolution" and the "cultural revolution" as it developed in the United States and to a less extent in Britain.

Love and Eroticism

The last section of the chapter outlining narratives of romantic love, considers some of the initial aspects of the "erotic revolution" and anticipates a fuller discussion of these in Chapter 6. The emergence of discussions around the erotic were reflected in Max Weber's work, as Featherstone (1998: 10) comments:

> In his famous 'Zwischenbetrachtung' essay, Max Weber (1948) refers to the differentiation of the cultural sphere into separate aesthetic, intellectual and erotic life-orders. For Weber, the aesthetic, intellectual and erotic spheres were unable to repair the loss of ethical totality and capacity to provide a meaningful ordered life . . . His negative view of aesthetics and erotics was based upon the assumption that the preoccupation with forms and immersion is the irrational force of sexual life "the only and the ineradicable link to animality". (Weber 1948: 347)

Perhaps surprisingly, Weber was influenced in his thinking about the erotic sphere by his association with Otto Gross and Else Jaffe who had become involved in 1907. Jaffe wanted to bring Weber and Gross together. Weber was suspicious of the blend of: "psychoanalysis, Lebensphilosophie and bohemianism which Gross advocated and saw it as a threat of science and civilization, which necessarily depended on sublimation" (Featherstone 1998: 10).

Weber did visit the communes that Gross had established in 1913 and 1914 in Switzerland and did shift his position somewhat in maintaining that eroticism could offer an inner-wordly form of salvation. However, Weber maintained his distance from the excesses of Gross's lifestyle.

Erotic attraction in the twentieth century became increasingly to be defined in terms of sexual desirability or sexiness and a shift in emphasis to physical attractiveness and beauty and away from the moral world of values. While erotic attraction has always implicity acknowledged sexuality and beauty, Illouz (2012) maintains that its deployment as a pervasive cultural category is modern. Illouz (2012: 42) highlights the contrast between nineteenth and twentieth century conceptualisations of love, sexuality and beauty:

> As a cultural category, sexiness is distinct from beauty. Nineteenth-century middle-class women were viewed as having physical and spiritual attributes (This is why Robert Browning could fall in love with Elizabeth Barrett, who was an invalid, precisely because he could subsume her physical

appearance under her inner beauty. Her invalidity did not seem to pose a particular problem in his account of his love for her).

The shift in emphasis to beauty and physicality in the twentieth century is seen by Illouz as part of the cultural commodification of beauty and sexuality. As Illouz (2012: 42) comments: ". . . nineteenth-century notions of beauty did not contain an explicit reference to sex or sexuality. Quite the contrary, beauty was relevant to the extent that it reflected character. Victorian morality viewed cosmetics with suspicion because they were perceived to be an illegitimate substitute for 'real' inner moral beauty." These debates will be explored more fully in Chapters 5 and 6.

Conclusion

The history of the narratives of romantic love are diverse, contested, painful and seductive. There is no single ideology of romantic love but a nuanced and varied range of discourses. As Evans (1998: 274) observes:

> The social tragedy of romance (unlike its many personal tragedies) is that just as it seemed possible to recognize the loneliness of the human condition (and Frankenstein's monster in Mary Shelley's novel spoke for everyone when he cried out for human companionship) and to attempt to build an ethic of love which would diminish that loneliness, social and material factors usurped romance and love forced them into the endlessly infantilizing constructions that we know as 19th and 20th century love and romance.

Notes

1. *Cosi fan Tutti* is an Italian-language opera in two acts by Wolfgang Amadeus Mozart first performed in 1790. The libretto was written by Lorenzo Da Ponte, who also wrote *Le nozze di Figaro* and *Don Giovanni*. The title, *Così fan tutte*, literally means "Thus do all [women]" and is popularly used to mean "Women are like that".
2. Illouz (2012: 190) explains what she means by an "architecture of choice". She shows how it contains a number of cognitive and emotional processes, and, more especially, it has to do with the ways in which emotional and rational forms of thinking are valued . . . in making a decision.
3. Historically, especially in late eighteenth and early nineteenth century Britain, a dandy, who was self-made, often strove to imitate an aristocratic lifestyle despite coming from a middle-class background.

Bibliography

Baudelaire, Charles. 1964a/1863. *The Painter of Modern Life*. New York: Da Capo Press.
Baudelaire, Charles. 1964b/1863. "The Painter of Modern Life." In Jonathan Mayne (trans and ed.). *The Painter of Modern Life and Other Essays*. Oxford: Phaidon Press.

Baudelaire, Charles. 1965a. "The Salon of 1845." In *Art in Paris 1845–1862*. Oxford: Phaidon Press.
Baudelaire, Charles. 1965b. "The Salon of 1846." In *Art in Paris 1845–1862*. Oxford: Phaidon Press.
Bauman, Zygmunt. 1988. "Love as Passion: The Codification of Intimacy by Niklas Luhman" *American Journal of Sociology* 93(5): 1240–1243.
Benichou, Paul. 1992. *L'Ecole du desenchantement: Sainte-Beuve, Nodier, Musset, Nerval, Gautier*. Paris: Gallinard.
Benjamin, Walter. 1973. *Charles Baudelaire: A Lyric Poet in the Era of High Capitalism*. London: New Left Books.
Benjamin, Walter. 1985. "Central Park. Trans. Lloyd Spencer" *New German Critique* 34: 1–27.
De Rougemont, Denis. 1983. *Love in the Western World*. Princeton, NJ: Princeton University Press.
Elias, Norbert. 1983. *The Court Society*. Oxford: Blackwell.
Elias, Norbert. 1994/1939. *The Civilizing Process: The History of Manners and State Formation*. Oxford: Basil Blackwell.
Evans, Mary. 1998. "'Falling in Love with Love Is Falling for Make Believe': Ideologies of Romance in Post-Enlightenment Culture" *Theory, Culture, Society* 15(3–4): 265–275.
Featherstone, Mike. 1995. *Undoing Culture: Globalization, Postmodernism and Identity*. London: Sage.
Featherstone, Mike. 1998. "Love and Eroticism: An Introduction" *Theory, Culture Society* 15(3–4): 1–18.
Gautier, Theophile. 1874. *Historie du Romantisme*. Paris: Charpentier.
Gautier, Theophile. 1966. *Mademoiselle de Maupin*. Paris: Garnier-Flammarion (orig. 1835).
Giddens, Anthony. 1991. *Modernity and Self-Identity: Self and Society in the Late Modern Age*. Cambridge: Polity Press.
Giddens, Anthony. 1992. *The Transformation of Intimacy*. Stanford, CA: Stanford University Press.
Illouz, Eva. 1998. "The Lost Innocence of Love: Romance as a Postmodern Condition" *Theory, Culture, Society* 15(3–4): 161–186.
Illouz, Eva. 2012. *Why Love Hurts: A Sociological Explanation*. Cambridge: Polity.
Luhmann, Niklas. 1986. *Love as Passion: The Codification of Intimacy*. Cambridge, MA: Harvard University Press.
Moers, Ellen. 1977. *Literary Women*. New York: Anchor Press.
Paz, Octavia. 1996. *The Double Flame: Essays on Love and Eroticism*. London: Haverill.
Poster, Mark. 1988. "Love as Passion: The Codification of Intimacy by Niklas Luhmann" *American Historical Review* 13(5): 1294–1295.
Sand, George. 1832/1870. *Indiana*. Trans. George W. Richards. Philadelphia: T.B Peterson and Brothers.
Sand, George. 1833. *Lelia*. Paris: Henri Dupuy.
Sand, George. 1837/1998. *Mauprat*. Oxford: Oxford University Press.
Sand, George. 1842a/1992. *A Winter in Majorca*. Chicago: Academy Chicago Publishers.
Sand, George. 1842b/1889. *Consuelo*. Trans. Frank H. Potter. New York: Dodd, Mead and Company.

Sand, George. 1847/1993. *Lucrezia Floriani.* Trans. Julius Eker. Illinois: Academy Chicago Publishers.
Sand, George. 1849/1900. *La Petite Fadette.* Trans. Henry Holt and Company. Boston: Henry Holt and Company.
Sand, George. 1852a/1995. *The Miller of Angibault.* Oxford: Oxford University Press).
Sand, George. 1852b/1994. *The Master Pipers.* Oxford: Oxford University Press.
Sand, George. 1861/2012. *Valvedre.* New York: SUNY Press.
Simmel, George. 1950a. "The Stranger." In Kurt H. Wolff (ed.), *The Sociology of George Simmel.* New York: Free Press.
Simmel, George. 1950b. "The Metropolis and Mental Life." In Kurt H. Wolff (ed.), *The Sociology of George Simmel.* New York: Free Press.
Stone, Lawrence. 1977. *The Family, Sex and Marriage in England, 1500–1800.* New York: Harper and Row.
Swidler, Anne. 2001. *Talk of Love: How Culture Matters.* Chicago: University of Chicago Press.
Weber, Max. 1948. "Religious Rejections of the World and Their Directions." In H.H. Gerth and C. Wright Mills (eds), *From Max Weber.* London: Routledge.
Wilson, Elizabeth. 1998. "Bohemian Love" *Theory, Culture and Society* 15(3–4): 111–127.
Wolff, Janet. 1985. "The Invisible Flaneuse: Women and the Literature of Modernity" *Theory, Culture and Society* 2(3): 37–46.

4 "Mapping Intimacy through Sex in Twentieth Century Colonial Cultures"
The Work of Laura Ann Stoler and Anne McClintock

Introduction

This chapter focuses on the role of sex in colonial cultures and draws on the work of some of the major feminist historians, anthropologists and social theorists who have researched the area and provided a multidisciplinary analysis of the field. The particular focus of the chapter is on the significant and exciting contribution of Laura Ann Stoler's work, whose work in the area of sex and intimacy in twentieth century colonial cultures has been powerful both theoretically and empirically. However the analysis of sex cannot be taken in isolation and is intersected by issues of gender, race, nation and class. In this regard the work of Anne McClintock (1995, 1997) has provided further analysis of discourses of race, gender and nation and provides a powerful additional contribution to the debate. In this chapter I first contextualise Stoler's research by looking initially at the historical field of sex and sexuality in colonial cultures developed in the work of Philippa Levine (2004a) and Kathleen Wilson (2004) among others, who provide a historical framework to the development of relations of power, sex, gender and Empire in different historical periods. In the second part of the chapter I analyse the contribution of Stoler (1997, 2002, 2006) to discourses around the analysis of power, which she develops from the work of Michel Foucault, as well as to her extensive empirical analysis of Dutch, French and British imperial cultures. The third part of the chapter focuses on McClintock's analysis of gender, race and nationalism.

Sex and Sexuality in Colonial Contexts

In "Sexuality, Gender and Empire," Levine (2004a) shows that sex and sexual fantasy were a critical part of relations between colonizer and colonized, and that race and sex were closely connected in the shaping of relationships in the colonies. One of the clearest expressions of this was concubinage and Levine shows that it was widespread in the Caribbean, India, parts of Africa and in the

Pacific in the eighteenth century. While attitudes varied from one country to another, Levine (2004c: 138) indicates that:

> . . . the arrangement sometimes allowed women to rise in status or wealth . . . women provided domestic and sexual services, often bore a man's children, and were sometimes supported materially after men returned to Europe . . . Though in the Dutch East Indies concubinage survived as "the dominant domestic arrangement" into the twentieth century, enjoying formal "recognition in the civil law code," this was not so in the British colonies . . . The East India Company prohibited senior employees from marrying Indian women by 1835.

The intersection of race and sex were a feature of what was seen as the "over-sexedness" of colonial peoples as Levine (2004c: 137) notes the key to maintaining superiority in the Empire was the regulation and management of sex:

> . . . there was far more regulatory activity around practices which might harm or jeopardize the standing of the Empire and its maintenance than around those harmful to colonized women. Thus while prostitution was, in almost the whole Empire, subject to stringent management, the trafficking of women for sexual gain was of only nugatory interest in the imperial state.

Another dimension of inter-racial relationships was that between a white woman and non-white colonial man. As Levine comments white women were excluded from white society if they were involved in "inter-racial liaison". At the outset of colonial settlement, the East India Company had encouraged inter-racial marriage to avoid the additional cost of shipping out white women. However, this changed and the state played a significant role in intervening in marriages, as Levine (2004c: 141) shows:

> The colonial state frequently intervened in marriage practices, affecting contracts between husband and wife as well as with their kin, the status of wives, the property that accompanied marriages and the age of marriage . . . In many instances, colonial intervention worsened women's lot. The 1856 Widow Remarriage Act in India which attempted to facilitate women re-marrying when widowed, assumed high-caste Hindu practice to be widespread. Yet though the high-caste Hindu widow was expected to live in chastity and seclusion following the death of her husband (a situation which often led to poverty and isolation for women likely to have been married at a very young age), other Hindus rejected the practice. As a result of its focus on the high-caste, the Act hurt poorer women hitherto unaffected by these constraints. . . .

A third element in the sexualisation of the Empire was that of prostitution. Levine reports that colonial officials were condemnatory of many colonial cultures for "the sexual enslavement of women," these included the Chinese who enslaved poor women in brothels and Indian culture which practiced temple prostitution (see Bush 1990). As a result, by the middle of the nineteenth century, there were systems for regulating prostitution throughout the Empire (Howell 2000).

Levine notes that the registration of brothels became a requirement for colonial authorities and this was accompanied by the racial segregation of brothels. She indicates that by the late nineteenth century, European prostitutes worked in most parts of the Empire, although she notes that few were English. Colonial officials, however, were alarmed that the implication of this was that all white women would be seen as sexually available. Levine also notes that: "white colonial customers disliked the idea that the women they purchased might service men of other races" (Levine 2004c: 145). Eventually, as regulation proved difficult, a shift was made to suppression, with commercial sex being banned in India, the Malay penninsula and Hong Kong.

In addition to sex, conceptualisations of nation also played an important role in reinforcing gender divisions within colonial cultures, as Wilson (2004: 17, 20) comments:

> Ideologies of nation brought gender and sexual practice, as sources and symbols of a common inheritance, to the forefront of social and political theories . . . In contrast to the sixteenth and seventeenth centuries, when gender was understood to be the stable marker of a cosmic and largely inscrutable divine order, it emerged in the eighteenth century as both "natural"- the product of the universal and discernible . . . laws of human nature and society, akin to other phenomena in natural science . . .
>
> In the 1770s, women's role in Empire and patriotism was represented as more beneficial if less direct than previously, as their domestic virtue was promoted as a source of moral authority in the broader imperial polity.

Wilson develops an interesting approach to gender and Empire through the concept of "sensibility". Sensibility on the one hand could be seen as the hallmark of a "modern" civilised nation in its relationship with Empire, and as Wilson notes, women were central to sensibility's foundation. An example of this could be seen in the late 1780s, as Wilson (2004: 21) shows:

> . . . the much vaunted moral influence of English women saturated colonial reform initiatives such as anti-slavery. Deploying the language of sensibility, British women brought their supposed feminine compassion and sympathy to bear on the sexual exploitation of black women and the break-up of families, slavery enjoined (see Midgely 1992, Sussman 2000)

However the implications of such sensibility, also brought with it a sense of superiority and the view that white English women embodied the highest levels of civilisation and thus "entitled" to represent the moral and ethical face of Empire:

> ... they felt entitled to dominate other women of the Empire, to serve as "teachers of nations" and manners to the less well-positioned. Those who failed to exhibit these qualities—which by the 1780s and 1790s included working-class women within Britain, as well as colonized and enslaved women—were denigrated as savage or depraved, redeemable only by acquiescing in the division of labour and standards of domesticity set for them by their betters.
> (Wilson 2004: 22)

Wilson shows how in eighteenth century America, sexual relationships between English settlers and Native Americans also highlighted this pattern of movement from "savagery" to "civility". As Wilson (2004: 24) outlines:

> Male authority ... seemed conspicuous in Indian communities by its lack. The women's sexual 'libertinism,' the effortlessness with which they gave birth ... and the ease with which heterosexual partnerships were made and dissolved underscored the problem of masculine deficiency and debased femininity.

As in many colonised cultures, Wilson shows that Indian women served more than as sexual partners, they acted as "sleeping dictionaries" for the male coloniser, providing "access to gossip circulating through nearby or rival settlements and across plantations" (Wilson 2004: 25), and producing mixed-blood offspring. It was a combination of colonisation and patriarchy which acted to manage both colonised and white women in the colonies.

Settler women did sometimes breakthrough to establish themselves in colonial cultures and Wilson shows that in the Caribbean or New South Wales, white British women could establish themselves in good marriages:

> "Widowarchy" prevailed in other Atlantic colonies too, from Virginia to St Helena, where the regulation of marriage as a means of transmission of property was of critical import. Even the penal colony of New South Wales afforded social mobility. Esther Abrahams, a Jewish convict transported for stealing lace, became the mistress and then wife of a future Governor of the colony, serving as a beacon of hope to other convict women.
> (Wilson 2004: 28)

Perhaps the most harsh dimension of colonisation was "chattel slavery" which was controlled by Europeans in the New World. As Wilson shows in British

America, the vast majority of slaves were of African descent and most worked (men and women) on the sugar, rice and tobacco "plantations in the Caribbean, Chesapeake and North American Low Country" (Wilson 2004: 28). The levels of control employed by Europeans on plantation slaves brought together systems of gender and racial power, sexualised, racialised and managed to establish "the reproduction of plantation slavery" (Wilson 2004: 29). Wilson (2004: 29) shows how gender and racial power intersected in the case of plantation slaves:

> Plantation slavery not only transgressed West African gender occupations (and West African patterns of bondage, where slaves were predominantly women and more highly valued than men); it also reversed the custom of male lineage typical of British law. For in order to ensure a future supply of slaves, all children at birth took their legal status from their mother. This meant that white women, white men, and black men, free or slave, could, at least theoretically, produce free children, but enslaved mothers could only produce more slaves.

Beyond the sexualised and racialised patterns of control was also the claim that Europeans were more "superior" to colonised peoples, as Wilson (2004: 29) comments "religiously, culturally and phenotypically superior." However, Wilson also shows how enslaved women and men did what little they could to assert their position:

> Mulatto women, in particular, used their colour and attractiveness to ensure a favourable place within hierarchies of plantation life, in the West Indies they almost never worked in the fields but were favoured servants in the household. Enslaved women of all hues could exploit their sexual or emotional intimacies to acquire property or established themselves in trade and freedom.
>
> (Wilson 2004: 31)

> By exerting rights and power over their own persons and fates, enslaved men and women made perfectly clear that they were not property but human beings. Their success ultimately led planters to adopt pro-natalist policies to encourage reproduction. Beginning in the 1770s, slaves were encouraged to form Christian-style marriages, pregnant slaves were given reduced work-loads, and financial payments for successful live births to enslaved mothers and enslaved mid-wives became commonplace
>
> (Wilson 2004: 33) (see also Bush 1990)

The enslavement of black women also impacted on white women and "mistresses" in the rarified environment of colonial culture. White women "mistresses" were cruel with their slaves and as Wilson states, brooked no subordination, the result of the way they were regarded and treated by men.

Gender differentiated patterns were not universalised in different colonial cultures. The response of white men to native women varied enormously and in relation to context. For example, Wilson shows that within British settlements in India, officers working for the East India Committee, had established "connections" rather than relationships with "native" women. Wilson (2004: 36) reports that they were less romantic and recognised as a more complex and sophisticated ancient nation, although one regarded as "barbaric" by white Europeans. As she shows:

> In this setting, romance and marriage among high-ranking Company officials and Indian noblewomen, such as that of the orientalist James Kirkpatrick, resident of the Hyderabad Court, and Khair-un-Nissa, added to the mystique. Having and maintaining "bibis," as they were called, was widespread among Company officials and servants. (Teltscher 2004)

At a later point such relationships were discouraged by Cornwallis and Wellesley to make sure the boundaries between the British and natives were clear as well as to prevent people of colour from becoming a factor in local politics. However, as will be shown later in the chapter, the practice of maintaining mistresses and concubines continued into the nineteenth century. Most were left behind after the army returned to Britain:

> Native women who "married" a soldier or Company servant through a secret ceremony were left behind when the man returned "home", as were their children. By an order of 1783, only children with two parents of European birth could be removed to England. (see Chatterjee 1999) (Wilson 2004: 37)

Military orphanages were established for "half-caste" children in the late eighteenth century and girls were trained to become domestic servants in the homes of Company officers and other employees. Wilson points out that some were selected to be "wives" despite the fact they were still children. This "trafficking" of girls and women was hidden from the view of those in Britain with the East India Company acting as the gatekeeper, maintaining boundaries between home and abroad.

By contrast from the 1770s onwards, increasing numbers of women moved to the subcontinent to marry "Company" men. As Wilson (2004: 38–39) notes, white European women served a number of "political" and social functions for Empire:

> ... white, Christian, and properly married or chaperoned British ladies did give visible embodiment to the demarcations of national and lineage politics and the personal and political boundaries of rule. Their presence also offered an implicit critique of the arranged marriages of Indian society

and the miscegenated alliances and cultural practices of Company officers and servants. As elsewhere in the Empire, British women held social and symbolic positions that defined appropriate relations of power and subordination and clarified who was entitled to claim the "rights and privileges" of British people and who was not.

The presence or absence of European women was significant for colonial cultures, as shown by Stoler (2002 and see below):

> In settings where European women were absent such as the South Pacific prior to the late 1780s, gender and sexual practices provided crucial but mutable markers of identity, difference, and dispossession for British men and Oceanic men and women alike. Indeed the South Seas was a place where the "sexual interface" of the colonial encounter generated endless fascination both at the time and in generations to come.
>
> (Wilson 2004: 39)

"Mapping Intimacy through Sex in Colonial Cultures": Laura Ann Stoler

The relationship between sex, gender and power is of course implicit in the work of many of the historians and feminist theorists outlined above. The difference between Stoler and the other theorists of Empire is that she explicitly confronts the issue of power and seeks to theorise power by drawing on the work of Michel Foucault. The relationship between sex and power is an important dimension of the analysis of intimacy, gender and emotions in colonial cultures. Fundamental to both Foucault and Stoler is the analysis of power and in particular the relationship between sex and power. Stoler is particularly interested in Foucault's concept of "biopower," but while her theoretical position is influenced by Foucault she does offer a critique of Foucault which is developed in Chapter 1 and is further developed below. I analyse Stoler's contribution to the debate on the relationship between intimacy, sex, power and colonial cultures and her analysis is assessed for the significance of intimacy as a driver of emotional and historical change. In her analysis Stoler draws on the intersection of gender, race and class in explaining the relationship between "carnal knowledge and imperial power."

In "Making Empire Respectable: the Politics of Race and Sexual Morality in Twentieth Century Colonial Cultures" Stoler (1997) explores the underpinnings of the racial and sexual politics of Empire and considers European women's impact on Dutch, French and British imperial cultures. Stoler (1997: 344) raises the question: "In what ways were gender inequalities essential to the structure of colonial racism and imperial authority?" She shows how in colonial cultures of French, Indochina and Dutch East Indies in the early twentieth century that the terms "colonizer" and "colonized" "were secured through forms of sexual control that defined the domestic arrangements of Europeans" (Stoler 1997: 345).

In this article, Stoler (1997: 345) focuses on how the management of sexual activity, reproduction and marriage "related to the racial politics of colonial rule." She shows that colonial authority was based on two false premises, the first was that Europeans in the colonies made up a clearly identifiable and biologically and socially distinct grouping. In other words, that they could be seen as a "natural community" with class, racial, political and cultural interests. The second false premise was the idea that there were easily identifiable boundaries between coloniser and colonised (see Stoler 1989).

In fact Stoler (1997: 345) shows that categories were complex, interrelated and regulated:

> Sexual unions in the context of concubinage, domestic service, prostitution, or church marriage derived from the hierarchies of rule; but these were negotiated and contested arrangements, bearing on individual fates and the very structure of colonial society. Ultimately inclusion or exclusion required regulating the sexual, conjugal, and domestic life of both Europeans in the colonies and their colonized subjects.

Stoler is in no doubt that "European pornographic fantasies" which she claims existed prior to colonization and the: "sexual prescriptions by class, race, and gender became increasingly central to the politics of rule and subject to new forms of scrutiny by colonial states . . . " (Stoler 1997: 345).

She shows how sexual domination as a "social metaphor" for European control is not new and Edward's Said's (1979) treatment of "Orientalist discourses" and the "sexual submission . . . of Oriental women by European men 'stands for the pattern of relative strength between East and West' (1979: 6)" (Stoler 1997: 346). Stoler highlights how the " 'politics of sex' has been a neglected area and is a fundamental class and racial marker implicated in a wider set of relations of power . . . " (Stoler 1997).

Beyond the raw politics of sexual exploitation by Europeans within colonialist frameworks, is what Stoler (1997: 346) identifies as:

> . . . [a]n overlapping set of discourses [which] has provided the psychological and economic underpinnings for colonial distinctions of difference, linking fears of sexual contamination, physical danger, climatic incompatibility and moral breakdown to a European colonial identity with a racist and class-specific core.

The Domestic Politics of Colonialism: Concubinage and the Restricted Entry of European Women

Stoler shows that sexual relations were a central element in the development of colonial settlements:

> From the early seventeenth through the twentieth century, the sexual sanctions and conjugal prohibitions of colonial agents were rigorously

debated and carefully codified. In these debates over matrimony and mortality, trading and plantation company officials, missionaries, investment bankers, military high commands and agents of the colonial state confronted one another's vision of empire, and settlement patterns on which it would rest.

(Stoler 1997: 347)

She shows how the Dutch East Indies Company restricted the immigration of European women to the East Indies for two hundred years. As Stoler (1997: 347) notes: " Enforcing the restriction by selecting bachelors as their European recruits, the Company legally and financially made concubinage the most attractive option for its employees."

The operation of concubinage is outlined in Chapter1, and provided a useful mechanism to keep European men focused on their work:

> Native women (like European women in a later period) were to keep men physically and psychologically fit for work and marginally content, not distracting or urging them out of line, imposing neither the time-consuming nor the financial responsibilities that European family life was thought to demand . . .

(Stoler 1997: 348)

The shift in sexual relations in colonised cultures frequently occurred with the arrival of sizeable numbers of European women, as Stoler (1997: 35) shows:

> The arrival of large numbers of European women thus coincided with an embourgeoisement of colonial communities and with a significant sharpening of racial lines. European women supposedly required more metropolitan amenities than men and more spacious surroundings to allow it; their more delicate sensibilities required more servants and thus suitable quarters—discrete and enclosed. In short, white women needed to be maintained at elevated standards of living, in insulated social spaces cushioned with the cultural artefacts of "being European" . . . Segregationist standards were what women "deserved" and more importantly were what white male prestige required that they maintain.

European women brought cultural and class prejudices with them and also reinforced "new racial antagonisms" and were "hard-line operatives who put them into practice . . ." (Stoler 1997: 352). They opposed concubinage for a variety of reasons and reshaped at least some of the colonial discourse as Stoler outlines:

> If white women were the primary force behind the decline of concubinage, as is often claimed, then they played this role as participants in a broader racial realignment and political plan . . . This is not to suggest that

European women were passive in this process, as the dominant themes of novels attest . . . Many European women did oppose concubinage not because of their inherent jealousy of native women, but as they argued, because of the double standard it condoned for European men . . . The voice of European women, however had little resonance until their objections coincided with a realignment in racial and class politics.

As is also shown in Chapter 1, native men were seen as a threat to European women, despite the trivial nature of many of the "threats". This pattern was not restricted to cultures colonised by Europeans, as can be seen in the southern states of America:

> As in the American South etiquettes of chivalry controlled white women's behaviour even as [it] guarded caste lines. A defense of community, morality and white male power affirmed the vulnerability of white women and the sexual threat posed by native men and created new sanctions to limit the liberties of both.
>
> (Stoler 1997: 354)

Beyond their part in changing the role of concubinage in colonial cultures, European women also contributed to colonial economic cultures by working in the community. Stoler indicates that French women in Algeria and Senegal ran farms, boarding houses and shops. Women were also posted to colonial cultures as nurses, missionaries and teachers. Stoler shows that professional competence did not protect women from prejudice and marginalisation. She notes that contempt was shown towards single women as well as prostitutes.

At the turn of the twentieth century, concubinage was seen as part of an imperial politics which was grounded in a "metropolitan bourgeois discourse" which was accompanied by an ideology of racism and "degeneracy." Stoler (1997: 360) shows how the children of such relationships were treated:

> Concubines' children posed a classificatory problem, impinging on political security and white prestige. The majority of such children were not recognised by their fathers, nor were they reabsorbed into local communities as authorities often claimed. Although some European men legally acknowledged their progeny, many repatriated to Holland, Britain or France and cut off ties and support to mother or children . . . Native women had responsibility for, but attenuated rights over their own offspring. They could neither prevent their children from being taken from them nor contest paternal suitability for custody.

As shown in Chapter 1, and as outlined by Stoler here: "the political etymology of colonizer and colonized was gender—and class specific" (1997: 365). She notes that changes in both sexual protocol and morality were directly linked to the tenuous nature of colonial control by European communities.

Stoler's (2002) *Carnal Knowledge and Imperial Power: Race and the Intimate in Colonial Rule* makes a significant theoretical contribution to the analysis of intimacy through sex in colonial cultures. She shows how sexuality and power are inextricably linked in the way relationships were structured to reinforce the nature of power relationships under colonial rule. As shown in Chapter 1, Stoler draws on Foucault's analysis of sex and power to show how colonial power relations operated at every level of society, including at the level of sexual power relations. The use of Foucault's concept of "biopower" is particularly valuable as a methodological device to facilitate this analysis (see Chapter 2).

Stoler's (2002) "Colonial Reading of Foucault" builds on Foucault's analysis of sexuality as "an especially dense transfer point for relations of power" (Foucault 1978: 103) and as she says, her analysis of colonial power and the management of sex, draws on Foucault's analysis of sexuality and power in *The History of Sexuality, Volume 1: An Introduction*. She is however not uncritical of Foucault, particularly in the absence of race in his analysis, as Stoler (2002: 141) notes:

> My colonial reading of Foucault draws on cumulative contributions to colonial studies to ask what implications such a rereading might have for how we think about the intimacies of empire, European history, and the colonial etymologies of race.

Stoler is keen to draw on Foucault but also to push beyond his analysis. In particular, Stoler claims that Foucault's emphasis that "sexuality was originally historically bourgeois" negates the significance of race, which she contests. Stoler (2002: 144) maintains:

> ... I argued that racial entailments were not relevant in the colonies alone. By bringing anxieties and citizenship and nation back within our frame (as Foucault did not), bourgeois identities in metropole and colony emerge as tacitly and emphatically coded by race. In rerouting the history of sexuality through the history of empire, modern racism appears less "anchored" in European technologies of sex than Foucault claimed. Both racial and sexual classifications appear as ordering mechanisms that *shared* their emergence with the bourgeois order of the early nineteenth century. Racial thinking was not subsequent to the bourgeois order but constitutive of it.

In *The History of Sexuality, Volume 1: An Introduction*, Foucault challenges the idea of nineteenth century European sexuality as being a repressed discourse, as Foucault (1978: 3) notes: "the image of the imperial prude . . . emblazoned on our restrained, mute and hypocritical sexuality" was as Stoler shows an incorrect view of sexuality and its relationship with power. She indicates that for Foucault, sexual discourse is not opposed to power but as Foucault observes a "dense transfer point of it." Stoler (2002: 145) indicates this can be seen in the operation of sexuality in colonial cultures:

> ... the management of the sexual practices of colonizer and colonized was fundamental to the colonial order of things and that discourses on sexuality at once classified colonial subjects into distinct human kinds while policing the domestic recesses of imperial rule.
>
> (see McClintock 1995 below)

Foucault drew on a simple binary model of sexuality and its deployment in analysing sexuality in Europe comparing as Stoler shows the "pat binary world of *ars erotica* (the Orient) and *scientia sexualis* (the West)" (Foucault 1978: 57–58) (cited in Stoler 2002: 146). Nevertheless, Stoler sees Foucault as useful for opening up a debate around colonial studies as she comments:

> Foucault's impulse to write a history of Western desire that rejects desire as a biological instinct or as a response to repressive prohibitions pushes colonial studies in a direction feminism has long urged, to question how shifts in the imperial distribution of desiring male subjects and desired female objects might shape that story as well.
>
> (Stoler 2002: 146)

Stoler uses race and racial discourse as part of Foucault's genealogical approach, where it formed part of "the technologies of sex that arose in the eighteenth century to regulate sexual conduct and by which populations could be expanded and controlled" (Stoler 2002: 149). Perhaps most profoundly, Foucault identified the discursive site for bourgeois culture within the family: "It was a discourse in which the distribution and education of desire was lodged in the home, as Foucault put it, in that 'tiny sexually saturated familial space' (Foucault 1978: 47)" (Stoler 2002: 155).

Carnal Knowledge and Imperial Power formulates more theoretically Stoler's analysis of sexual relations in colonial cultures, which she sees "not as a metaphor for colonial inequities but as foundational to the material terms in which colonial projects were carried out" (Stoler 2002: 14). The book provides a broad "etymology of the 'carnal' that includes the sensual and affective passion, and compassion, and the unsanctioned and the flesh" (Stoler 2002: 18).

In building her theoretical model, Stoler draws on Foucault's analysis of sexuality outlined in *The History of Sexuality, Volume 1: An Introduction*, in particular his use of genealogy. More specifically, Stoler (2002: 19) draws on Foucault's:

> ... methodological insights that Foucault's histories of racial discourse and biopower afford by underscoring both the 'polyvalent mobility' of racial discourse and what might be gained by attending to racial discourses as historical processes of rupture and recouperation. It makes

theoretically explicit a theme that informs . . . how and why microsites of familial and intimate space figure so prominently in the micropolitics of imperial rule.

Gender and Sex: Asymmetries in Colonial Intimacy

The micropolitics of imperial rule frames Stoler's analysis of the intersection of intimacy and power as she observes: "In them I locate the affective grid of colonial politics" (Stoler 2002: 7). As shown in Chapter 1, some colonial historians, such as Hyam (1986) have gone so far as to equate colonial expansion with what he calls the "export of male sexual energy." Said (1979) had long before established the sexual politics of what he called "Orientalism." The issues are developed in Chapter 1 and in this chapter, as Stoler (2002: 56) comments: "Sex was not a levelling mechanism but a site in which social asymmetries were instantiated and expressed" (see Strobel 1987).

The role of European women in buttressing colonial rule is outlined earlier and while some European women did have skills as missionaries, nurses and teachers, many had very few skills (see Ralston 1977). Some colonial widows, such as the editor of a major Saigon Daily, succeeded in their own ambitions, as Stoler points out, most were shipped out to Indochina at the expense of the government, regardless of skill. In addition, married European women were also put in a difficult situation, as Stoler shows and had to face hard choices: ". . . separation from their children or separation from their husbands. Frequent trips between colony and metropole not only separated families but also broke up marriages and homes" (Stoler 2002: 75).

The Politics of Intimacy

The issues raised by Stoler regarding the politics of the intimate is an important dimension in understanding power and dominance in the politics of intimacy in a broader sense. While Stoler (2006: 16) recognises it is not the sole or dominant dimension, she shows the importance and value of "affective politics":

> . . . giving weight to the intimate is not to suggest that these are the sites of deeper truths where the secrets of the state are stored. What it does allow is a call to question cherished assumptions: that the intimate is located primarily in the family, that the family is a ready model for, and microcosm of the state, and that affective ties are inherently tender ones.

Indeed in "Tense and Tender Ties: The Politics of Comparison in North American History and (Post) Colonial Studies" Stoler (2006a: 24) expands the framework and draws comparison between post-colonial studies and North American history. She draws on:

> . . . what Albert Hurtado refers to as "the intimate frontiers" of empire, a social and cultural space where racial classifications were defined and

defied, where relations between colonizer and colonized could powerfully confound or confirm the structures of governance and the categories of rule.

Stoler shows how many of the same issues around affective politics and racial discourses can be seen in the history of North America:

> ... Ramon A. Gutierrez [1991] has shown how marriage structured racial inequalities in New Mexico, as Jennifer L. Morgan [1997, 2001], in her survey of 16th century travel literature, has detailed how gender was imbricated in the racial ideologies and strategies of rule. Such studies as Kathleen M. Brown's [1996] on gender, race and power in colonial Virginia speak directly to Jean Geltman Taylor's [1983] ethnographic history of the same issues in seventeenth-century colonial Java, halfway around the world.
>
> (Stoler 2006a: 33)

Stoler shows that despite differences in the racial and cultural structures of dominance, the patterns of exploitation both sexual and economic were the same:

> Although the plantation households of the Old South depended on slave labor and the colonial households of the Dutch, French and British in Asia employed "contract coolies" and wage labor, anxieties within European colonial communities over intimacies and fear of contamination by those who performed domestic service were strikingly similar.
>
> (Stoler 2006a: 35)

In drawing parallels between European colonial history and North American history, Stoler shows that taken at the level of the politics of intimacy there were significant similarities. As Stoler (2006a: 55) indicates: "Sexual violence was fundamental to conquest, but so was colonizing the hearts and minds of women, children and men." Gordon (2006: 439) raises some interesting differences in the patterns of Hispanic exploitation by North American white men. She shows that an "Orientalist" reading of sexual relations in the case of Mexican women was not entirely accurate:

> An "Orientalist" construction of Mexican women made them simultaneously submissive and exotically sexually attractive. But this white male perception of Mexican women intersected with the status of Mexican women handsomely dowried with property, or even as property heirs under the Spanish—Mexican law that governed south western realty property in the nineteenth and early twentieth centuries, so that they became also economically attractive partners for the ambitious white men who were migrating to the Southwest in the nineteenth century. Moreover, Mexican women were not merely exchanged. They often preferred or even sought

out marriages with white men because of their reputation of being more egalitarian, less controlling than Mexican men and because of their better jobs and greater resources.

This highlights a far greater capacity for agency on the part of Mexican than many other colonised women. In addition, the role of white "settler" women acted in the same way as the arrival of European women into the colonies, as Gordon (2006: 440) notes:

> Like the metropolitan and settler women in transoceanic colonies, white elite women in internal colonies frequently interpreted the alleged benefits of imperialism in terms of the gender system in which they functioned. They championed their dominion over underdeveloped populations as a necessary historical process of female emancipation and uplift . . .
> Female elite discourse treated "native" women as alternatively victimized or morally "fallen", but in either case low . . .

White colonizer or "settler" women shared the same attitude towards native women and in Asia, Europe and North America that attitude extended into the twentieth century and remains the case today:

> . . . female elites depended on the cheap domestic labor of colonized women to buy their own leisure and freedom of movement, within as well as outside the United States. Indeed, the relation between mistress and domestic was in some ways as central to the colonial relation as was that between landlord and peasant . . .
>
> (Gordon 2006: 440)

As Gordon observes white women settlers had a vested interest in maintaining the subordination of colonised women. In fact settler women acted to prevent native women from changing their status as when they argued that schools had to train women for domestic service. White women served to stabilise and reinforce the interests of the colonial state across a number of different countries and over different periods of time.

Imperial Liaisons: Intimacies, Race and Nationalism

The last section of this chapter focuses on the work of Anne McClintock (1995, 1997) and shows how her work brings the intersection of nationalism, race and gender into play in the analysis of intimacies. McClintock's work provides an analysis of epistemologies of intimacy across discourses of race, gender and sexuality in colonial and post-colonial contexts. Her work covers discourses of psychoanalysis, nationalism and hybridity.

Before looking at McClintock's work it is useful to contextualise some of the broader debates around gender, race and nationalism which underpin her work. Bush (2004) argues that gender was an integral feature of articulating "whiteness" within Empire and strengthening race and sex boundaries, but she also notes that gender could not be taken in isolation and had to be seen alongside other social phenomena in understanding historical change including national belonging and imperial identities.

So how was the notion of national belonging and imperial identity established? This was partially through the establishment of a domesticated normativity, as domesticity, marriage and appropriate gender roles remained central to imperial stability. As Bush (2004: 85) comments: "Eugenicists believed that single men and women who delayed marriage were failing in their racial duty to reproduce the white race. Single women were regarded as an economic and sexual threat ('amazons' and 'flappers') and masculinity was still defined through marriage . . . ".

Imperial identities were reinforced through negative images of anything that went outside the frame of domestic normativity. Bush shows how this was encouraged in everyday and popular culture:

> Popular narratives of miscegenation evoked images of predatory 'oriental' men mingling on the "dark side" of London and other British ports with the new sexually "loose" flappers and degenerate "dope" girls. The Chinese opium dens of London's Limehouse were constructed as a site of the corruption of white women, and the predatory sexuality of Chinese men was "a relentlessly reiterated theme" in popular culture. (Bickers 1999: 44–45, 51–53)
>
> (Bush 2004: 86)

Press reports and popular literature led to the media amplification of anxiety regarding Asian men and the threat they posed to white women:

> Representations of Asian men as a threat to white women were fuelled by sensational press reports of violent abductions of European women and girls in China . . . White representations of such men as inherently bestial and emblematic of forbidden sexuality were also reinforced in the new "desert romance" genre, where the handsome but brutal "oriental" forced white women into submission and sexual slavery. (Melman 1986: 137)
>
> (Bush 2004: 86)

By contrast, as Bush notes the "Empire Romance" presented the superiority of Anglo-Saxon identities and central in this was white womanhood. They represented the normalisation of Empire, emphasising stability and racial purity. The contrast between white and colonised women was pronounced as Bush (2004: 94) shows: "In white women's memoirs, African women are silent, nameless ciphers most commonly represented as beasts of burden . . . This distance increased the risk of cultural misunderstanding and reinforced white women's sense of superiority."

White women did have more social contact with colonised women in Malaya, Hong Kong and India but popular representations continued to contrast white women's freedom with the drudgery and subservience of Asian women. As Bush (2004: 109) notes: "Superior imperial masculinities and white domesticity were central to white prestige and power and the strengthening of racial boundaries."

McClintock (1995, 1997) has focused throughout her work on the intersection of gender, race and nationalism and she is uncompromising in her account of nationalism and the "institutionalization of gender *difference*" (1997: 89). She sees nationalism as a masculinised experience and argues that male theorists of imperialism and post-colonialism have neglected to explore gender within their analysis. As she comments: "Even Edward Said's enormously important and influential *Orientalism* does not explore gender as a category constitutive of imperialism" (McClintock 1995: 397N4).

In "No Longer in a Future Heaven: Gender, Race and Nationalism" McClintock (1997) provides a powerful analysis of gender within nationalist discourses and considers the contributions of some of the key theorists in the field, including Bhabha (1990), Fanon (1965), Yuval-Davis and Anthias (1989). They outline how women have been implicated in nationalist discourses particularly as "reproducers" and through active "transmitters and producers of the national culture." She also notes that in Homi Bhabha's work: "Except for a cursory appearance in one paragraph, women haunt Bhabha's analysis as an elided shadow-deferred, displaced and dis-remembered" (McClintock 1997: 95).

In a fascinating analysis of Fanon's (1965) "Algeria Unveiled" McClintock (1997: 96), citing Fanon, comments:

> . . . Fanon ventriloquizes–only to refute—the long Western dream of colonial conquest as an erotics of ravishment. Under the hallucinations of empire, the Algerian woman is seen as the living flesh of the national body, unveiled and laid bare for the colonials' lascivious grip, revealing "piece by piece, the flesh of Algeria laid bare". (Fanon 1965: 42)

She shows how Fanon's analysis of colonialism leads to the "domestication" of the colony through its repression and exploitation of both the labour and sexual economy which serves the purpose of diverting "female power into colonial hands and disrupt[ing] the patriarchal power of colonized men" (McClintock 1997: 97). Fanon recognises that women are visible markers of national homogeneity. In other words, colonised women can be used to challenge nationalism and its power in colonial cultures by undermining men's power both physically and sexually.

The veil is a significant symbolic and cultural expression of both repression and resistance and McClintock (1997: 97) highlights its potency in Fanon's work:

> From the outset, colonials tried to grant Algerian women a traitorous agency, affecting to rescue them from the sadistic thrall of Algerian men. But as Fanon knows, the colonial masquerade of giving women power

by unveiling them was merely a ruse for achieving "a real power over the man". (Fanon 1965: 39)

However, militant Algerian women started unveiling themselves "mimicking the colonial masquerade," and the colonialists assumed they were converts to the colonial discourse. But the Algerian women had a different agenda as McClintock (1997: 97) shows: "For the *fidai*, however, the militant woman was 'his arsenal', a technique of counter-infiltration, duplicitously penetrating the body of the enemy with the armaments of death." Fanon's failure to comprehend gender politics leads him to fail to recognise the significance of the veil in the gender dynamics of Algerian society. As McClintock (1997: 97) shows: "Fanon denies the 'historic dynamism of the veil' and banishes its intricate history to a footnote, from where, however it displaces the main text, with the insistent force of self-division and denial."

Fanon's analysis has always been masculinized and this is shown in his representation of Algerian women. He presents an image of the Algerian woman as both eroticised and militarised, in "carrying the men's pistols, guns, and grenades beneath her skirts". In doing so, as McClintock points out: "Fanon masculinizes the female militant, turning her into a phallic substitute, detached from the male body but remaining, still, the man's 'woman-arsenal'" (1997: 98).

Beyond her critique of the intersection of gender and nationalism, McClintock sees women as the "boundary-makers" of Empire, but the exact form varied depending on the cultural context, as she (McClintock 1995: 31) shows:

> . . . the gendering of imperialism took very different forms in different parts of the world. India, for one, was seldom imagined as a virgin land, while the iconography of the harem was not part of the Southern African colonial erotics. North African, Middle Eastern and Asian women were, all too often, trammelled by the iconography of the veil, while African women were subjected to the civilizing mission of cotton and soap. In other words, Arab women were to be "civilized" by being undressed (unveiled), while sub-Saharan women were to be civilized by being dressed (in clean, white British cotton). These sumptuary distinctions were symptomatic of critical differences in the legislative economic and political ways in which imperial commodity racism was imposed on different parts of the world.

In this analysis McClintock raises an important dimension in her conceptual framework, the link between race and the "iconography of degeneration." She draws on Stoler's framing of the dangers of racial deterioration and contamination in the colonies:

> *Metissage* (interracial unions) generally and concubinage in particular, represented the paramount danger of racial purity and cultural identity in

> all its forms. Through sexual contact with women of color European men "contracted" not only disease but debased sentiments, immoral proclivities and extreme susceptibility to decivilized states.
>
> (Stoler 2002: 78)

McClintock draws parallels between how women who "transgressed" the private/public divide in the Victorian era and racial regression. "Female domestic servants were frequently depicted in the iconography of degeneration—as 'plagues', 'black races', 'slaves', and 'primitives'" (McClintock 1995: 42).

McClintock shows there was a direct link between the stabilisation of relations within the Empire and controlling women's sexuality and this was in turn linked to "the discourse of degeneration". She indicates that in the Victorian era, social Darwinism was a strong element in social thinking and social planning and the idea of "contagion" was a strong feature in thinking both home and abroad:

> Controlling women's sexuality, exalting maternity and building a virile race of empire builders were widely perceived as the paramount means for controlling the health and wealth of the male imperial body politic, so that, by the turn of the century, sexual purity emerged as a controlling metaphor for racial, economic and political power. (Davin 1978)
>
> (McClintock 1995: 47)

The Victorians saw domestic discipline, sexual probity and moral sanitation as central to maintaining standards of behaviour in the metropolis and in the empire. Those who fell "outside" or "beneath" these standards face particular opprobrium as McClintock (1995: 56) outlines:

> Domestic workers, female miners and working class prostitutes (women who worked publicly and visibly for money) were stationed on the threshold between the white and black races, figured as having fallen farthest from the perfect type of the white male and sharing many atavistic features with "advanced" black men. Prostitutes—as the metropolitan analogue of African promiscuity—were marked as especially atavistic and regressive . . . Prostitutes visibly transgressed the middle-class boundary between private and public, paid work and unpaid work and in consequence were figures as "white negroes" inhabiting anachronistic space, their "racial" atavism anatomically marked by regressive signs . . .

Drawing on a range of psychoanalytic and feminist theorists including Lacan, Kristeva and Irigaray, McClintock draws on a range of psychoanalytic and post-colonial concepts to understand the role of gender within colonial relations. One of these concepts is "abjection". McClintock (1995: 72) argues for the "development of a *situated psychoanalysis*—a culturally contextualized psychoanalysis that is simultaneously a psychoanalytically informed history." She sees imperialism as providing a wide ranging set of examples of abjection:

> Under imperialism, I argue, certain groups are expelled and obliged to inhabit the impossible edges of modernity: the slum, the ghetto, the garrett, the brothel, the convent, the colonial Bantustan and so on. Abject peoples are those whom industrial imperialism rejects but cannot do without: slaves, prostitutes, the colonized, domestic workers, the insane, the unemployed, and so on. Certain threshold zones become abject zones and are policed with vigor: the Arab Casbah, the Jewish ghetto, the Irish slum, the Victorian garret and kitchen, the squatter camp, the mental asylum, the red light district, and the bedroom . . .
> (McClintock 1995: 72)

McClintock's critique of Lacan is as emphatic as her critique of Fanon and she sees Lacan's vision as bearing: "an uneasy affinity to nineteenth–century discourse on degeneration, which figured women as bereft of language, exiled from reason and properly inhabiting the prehistory of the race" (McClintock 1995: 193). Lacanian psychoanalytic theory has always denied women's agency as McClintock shows: "Just as, in imperial discourse, white men were the sole heirs to the grand narrative of historical progress, so in Lacanian discourse, men are the sole heirs to the Symbolic." She shows how the parallels between the Lacanian vision of women and the imperial discourse: "relegated women and the colonized to the realm of the unrepresentable, the prehistoric, the Dark Continent" (McClintock 1995).

Conclusion

This chapter has focused on the intersection of gender and sex in colonial and post-colonial cultures as represented in the work of two leading feminist theorists Laura Ann Stoler and Anne McClintock whose analysis has contributed enormously to an understanding of intimacy and desire both historically and contemporaneously. This chapter further draws on the contribution of a number of leading feminist historians whose work has illuminated the history of imperial cultures.

Bibliography

Bhabha, Homi. 1990. *Nation and Narration*. New York: Routledge.
Bickers, Robert. 1999. *Britain in China: Community, Culture and Colonialism, 1900–1949*. Manchester: Manchester University Press.
Brown, Kathleen. 1996. *Good Wives, Nasty Wenches, and Anxious Patriarchs: Gender, Race and Power in Colonial Virginia*. Chapel Hill: University of North Carolina Press.
Bush, Barbara. 1990. *Slave Women in Caribbean Society 1650–1838*. Bloomington: Indiana University Press.

Bush, Barbara. 2004. "Gender and Empire: The Twentieth Century." In Philippa Levine (ed.), *Gender and Empire*. Oxford: Oxford University Press, 77–111.

Chatterjee, Indrani. 1999. "Colonial Subalternity: Slaves, Concubines and Social Orphans in Early Colonial India." In Guatam Bhandra, Glyn Prakash and Susie Tharu (eds), *Subaltern Studies X*. Delhi: Oxford University Press, 49–97.

Davin, Anna. 1978. "Imperialism and Motherhood" *History Workshop* 5: 9–65.

Fanon, Franz. 1963. *The Wretched of the Earth*. Trans. Constance Farrington. London: Penguin.

Fanon, Franz. 1965. "Algeria Unveiled." In Haakon Chevalier (trans.), *A Dying Colonialism*. New York: Grove Press, 35–67.

Fanon, Franz. 1986. *Black Skin, White Masks*. Trans. Charles Markman. London: Pluto Press.

Foucault, Michel. 1978. *The History of Sexuality, Volume 1: An Introduction*. New York: Vintage.

Gordon, Linda. 2006. "Internal Colonialism and Gender." In Laura Ann Stoler (ed.), *Haunted by Empire: Geographies of Intimacy in North American History*. Durham, NC and London: Duke University Press.

Gutierrez, Ramon, A. 1991. *When Jesus Came, the Corn Mothers Went Away: Marriage, Sexuality and Power in New Mexico, 1500–1846*. Stanford, CA: Stanford University Press.

Howell, Philip. 2000. "Prostitution and Radicalized Sexuality: The Regulation of Prostitution in Britain and the British Empire Before the Contagious Diseases Act" *Environment and Planning Dr Society and Space*, XVIII: 321–339.

Hyam, Ronald. 1986. "Concubines and the Colonial Service: The Crew Circular . . ." *Journal of Imperial and Commonwealth History* 14(3): 170–186.

Levine, Philippa (ed.). 2004a. *Gender and Empire*. Oxford and New York: Oxford University Press.

Levine, Philippa. 2004b. "Introduction: Why Gender and Empire?" In *Gender and Empire*. Oxford and New York: Oxford University Press, 1–13.

Levine, Philippa. 2004c. "Sexuality, Gender and Empire." In *Gender and Empire*. Oxford and New York: Oxford University Press, 134–155.

Melman, B. 1986. *Women and the Popular Imagination in the Twenties: Flappers and Nymphs*. Basingstoke

Midgely, Clare. 1992. *Women Against Slavery: The British Campaigns, 1780–1870*. London: Routledge.

Morgan, Jennifer L. 1997. "Some Could Suckle over Their Shoulders: Male Travellers, Female Bodies and the Gendering of Racial Ideology, 1500–1700" *William and Mary Quarterly* 54: 167–192.

McClintock, Anne. 1995. *Imperial Leather: Race, Gender and Sexuality in the Colonial Contest*. New York and London: Routledge.

McClintock, Anne. 1997. "No Longer in a Future Heaven: Gender, Race and Nationalism." In A. McClintock, A. Mufti and E. Shohat (eds), *Dangerous Liaisons: Gender, Nation and Postcolonial Perspectives*. Minneapolis: University of Minnesota Press.

Ralston, Caroline. 1977. *Grass Huts and Warehouses: Pacific Beach Communities of the Nineteenth Century*. Canberra: Australia University Press.

Said, Edward. 1979. *Orientalism*. New York: Vintage.

Said, Edward. 1993. *Culture and Imperialism*. London: Chatto and Windus.

Strobel, Margaret. 1987. "Gender and Place in Nineteenth and Twentieth Century British Empire." In R. Bridenthal, C. Koonz and S. Stuard (eds), *Becoming Visible: Women in European History* 2nd ed. Boston: Houghton Mifflin, 389–414.

Stoler, Laura Ann. 1989. "Rethinking Colonial Categories European Communities and the Boundaries of Rule" *Comparative Studies in Society* 13(1): 134–161.

Stoler, Laura Ann. 1997. "Making Empire Respectable: The Politics of Race and Sexual Morality in Twentieth Century Colonial Cultures." In A. McClintock, A. Mufti and E. Shohat (eds), *Dangerous Liaisons: Gender, Nation and Postcolonial Perspectives*. London and Minneapolis: University of Minnesota Press, 344-373.

Stoler, Laura Ann. 2002. *Carnal Knowledge and Imperial Power: Place and the Intimate in Colonial Rule*. Berkeley: University of California Press.

Stoler, Laura Ann (ed.). 2006a. *Haunted by Empire: Geographies of Intimacy in North American History*. Durham, NC and London: Duke University Press.

Stoler, Laura Ann. 2006b. "Tense and Tender Ties: The Politics of Comparison in North American History and (Post) Colonial Studies." In *Haunted by Empire: Geographies of Intimacy in North American History*. Durham, NC and London: Duke University Press, 23–70.

Sussman, Charlotte. 2000. *Consuming Anxieties: Consumer Protest, Gender and British Slavery, 1713–1833*. Stanford, CA: Stanford University Press.

Taylor, Geltman, J. 1983. *The Social World of Batavia: European and Eurasian in Dutch Asia*. Madison: University of Wisconsin Press.

Teltscher, Kate. 2004. "Writing Home and Crossing Cultures: George Bogle in Bengal and Tibet, 1770–1775." In Kathleen Wilson (ed.), *A New Imperial History: Culture, Identity and Modernity in Britain and the Empire 1660–1840*. Cambridge: Cambridge University Press, 281–296.

Yuval-Davis, Nira and Floyd Anthias (eds). 1989. *Women-Nation-State* London: Macmillan.

Wilson, Kathleen. 2004. "Empire, Gender and Modernity in the Eighteenth Century." In Philippa Levine (ed.), *Gender and Empire*. Oxford and New York: Oxford University Press, 14–45.

5 Love and Intimacy in Late Modernity
The Transformation of Intimacy

Introduction

Sociological analysis of the relationship between intimacy, "detraditionalization," reflexivity and late modernity has occupied a central place in contemporary theoretical debates since the 1990s. Some of the key interrelationships between intimacy, social change and late modernity are outlined in Chapter 1. As shown in Chapter 1, key figures in the discipline have contributed significantly to the debates including: Bauman (2000), Beck and Beck-Gernsheim (1996), Giddens (1992) and Illouz (1997) among others. Chapter 1 also sets out the theoretical fields within the broader epistemological framework covering areas such as: intimacy and globalisation (Giddens 1992); intimacy and individualisation (Beck and Beck-Gernsheim 1996); the commercialisation of intimacy (Hochschild 2003, Illouz 1997, 1999); intimacy and "reflexive modernization" (Alexander 1996, Beck et al. 1994, Giddens 1992, 1994). This chapter amplifies some of these debates focusing further on these theoretical debates as well as on the work of Illouz (1997) and Jamieson (1998, 1999).

While the theories outlined above do diverge in their orientation, there is a general consensus around:

> ... an image of late modern intimacy as detraditionalized relative to 50 to 100 years ago. Modernity, to be sure, transformed intimacy in crucial ways, especially in the great urban centres, where new practices for mating and dating amid the anonymity of city life were developed and where bohemian writers, artists, and philosophers articulated new visions of love and eroticism.
>
> (Gross 2005: 287, Kern 1992, Seidman 1991, Wilson 1999)

Some of the main elements of what is known as "the detraditionalization thesis" include: the breakdown of traditional relationship patterns such as marriage for life and as the primary basis of procreation; the dominance of heterosexual relationships; male dominance in relationships; and the traditional gendered division of labour and caring roles. In addition to structural changes there is also a liberalisation of traditional constraints as well as a growth in autonomy and reflexivity.

While this changing framework of traditional relationships is said to be characteristic of the West, Gross (2005: 286) shows that American society's view of intimate relationships still view "couplehood" and marital intimacy as "a hegemonic ideal" and that: "Intimacy in the United States also remains beholden to the tradition of romantic love" (Gross 2005). These attitudes remain regardless of a divorce rate of 46% for the United States and similar patterns in other parts of the world (see Chapter 1). As Gross (2005: 288) indicates, American intimate relationship in subscribing to a tradition of romantic love follow: " . . . a cultural form that has its origins in 11th and 12th—century Europe. These forms of indebtedness to tradition impose cultural constraints on intimate practices that theorists of detraditionalization have largely ignored."

As shown in Chapter 1, Giddens (1992) argues that traditional narratives of romantic love have been replaced by "a new ideal" form of relationship which he calls the "pure relationship" which has a democratic frame of reference. To support this new form of relationship, Giddens shows how the mental health system and "psychotherapeutic ideologies . . . have helped foster a culture where individual self-fulfilment and growth are key factors in the development of intimacy in the 'pure relationship'" (Gross 2005: 289). Giddens defines "the pure relationship" as driven by the desire for satisfaction in self-development and of erotic needs. "Pure relationships, according to Giddens, whatever their drawbacks, are sites of extreme autonomy" (Gross 2005: 289–290). By contrast Foucault (1978) saw globalisation and the form of interaction emerging from it "as an encroachment on autonomy."

Giddens's analysis of intimacy in the context of late modernity is shared by other leading figures in sociology, particularly Ulrich Beck and Elizabeth Beck-Gernsheim (1996) (see also Chapter1). They share Giddens's interest in "the pure relationship" but argue that its emergence is based on the growth of individualisation in late modernity. Gross (2005: 290) contextualises the significance of individualisation in late modernity by distinguishing it from the concept of individualisation in classical versions of modernization theory: "In the vocabulary of Margaret Archer (2000), 'personal identity' becomes more significant than 'social identity' in an era where post-Fordist consumer and work identities loom large and where people are disembedded from stable local social networks."

Allied to this is a breakdown in normative structures in the formation of intimate relationships. As outlined in Chapter 1, Beck and Beck-Gernsheim claim that there is more variability and flexibility in "biographies of love" which are now more ad hoc and as defined by Beck and Beck-Gernsheim "do-it-yourself biographies". However in a more recent analysis of transnational relationships, *Distant Love: Personal Life in a Global Age*, Beck and Beck-Gernsheim (2014) have embedded their research in empirical analysis, and have moved away from their previous position. As Beck and Beck-Gernsheim (2014: 1–2) indicate: "In *The Normal Chaos of Love* we showed how individualism aided by a romanticizing idea of absolute love, has undermined the traditional form of living together ... In our new book we open up the horizon on the global chaos of love ...".

Beck and Beck-Gernsheim argue that religion and religious wars are a significant factor in understanding intimacy and they maintain that this has not been considered by some of the key theorists of intimacy and love:

> All universalist social theories of love overlook these religious wars when they speak about the nature of intimacy in "modern life" in general as did Anthony Giddens (1992), Eva Illouz (2012) and Niklas Luhman (1986), and we too are guilty of this in *The Normal Chaos of Love* (1995) ... what they regard as the universalism of modern love with its various paradoxes of freedom is only one of many possible developments, namely the version that has emerged in the historical, cultural, political and legal context of the West.
>
> (Beck and Beck-Gernsheim 2014: 3)

Beyond Giddens and Beck and Beck-Gernsheim, a number of other theorists have also contributed to an understanding of the changing nature of intimacy in late modernity. Manuel Castells (1997: 156) argues that social movements are a key factor in leading to change and in particular to patriarchy, because they have resulted in a restructuring of everyday life and "a substantial decline of traditional forms of patriarchal family."

Zygmunt Bauman (2000) links changes in the nature of intimacy with postmodernity and a general breakdown of codes and regulative structures. In particular, and showing parallels with Castells, Bauman argues that the nuclear family, typical of modernism has lost its appeal in a postmodern society.

A major group of theorists who have been central in the development of the genealogy of intimacy draw on feminist (and Marcusian) theoretical perspectives. They include Eva Illouz (1997, 1999) (see below and Chapter 6) who explore the relationship between romance and consumption; Arlie Hochschild (2003) who analyses the "commercialization of intimate life"; and Laura Kipnis (2003) who provides a polemic against contemporary perspectives of marital love. Gross (2005: 291) argues that Kipnis views "transcendent eroticism [a]s downgraded and virtue made of doing the arduous 'work' required to stay together over time." Gross also maintains that all the theorists see a process of "ideologicization of intimacy" as having developed in the twentieth century and traditional values characteristic of modernity as having been superceded.

In the UK one of the key critics of Giddens's work is Lynn Jamieson (1998, 1999). As shown in Chapter 1, Jamieson (1999) has criticised Giddens's concept of "the pure relationship" and more generally his analysis of intimacy. While a "popular" understanding of the transformation of intimacy, supports Giddens's view of the democratisation of heterosexual relationships, Jamieson (1999: 477) raises a number of concerns regarding this model. She shows that, while superficially, changes in heterosexual relationships are seen as becoming more egalitarian: "Much of personal life remains structured by inequalities."

In addition, Jamieson maintains that: ". . . much more, creative energy goes into sustaining a sense of intimacy, *despite* inequality than into a process of transformation" (Jamieson 1999).

An important dimension, that Jamieson (1999: 479) focuses on, is therapeutic discourse. She argues that:

> . . . the rhetoric of the "pure relationship" may point people in the wrong direction both personally and politically. It feeds on and into a therapeutic discourse that individualises personal problems and downgrades sociological explanations.

"Plastic Sexuality" and "Confluent Love"

In addition to the move to "the pure relationship," Giddens also identifies what he calls "plastic sexuality" which is defined by a move away from traditional sexual behaviour and relationships. The link between sexuality and intimacy is redefined as being about pleasure. As Jamieson (1999: 478) comments: ". . . Giddens suggests that preoccupation with the body and exploring sexual pleasure is increasingly . . . part of both self-construction and 'the pure relationship.'" As Giddens (1992: 84) notes "confluent love" expresses a much closer bond between "sexuality and intimacy."

One of the key elements of Giddens's theory which has attracted significant criticism is his uncritical reliance on therapeutic literature "as documents about and symptoms of personal and social change (Giddens 1992: 86)" (Jamieson 1999: 480). Giddens' commitment to therapeutic discourse, leads him to ignore significant social theorists who have been critical of the implications of therapy:

> Giddens explicitly counters Foucault's discussion of therapy as a mechanism of extending subtle forms of regulation and control (Giddens 1992: 28–34). In the process, Giddens also silently lays aside accounts such as those of . . . Bauman (1990) which focus on the negativity of dependency on experts for self-direction, self-creativity and unmediated social interaction.
>
> (Jamieson 1999: 480–481)

Jamieson is also critical of Giddens for his failure to recognise the damaging nature of therapeutic discourse for gender equality:

> The contribution of therapeutic discourse to damaging gender stereotypes is also unremarked, reflecting a more general underplaying of structures of gender inequality in *The Transformation of Intimacy*. Feminist work has documented how women carrying the burdens of systematic gender inequality have been recast by medical and therapeutic experts as pathological individuals.
>
> (Jamieson 1999: 481)

Beyond Giddens's failure to recognise and engage with feminist scholarship across a range of theoretical and empirical issues, Jamieson is also critical of how far his theory resonates with broader patterns of gender inequality. As she (1999: 482) notes: "It is not clear, for example that change in the quality of heterosexual relationships would shatter the interconnection of gendered labour markets, gendered distributions of income and wealth, and gendered divisions of domestic labour."

Jamieson maintains that *The Transformation of Intimacy* is cut off from feminist research and there is no attempt to embed wider debates around feminism and gender within the structure action model.

As indicated in Chapter 1, Jamieson suggests that as regards heterosexual relationships, the promise of increased democratisation of gender relationships within heterosexual partnerships as outlined by Giddens is not reflected in empirical research showing traditional power relationships operating in such partnerships which include financial, caring and household work responsibilities.

Giddens maintains that same-sex couples, particularly lesbians, are in the forefront of those having a "pure relationship" and thus prone to the breakdown of relationships. However, as Jamieson (1999: 487) states:

> There is a body of work which suggests that some same-sex couples, and particularly lesbians, tend to have and to see themselves as having more equal relationships than heterosexual couples (Dunne 1997; . . . Weeks *et al.* 1998; . . .) and that, moreover, lesbian relationships are particularly characterised by high levels of intimacy and communication. (Dunne 1997: 201)

Despite this, Jamieson says that she is not convinced that same-sex relationship are characterised by "pure relationships".

Another dimension of the debate outlined in *The Transformation of Intimacy* concerns parenting. Giddens argues that relationships between parents and children are also tending towards "the pure relationship". Jamieson (1999: 489) maintains that the so-called "democratization" of heterosexual relationships has consequences for parenting, particularly in situations of divorce:

> . . . Ben Neale and Carole Smart (1997) have found fathers claiming their right to custody of their children following divorce on the grounds that "everyone's talking about new age man." Their study revealed that men's interest in custody sometimes reflects a competitive approach to their wives rather than their prior relationship with their children.

Far from reflecting a situation of democratisation in their attitude to their partners and children, this research shows an antagonistic attitude to their partners: ". . . men used ideas of gender equality to do their wife down, claiming that because women in general have equality, then their wife should forfeit any special claim to children even if she had been a full-time wife and mother" (Jamieson 1999: 489).

Jamieson (among others) feels that Giddens has been too optimistic about the so-called "transformation of intimacy" and fails to recognise the negative implications. As she (1999: 490) comments: "Extolling the values of mutual self-disclosure and 'the pure relationship' feeds into a therapeutic discourse that has sometimes been the antithesis of empowering for women and gays."

Eva Illouz: How Intimacy Is Structured by Its Encounters with Late Capitalism

As previous chapters have shown, definitions of emotions, intimacy and love underwent a significant change within and outside marriage in the move to modernity. The change from the nineteenth to twentieth centuries proved to be a seismic shift not only in terms of how marriage was viewed but in the very definition of love and intimacy. The rapidity of the changes and the ramifications throughout society led to a change in the cultural infrastructure of society with the growth of *psy*-disciplines contributing and amplifying discourses around emotion and intimacy. Illouz's (1997, 1998/9, 2008, 2012) work charts the shift in these discourses and contributes significantly to the debate concerned with the transformation of intimacy in late modernity.

The Victorian family of the nineteenth century was characterised by an emphasis on piety and a devotion to children and on clearly defined gender identities and roles. Intimacy was largely absent from Victorian marriages and where intimacy did exist it was outside of marriage. The widely documented collapse of the Victorian marriage in the twentieth century is seen by Illouz (1997) as a result of a variety of pressures including secularisation, consumption and the emergence of democratic expectations of relationships.

The pace of change in the early years of the twentieth century was rapid and as Illouz (1997: 45) shows this was partly related to the growth of popular magazines which discussed new expectations regarding marriage, particularly for women. The emphasis shifted to viewing marriage as a joint emotional enterprise and in the process, women's expectations of men changed:

> With the demise of networks of social support brought about by an expanding market (Coontz, 1998) and with changing definitions of marriage as an exclusively emotional enterprise, women turned to men to satisfy emotional needs and started to suggest that men be expressive, attentive and caring in a way that was unprecedented in U.S. history.
>
> (Illouz 1997: 46)

Along with changing definitions of marriage came different definitions of intimacy and love. The sociologist Francesca Cancian characterises the change within the now popularised phrase the "feminization of love" (see Cancian 1987).

The Crisis of Marriage and the Growth of Psychology

There were pressures in and around marriage as the emphasis shifted to discourses relating to the equation of love, marriage and happiness. As Illouz (1997) shows women's magazines focused on changing expectations of marriage and both the causes of and solutions to the crisis of marriage. This left the way open for explanations to emerge to explain marital crises. These explanations came from the *psy*-disciplines, particularly psychology. As Illouz (1997: 47) shows, psychology and other psy-disciplines led to a focus on the association of happiness and "mental health":

> Following this new faith in "mental health" and psychology, the widely popular magazine, *Ladies Home Journal* started a column 'Can this Marriage be Saved? Authored by Dr Popenoe, who was head of the newly founded and very popular Institute for the Mental Health of the Family. The column presented the conflicting viewpoints of an estranged husband and wife, and proceeded to show how the conflict resulted from each one's unhappy childhood. The basic idea that was promoted and that was increasingly taking hold of American culture was that marital happiness was a matter of mental health and that experts and scientific knowledge could help remedy problems of unhappiness and marital discord.

Before going on to explore the impact of psychology and the *psy*–sciences in relation to the growth of the "therapy industry" in late modernity. It is important to understand the history and significance of clinical psychology and its impact in understanding love and the emotions.

Making Love into a Science

The emergence of the *psy*-disciplines in the twentieth century and their continuance into the twenty-first century, including psychology, psychoanalysis, biology and others, have had a significant impact in how we understand relationships and not to the benefit of the development of mature psyches. As Illouz (2010: 24) shows the *psy*-disciplines have subsumed love "under such categories 'the unconscious', 'sex drive', 'hormones', . . . or 'brainchemistry', . . .". Freudian culture and clinical psychology have been central in giving scientific legitimacy to the idea that love is a re-enactment of early childhood conflicts. As Illouz (2010: 24) shows:

> . . . psychoanalysis claims love is caused by the ways in which we form attachments to early parental figures, and by the ways in which our psyche

faces and processes the Oedipus complex. Love is thus reduced to a universal psychic structure.

The emphasis on the fact that, based on this model, romantic misery was self-made, provided an opportunity for the *psy*-sciences to develop in a number of directions, expanding the professional fields in the area of psychoanalysis, psychologists, and therapists, all of whom reinforced the "scientific model" on which the *psy*-sciences were based:

> Moreover in prescribing models of intimacy based on negotiation, communication and reciprocity, the *psy*-sciences make intimate relationships highly *plastic*, to be fashioned out of the design and reflexive monitoring of an autonomous will and tailored to the particular needs and psychological make-up of an individual, thus liquidating the association of love with an absolute form of transcendence.
> (Illouz 2010: 24)

Underlying this is a model of health and well-being that insists that love is a prerequisite of happiness and well-being. Therapy and clinical psychology is frequently accompanied by medication and there is a close association between the psy-sciences and chemicals and chemical processes in providing explanations of behaviour and in thus treating this behaviour. Illouz (2010: 25) offers a comprehensive summary of the relationship between drugs and love:

> Biologists typically explain love through chemical processes, that, even more than psychology, reduce love to factors that are entirely extraneous to the sentiment of love itself. Studies in neuroscience have suggested that a consistent number of chemicals are present in the brain when people testify to feeling love. These chemicals include: Testosterone, Estrogen, Dopamine, Norepinephrine, Serotonin, Oxytocin, and Vasopressin. For example a dramatic increase in the amount of Dopamine and Norepinephrine is said to be present in the brain when one is infatuated with another person. More specifically, higher levels of Testosterone and Estrogen are present during the lustful phase of a relationship. Dopamine, Norepinephrine and Serotonin are more commonly found during that attraction phase of a relationship. The Serotonin effects of being in love have a similar chemical appearance to obsessive-compulsive disorder, which in turn would explain why we seem not to be able to think of anyone else when we are in love.

Thus as Illouz concludes, the impact of these scientific and pseudo-scientific explanations, "reduce love to an epiphenomenon, a mere effect of prior causes" (Illouz 2010: 26) and embedded in "mechanical—psychic or chemical-processes". Many feminist theorists including Illouz offer a critical view of this model showing that love and the pain that often accompanies it, is not a result of dysfunctional childhoods or immature psyches but social and cultural tensions and contradictions that define contemporary identities (see Chapter 6).

Despite the critique offered by Illouz of the Freudian model and *psy*-sciences more generally, she shows how this provided a direct opening for the development of the "therapeutic discourse". As Illouz (1997: 48) shows:

> Culturally, the most striking element of humanistic psychology was that it put happiness and self at the center of public discourse to "realise oneself," to discover one's "authentic self," to achieve emotional well-being and mental health inside the family as well as at work, became new categories of public awareness. And by the 1970s this idea had penetrated organizations, corporations as well as the family.

Within this context, intimacy was located in a matrix of emotional work and as Illouz notes, feminists quickly defined emotional satisfaction as a "right". Thus the therapeutic and rights discourse became closely connected. The therapeutic discourse operated in a domestic and work-life context. As Illouz (1997: 48) notes: "In the same way that the therapeutic ethos had introduced a vocabulary of emotions and a norm of communication inside the corporation, it ushered in a rational and quasi-economic approach to emotions in the domestic sphere."

The therapeutic discourse provided an infrastructural framework which put relationships and emotions centre-stage as the wider utilitarian socio-economic needs of marriage and family dropped away. This coincided with Giddens's (1992) definition of the "pure relationship" within the wider context of the reflexive modernisation debate.

Reflexivity, Modernity and the Transformation of Intimacy: Giddens and Beck

The "reflexive modernization" debate (see also Brooks 2008) has been a significant one for contemporary sociologists and as Illouz (1997: 34) shows, is characterised by a surprising convergence in the thinking of some of the key contemporary sociological theorists, Anthony Giddens (1992, 1994) and Ulrich Beck (with Elizabeth Beck-Gernsheim 1996). As shown earlier, they argue that in explaining relationships of intimacy in late modernity, there is a need to move away from traditional sociological conceptions of society defined in terms of class stratification and "emancipatory" struggles. Illouz (1997: 34) situates the debate within wider conceptualisations of emotion and intimacy:

> ... intimacy points to a broad-sweeping transformation of selfhood and gender relations ... I will argue that, in the context of contemporary American society, contemporary definitions of intimacy are intimately linked to the language of therapy and that this language has naturalized and legitimated the emotional and verbal style of the new middle class.

One of the most important aspects of this new model is the development of an affinity between spheres of work and intimacy and Illouz maintains that as a result of this, Freudian theory which equates psychic "liberation", intimacy and well-being needs to be revised. Illouz (1997: 34) shows that this is closely related to issues around gender equity issues and the role of women in the labour force:

> In the context of the greater equality between the sexes entailed by women's entry into the labour market, intimacy demands a complex symbolic and emotional work that is analogous to and even draws from the emotional and symbolic competence demanded by the contemporary corporation, a process that has been, if not initiated, at least facilitated by psychologists' intervention in these two spheres.

Emotional Capital, Intimacy and Therapeutic Discourse

As shown above, the emergence of capitalism and the demise of the family in late modernity has resulted in a more abstract ideal of intimacy emerging alongside "a different narrative of personal identity" (Illouz 1997: 54). As Illouz observes, this is particularly the case for women and this posed significant challenges to traditional conceptions of intimacy as well as "render[ing] obsolete the skills that made up traditional marriage" (Illouz 1997: 54).

Thus "the transformation of intimacy" emerges from the transformation of identity as a result of the onset of modernity. Despite the overall convergence of views, the views of the Becks (Ulrich and Elizabeth Beck-Gernsheim 1996) do differ in some critical areas to those of Giddens:

> As the Becks (1996) argue, the making of men and women into competitive economic actors has thrown intimacy into disarray. Love is in a state of 'chaos' because men and women are called upon by the market and the states to become self-reliant actors.
>
> (Illouz 1997: 54–55)

Thus while the key source of contradiction and "chaos" for the Becks is love arising from the disjunction between the nuclear family and the market, for Giddens it is biography, as Illouz (1998: 163) shows:

> . . . Giddens views romantic "biography" as the framework par excellence within which the self shapes itself in the face of the "disembedding mechanisms" of modernity. In a brilliant departure from the long standing moral discourse on fiction and reality, Giddens argues that historically romantic love has had an affinity with the novel and that it offers an overarching symbolic structure in which the self can orient itself, shape and "author" its autobiography reflexively.

Illouz however does not entirely agree with either Giddens or the Becks. She maintains that if economic survival was the *raison d'etre* of premodern marriage, then "emotional survival" is the mantra of the modern family who must deal with complexities of emotional intimacy in everyday life. The negotiation of this is not a straightforward one. This also has implications for the position taken by the Becks that "[love is] a kind of rebellion, a way of getting in touch with forces to counteract the intangible and unintelligible existence we find ourselves in" (Beck and Beck-Gernsheim, 1996: 178) (Illouz 1998: 169–170).

As Illouz (1998: 170) outlines, love is not just a kind of rebellion, but can be approached through different discourses, and contemporary analyses of love are deeply split:

> ... one way of experiencing love is indeed on the mode of "rebellion"; but another–on which self-help literature endlessly capitalises—is an attempt—unprecedented in the cultural history of love—to incorporate love in the discourse and phenomenological properties of daily life.

Love and Modernity

As has been shown earlier in this chapter, Illouz's work has focused in different ways on love and intimacy, and in particular, to show how "the structure of the romantic self has changed in modernity" (Illouz 2012: 6). But her fundamental contribution is to show how intimacy is structured by its encounters with late capitalism. Illouz (2012: 6) comments:

> ... my aim is to do to love what Marx did to communities; to show that it is shaped and produced by concrete social relations; to show that love circulates in a marketplace of unequal competing actors; and to argue that some people command greater capacity to define the terms in which they are loved than others.

Illouz, more than other theorists of late modernity, shows that gender politics in the form of gender equality and sexual freedom impacts directly on love and intimacy. Illouz (2012: 9) maintains that this contributes to the "profoundly split and dual aspect of love—both as a source of existential transcendence and as a deeply contested site for the performance of gender identity—that characterises contemporary romantic culture."

Late modernity is characterised by the intersection of the emotional and economic and is, captured in the "individualization of lifestyles", the "economization of social relationships" and "the pervasiveness of economic models to shape the self and its very emotions." In addition there is a disengagement of sex and sexuality from moral norms. Perhaps one of the most important dimensions of the intersection of the emotional and economic in late capitalism was the new role love played in social mobility. As Illouz (2012: 10) notes:

"One of the key cultural transformations accompanying modernity was thus the co-mingling of love with economic strategies of social mobility."

For both women and men, love provided a means of social mobility as: "the modern choice of mate progressively included and mixed both emotional and economic aspirations" (2012: 10). Choice of partner became part of the economic calculus which defines love in late modernity.

Conclusion: Love, Modernity and the Reflexive Emotional Self

Illouz adds an additional dimension to the "reflexive modernization" debate by focusing not just on the "reflexive self" but on the "reflexive emotional self" (see Illouz, 2008) which she shows is "centered on the management and affirmation of its feelings" (2012: 11). This new model of the self, reflected changes in the shift away from the model of romantic love to the model of relationships and the self of late modernity as Illouz (2012: 12) shows:

> Love put women under the tutelage of men, but it did so by legitimizing a model of the self that was private, domestic, individualistic and most of all demanded emotional autonomy. Romantic love thus reinforced within the private sphere the moral individualism that had accompanied the rise of the public sphere. In fact, love is the paradigmatic example and the very engine of a new model of sociability dubbed by Giddens as that of the "pure relationship" based on the contractual assumption that two individuals with equal rights unite for emotional and individualistic purposes.

However while Illouz shows that love in modernity has produced a number of positives, particularly for women, the claim that it is a steady development to emancipation is over optimistic. Illouz argues that this emerges from "the highly ambivalent normative character of modernity" (2012: 13). Thus, while modernity has disrupted the traditional economic basis of marriage and nature of sexual relationships, the framework of gender relations in capitalism remains problematic as Illouz (2012: 14) shows:

> ... much of the anger or disappointment in marriage has to do with the way in which marriage structures gender relations and mixes institutional and emotional logics: say, a desire for genderless fusion and equality, and the distance that inevitably emanates from the performance of gender roles.

Illouz's analysis of intimacy and love in late modernity has provided a perspective on relationships in late modernity absent from the analysis of Giddens and the Becks and more focused on the politics of gender. Chapter 6 focuses more directly on consumption and desire in late capitalism.

Bibliography

Alexander, Jeffrey. 1996. "Critical Reflections on 'Reflexive Modernization'" *Theory, Culture and Society* 13: 133–138.
Archer, Margaret S. 2000. *Being Human: The Problem of Agency.* Cambridge: Cambridge University Press.
Bauman, Zygmunt. 1990. "Modernity and Ambivalence." In Mike Featherstone (ed.). *Global Culture: Nationalism, Globalization and Modernity.* London: Sage, 143–169.
Bauman, Zygmunt. 2000. *Liquid Modernity.* Cambridge: Polity.
Beck, Ulrich. 1992. *Risk Society: Towards a New Modernity.* London: Sage.
Beck, Ulrich and Elizabeth Beck-Gernsheim. 1996. *The Normal Chaos of Love.* Cambridge: Polity.
Beck, Ulrich And Elizabeth Beck-Gernsheim. 2014. *Distant Love: Personal Life in a Global Age.* Cambridge: Polity.
Beck, Ulrich, Anthony Giddens and Scott Lash. 1994. *Reflexive Modernization: Politics, Tradition and Aesthetics in the Modern Social Order.* Stanford, CA: Stanford University Press.
Brooks, Ann. 2008. "Reconceptualizing Reflexivity and Dissonance in Professional and Personal Domains" *British Journal of Sociology* 59(3): 539–559.
Cancian, Francis. M. 1987. *Love in America: Gender and Self-Development.* Cambridge: Cambridge University Press.
Castells, Manual. 1997. *The Power of Identity.* Malden, MA: Blackwell.
Coontz, Stephanie. 1998. *The Way We Really Are: Coming to Terms with America's Changing Families.* New York: Basic Books.
Dunne, Gillian. 1997. *Lesbian Lifestyles: Women's Work and the Politics of Sexuality.* London: Macmillan.
Foucault, Michel. 1978. *The History of Sexuality, Volume 1: An Introduction.* New York: Vintage.
Giddens, Anthony. 1992. *The Transformation of Intimacy: Sexuality, Love and Eroticism in Modern Societies.* Cambridge: Polity.
Giddens, Anthony. 1994. "Living in a Post-Traditional Society." In Ulrich Beck, Anthony Giddems and Scott Lasch (eds), *Reflexive Modernization: Politics, Tradition and Aesthetics in the Modern Social World.* Cambridge: Polity, 56–109.
Gross, Neil. 2005. "The Detraditionalization of Intimacy Reconsidered" *Sociological Theory* 23(3): 286–311.
Hochschild, Arlie R. 2003. *The Commercialisation of Intimate Life.* Berkeley: University of California Press.
Illouz, Eva. 1997. *Consuming the Romantic Utopia: Love and the Cultural Contradictions of Capitalism.* Berkeley: University of California Press.
Illouz, Eva. 1998/1999. "The Lost Innocence of Love: Love as a Postmodern Condition." In M. Featherstone (ed.), *Love and Eroticism.* London: Sage" *Theory, Culture and Society*, 15(3): 161–186, http://tcs.sagepub.com/content/15/3.toc
Illouz, Eva. 2008. *Saving the Modern Soul: Therapy, Emotions and the Culture of Self-Help.* Berkeley: University of California Press.
Illouz, Eva. 2010. "Love and Its Discontents: Irony, Reason, Romance" *The Hedgehog Review*, 12(1): 18–32.
Illouz, Eva. 2012. *Why Love Hurts: A Sociological Explanation.* Cambridge: Polity.
Jamieson, Lynn. 1998. *Intimacy, Personal Relationships in Modern Society.* Cambridge: Polity.

Jamieson, Lynn. 1999. "Intimacy Transformed? A Critical Look at the 'Pure Relationship'" *Sociology* 33(3): 477–494.
Kern, Stephen. 1992. *The Culture of Love: Victorians to Moderns*. Cambridge, MA: Harvard University Press.
Kipnis, Laura. 2003. *Against Love: A Polemic*. New York: Pantheon.
Luhman, Niklas. 1986. *Love as Passion: The Codification of Intimacy*. Trans J. Gaines and D. Jones. Cambridge: Polity.
Neale, Barry and Carol Smart. 1997. "Experiments with Parenthood" *Sociology* 31: 201–219.
Seidman, Steven. 1991. *Romantic Longings: Love in America, 1830–1980*. New York: Routledge.
Weeks, Jeffrey, Catherine Donovan, and Brian Heaphy. 1998. "Everyday Experiments: Narratives of Non-heterosexual Relationships." In Elizabeth Silva and Carol Smart (eds), *The 'New' Family?* London: Sage, 83–99.
Wilson, Elizabeth. 1999. "Bohemian Love" In Mike Featherstone (ed.), *Love and Eroticism*. London: Sage, 111–127.

6 "The Intelligence of Emotions"

Intimacy, Emotions and the "Turn to Affect"—Feminist Interventions

Introduction

Theorising emotion and affect has become a central area of interest for social and cultural theorists including for many feminist theorists and the literature has been extensive (Berlant 1997; Damasio 1994, 2003; Massumi 2002; Ngai 2005; Nicholson 1999; and Nussbaum 2001). Much attention has focused on distinguishing between emotion and affect. As Gorton (2007: 334) shows: "some argue that emotion refers to a sociological expression of feelings whereas affect is much more firmly rooted in biology and in our physical response to feelings; others attempt to differentiate on the basis that emotion requires a subject while affect does not." However, not all feminist theorists see the need for a distinction as Probyn (2005: 11) indicates: "A basic distinction is that emotion refers to cultural and social expression, whereas affects are of a biological and physiological nature." One of the areas which has been central in these debates is the relationship between public and private domains.

The relationship between the personal and the political when it comes to intimacy and emotions has been addressed by a number of feminist theorists. Berlant (1997; and see Chapter 7) has been concerned with the way the private intrudes into the public sphere, which she calls the "intimate public sphere" (1997: 4). Berlant's work—as can be seen in Chapter 7—has made a significant contribution to the relationship between the intimate and the public sphere. As Gorton (2007: 336) argues, theorists find the explication of that relationship important in understanding the "relationship between emotion and the 'public sphere'".

In this regard Gorton recognises an important gap in the areas of theorising by feminists including Probyn (2005) and Ahmed (2004), which is the understanding of "desire" as a concept. As Gorton (2007: 345) comments: "how are we to theorize desire after the affective turn?" It is perhaps the preoccupation with a process of reflexivity in its own position which has led feminists to ignore desire in their analysis.

Feminism and feminist scholars are interested in the links between affect and feminism because they recognise the links between "affect and gendered, sexualised, racialised and classed relations of power" (Pedwell and Whitehead 2012: 116). Feminist engagement with emotion and affect are also part of an analysis of the "political, cultural, economic and psychoanalytic implications of affect and emotion [which] engages with a wider 'emotionalisation of society'" (Pedwell and Whitehead 2012: 116).

Part of this reassessment of the role of emotions and affect can be seen in a reconsideration of historical analysis of colonial relationships. As has been shown in the chapters of this book, the implications of historical analysis of colonialism are profound. For an analysis of intimacy Pedwell and Whitehead (2012: 116) indicate that:

> Affective frameworks also figure centrally in feminist and post-colonial analyses of the embodied and psychical legacies of colonialism and slavery, as well as the emotional politics of contemporary forms of nation building, migration and multiculturalism.

It is this which captures the distinction between emotion and affect and while outside the focus of this book, the distinction is important to understand the engagement of feminist and social theorists as outlined by Pedwell and Whitehead (2012: 116):

> Affect thus cannot be reduced to either "discourse" or "emotion" but rather exceeds these categories; it is a material intensity that emerges via the "in-between" spaces of embodied encounters, circulating power not primarily as a mode of discursive regulation but rather as the potential to "become otherwise". (Deleuze and Guattari, 1994)

One of the foremost feminist and cultural theorists of affect is Patricia Clough (2007). Her work points to changes in the way in which "the social" is conceptualised:

> Theories of affect and the deployment of affective capacity are valuable at this conjuncture, she suggests, "to grasp the changes that constitute the social and to explore them as changes in ourselves, circulating through our bodies, our subjectivities, yet irreducible to the individual, the personal and psychological". (Clough 2007: 3)
> (Pedwell and Whitehead 2012: 117)

Sara Ahmed's contribution to debates on emotion and affect has also been important and she shows how power works through affect to configure individual and social bodies (see Ahmed 2000). In *The Cultural Politics of Emotion* (2004) Ahmed's critical point is that emotions can tie us into conditions of subordination. She also recognises that change is difficult to achieve because relations of power are: "so intractable and enduring, even in the face of collective forms of resistance," and the reason for this "is the strength of our affective attachment to social norms" (Ahmed 2004: 11–12). As Pedwell and Whitehead (2012: 120) comment: "Feminist engagement with affective politics thus requires attention to the ways in which feelings can (re)produce dominant social and geo-political hierarchies and exclusions."

In recognising Ahmed's contribution to the debate, our primary indebtedness as feminists, sociologists and theorists of emotion has to be to Arlie Hochschild's (1983, 1997, 2003, 2008) work. Her analysis builds on the concepts of "emotional labour" and "emotionwork" and "feeling rules" (see also Brooks 2014) which established an entire generation of transnational feminists on a journey of theoretical and empirical work. Pedwell and Whitehead (2012: 121–122) provide a useful summary of her contribution:

> Hochschild's work was crucial in contributing to . . . theories of social construction of emotions and later analyses of their performative circulation in the context of gendered, classed, racialised and sexualized relations of power. It was also prescient in tracing the links between emotion, global capitalism and neo-liberalism . . . as well as laying the groundwork for analysis of their gendered articulation in relation to concepts of affective labour. (Adkins 2002; Swan 2008)

Pedwell and Whitehead's (2012: 124) analysis is important is framing some of the key issues raised by feminist theorists and: ". . . address the question of how affect travels within and across cultures, situating feminist debates about emotion and intimacy within international, transnational, cross-cultural and cross-racial contexts" (see also Brooks 2006; Brooks and Devasayaham 2011; Brooks and Simpson 2012).

They also show how feminist theory can be set alongside other theoretical analyses of power to provide a critical analysis of theories of affect:

> In the context of transnational capitalism, feminist and other critical theories of affect have been employed alongside Foucauldian notions of biopolitics to examine the politics of subject formation and neoliberal forms of governmentality (Adkins 2002; Fraser and Bedford 2008; Ong 2006; Pedwell 2012).
>
> (Pedwell and Whitehead 2012: 116)

One of the most important contemporary feminist theorists who has shown how intimacy and emotion and indeed love are defined by late capitalist modernity is Eva Illouz.

Eva Illouz: The Commercialisation of Intimacy: "Architectures of Choice" and the Emergence of Marriage Markets

Eva Illouz's (1997, 1998, 2010, 2012) work is concerned with how intimacy is structured by its relationships to late capitalism, in particular the relationship between romance and consumption. More recently, Illouz focuses on love in contemporary relationships and she investigates how it is shaped by the nature of relational and institutional arrangements and is critical of the cultural context of emotions in contemporary society.

1. Refashioning Love: From Premodern to Postmodern Love and Mate Selection

Across a range of work, Illouz outlines the transformation of love from premodern love to a postmodern mode of mate selection. She shows that while the modern mode of love and mate selection is more emancipated and more egalitarian than premodern love, Illouz (2010: 21) claims that: "it is also counter intuitively more rationalized than its premodern counterpart." She argues that: "The modern romantic condition more often resembles the process of 'sobering up' described by Marx than the fervour and frenzy of premodern love" (Illouz 2010).

This shift in emphasis can be described as a process of "disenchantment". This is in stark contrast to premodern love which Illouz characterises as "love at first sight". She defines this "enchanted" love of premodern society as opening up the self "to a quasi-religious sense of transcendence". As she further comments:

> "Love at first sight" contains a few consistent characteristics. It is experienced as a unique event, unexpectedly erupting in one's life. It is inexplicable and irrational. It is incited upon the first encounter and therefore not based on cognitive and cumulative knowledge on the other; rather it derives from a holistic and intuitive form of experience.
> (Illouz 2010: 21–22)

Despite the quasi-religious aspect of "enchanted love," Illouz shows that love in the Middle Ages was often characterised by amorous rhetoric characterising "the loved one as a divinity" and presenting the experience of love as "a total experience". Illouz compares this model to the postmodern experience which she claims is captured in Candace Bushnell's (1996: 2) *Sex and the City*:

> When was the last time you heard someone say, "I love you!" When was the last time you saw two people gazing into each others eyes without thinking, Yeah right? When was the last time you heard someone announce, "I am truly, madly in love," without thinking, just wait until Monday morning?
> (cited in Illouz 2010: 22)

Illouz claims that Bushnell's view is a self-conscious, ironic and disenchanted approach to love. Illouz, argues that Bushnell's work falls into a "chick-lit" genre which is oriented to women and focuses on the problems inherent in relationships. Illouz (2010: 22) claims that: "The rationalization of love is at the heart of the new ironic structure of romantic feeling, which marks the move from an 'enchanted' to a disenchanted cultural definition of love."

Central to Illouz's thinking is her view, consistent in all her work which is the cultural model of love, which shows how a range of cultural forces have refashioned love and have contributed to its "disenchantment" and its rationalization. She identifies science, technologies of choice and political values as instrumental in this process of refashioning.

We have already explored the impact of science on love in Chapter 5. As we saw and as Illouz (2010: 26) outlines;

> Scientific explanations reduce love to an epiphenomenon, a mere effect of prior causes that are unseen and unfelt by the subject, and that are neither mystical nor singular but rather located in involuntary and almost mechanical-psychic or chemical—processes ... Scientific interpretations of love do not replace traditional romantic conceptions of love, but rather compete with them, and in fact *undermine* them.

A further cultural dimension which has led to a refashioning of love is the growth of internet technology which Illouz argues overlaps with psychological knowledge and what Illouz identifies as "technologies of choice" that emerge with the growth of the market of choice in relationships.

Illouz argues that a characteristic of postmodern love is a shift of emphasis in the choice of a mate. As Illouz (2010: 27) shows:

> ... the premodern actor looking for a mate seems a simpleton in comparison with today's actors, who from adolescence to adulthood develop an elaborate set of criteria for the selection of a mate ... Psychology, internet technology, and the logic of the capitalist market applied to mate selection have contributed to create a self-conscious, manipulable personality, who uses an increasingly refined and wide number of criteria, presumably conducive to greater compatibility.

To provide an example of this model, Illouz undertook a study of online dating in 2006 and she shows that in responding to an open-ended questionnaire about the uses of Internet dating sites, respondents claimed that they would only correspond with people who closely suited their needs. Illouz (2010: 28) also shows that: "the majority of respondents reported that their tastes changed in the course of their search and that they aspired to 'more accomplished' people than they did at the beginning of their search."

Illouz maintains that these responses show that people use rational strategies to achieve their romantic aspirations and she maintains that her findings confirm the views of the sociologists Jeffrey Alexander (2003) and Neil Smelser (1997) who argue that technology has a rationalising effect which reinforces the process of disenchantment in modern life.

2. The Romanticisation of Commodities and the Commodification of Romance

Illouz's contribution to a contemporary analysis of love and intimacy has been substantial, both in terms of the analysis of qualitative empirical data and in terms of the experience of love. Her work also amplifies that of social theorists of late modernity including Giddens, Beck and Beck-Gernsheim. Turner (1998: 115) describes Illouz's work as "a sociology of romance" captured in the idea of "the romanticization of commodities and the commodification of romance" and this is certainly true of her recent work which focuses on an analysis of romance and consumerism in the twentieth century.

The process of "the romanticization of commodities" describes the way in which romance became popularised in the U.S. through the growth of advertising and the development of a mass market for romance. Romance becomes fundamentally linked to commodities and Illouz (1997: 115) maintains this can take two forms: "'Candid consumption' is the attachment of a romantic theme directly to the product; 'oblique consumption' is the indirect connection between the activity of the couple, their setting and the product."

Essentially, Illouz, sees romance as part of the growth of leisure and consumption. The growth of the film industry and the representation of romance in film was an important element in this as Turner (1998: 116) notes: "The use of close-ups in film and photography and the employment of movie stars to advertise commodities created a new cosmology in which icons represented the new lifestyle" (see also Leonard 2010 below). In addition, other aspects of lifestyle contributed to the importance of romance in the development of lifestyle. The growth of dating as a social phenomenon, against the backdrop of the growth of youth culture and the focus of having a social life outside the home in terms of "dining out" became part of how dating and courtship were defined.

This all contributed to the commodification of love and as Illouz notes is part of the American Dream. Love and romance are portrayed in advertisements as removed from domestic settings. Couples are never portrayed in the home with children but in a glamorous hotel or restaurant. Typical adverts are the advert for *Sandals* . . . the beach resort where love and romance are seen as an essential ingredient.

Turner (1998) in a critique of Illouz's analysis maintains that while Illouz acknowledges cultural contradictions in contemporary love, she fails to acknowledge the significance of adultery as a universal feature of contemporary marriage. Regardless of this criticism, Illouz's model of "the postmodern romantic condition" recognises how the romantic narrative has changed.

3. Postmodern Romance: The Love Affair

Illouz is an insightful observer of the changing nature of relationships. In "The Lost Innocence of Love: Romance as a Postmodern Condition" (1998), Illouz recognises that the life-long romantic narrative has largely collapsed and that "the affair" is now the more compressed romantic narrative form.

Illouz acknowledges that the rise of "the affair" is directly related to the transformation of the role of sex in relationships since the Second World War. She shows how sex as a central aspect of pleasure in relationships was legitimised by feminist and gay groups. As Illouz (1998: 176) notes:

> In contradistinction to the teleological, absolute and single-minded Romantic narrative of "grand amour," the affair is a cultural form that attempts to immobilize and repeat, compulsively, the primordial experience of "novelty". Moreover the affair is undergirded by a consumerist approach to the choice of a mate. During the Victorian era, people chose from a very narrow pool of available partners and often felt compelled to marry their first suitor.

The principle on which the affair is based is choice and a market framework within which to choose. As Illouz shows the experience of "waiting" which was the pattern of Victorian women's lives is now eliminated. This is replaced by periods of sporadic romantic intensity and as Illouz describes them, have the character of postmodern fragmentation. As Illouz (1998: 177) notes:

> Affairs then, are self-contained narrative episodes disconnected from one another in the flow of experience, resulting in a fragmenting of experience of love into separate emotional units (the transitory settings of so many of these stories exhibit a corresponding spatial fragmentation).

Illouz makes it clear that sex has always been a feature of relationships outside marriage but she claims that the character of these contemporary affairs is distinctively postmodern for the following reasons, "First like so much else in postmodern culture (Lash 1990) they institutionalize liminality" (Illouz 1998: 177). In other words, the affairs were located away from home and work, removed from marriage, family and domestic responsibilities.

Secondly, Illouz claims that the character of sexual pleasure is more about "liberation" than previous embodiments of sexual pleasure captured in the dominance of such pleasures by males such as Don Juan or Casanova. As she observes; "Contemporary affairs are most likely to be lived as sexual pleasure by both sexes, and in that respect, reflect the diffuse androgyny of postmodern culture" (Illouz 1998: 177).

Thirdly, Illouz argues that affairs are not about a deliberate statement of transgression and they do not set out to challenge normative or moral imperatives. The final point raised by Illouz is that the underpinnings of the postmodern affair which is how identity is being redefined is based on choices and consumer rationality. The affair is of course linked to adultery and whereas traditionally adultery was seen as being initiated by men, increasingly women are seen to initiate adulterous affairs.

4. Adultery and its Representation in Film

One of the classic analyses of adultery is Laura Kipnis's (1998) paper "Adultery". Kipnis argues from a Marxist perspective and draws parallels between marriage and work, using concepts such as "intimacy labour" or "relationship labour" to describe the experience of marriage as similar to alienated labour populated by "conjugal workers". Within this context Kipnis sees adultery as a protest against marriage and beyond this as a rejection of capitalist society. She seems marriage as an aspect of the disciplinary impact of capitalism and adultery is a form of resistance to the domestic drudgery of marriage. Kipnis claims that it is the work aspect of marriage which drives people into adulterous marriages.

The shift in emphasis to women initiating adulterous affairs has been represented in contemporary cinema with new film genres focusing on "the female adultery narrative." Leonard (2010: 108) identifies the following films as part of this genre: "American Beauty (1999); A Walk on the Moon (1999); Lovely and Amazing (2001); The Good Girl (2002); Unfaithful (2002); The Secret Lives of Dentists (2003); Closer (2004); We Don't Live here Anymore (2004) and Being Julia (2004)."

One of the main dimensions of this film genre is the focus on punishing the adulterous woman directly. As Leonard (2010: 111) notes: "In such cases, the female adultery narrative is deployed in order to explore the threat that the unfaithful woman poses, in general to the patriarchal order."

One of the ways in which this film genre represents this is through showing the impact of adultery on others particularly on the spouse. Leonard (2010: 111) shows how this is conveyed in the film *Unfaithful*:

> One variation on this theme explores the profound destabilization that ensues when men suspect their wives have betrayed them, an exploration typically accomplished by focusing not on the adulteress herself, but on the forms of male anxiety she instigates. In *Unfaithful* for example, Edward Sumner's (Richard Gere) confirmation of his wife's infidelity is linked to an unstoppable act of heinous criminality. Specifically when faced with the unsettling discovery that his wife Connie (Diane Lane) has given an anniversary present from him to her French lover, Edward brutally murders his sexual rival. The film, however, also implicitly normalizes this murder by making Edward a highly sympathetic figure, a choice that renders plausible the idea that finding out about a wife's betrayal is so profoundly disruptive that it causes an otherwise righteous and principled man to suddenly do the unthinkable.

Interestingly Leonard points to Flaubert's *Madame Bovary*, who she argues epitomises the bored adulteress. She maintains that: "Adultery, as a literary and historical construct, might be understood as a mode that articulated the boredom and restlessness that were the inevitable by-product of a social order which mandated women's estrangement from the economies of public labor and productivity" (Leonard 2010: 112).

5. "Architectures of Choice" and the Emergence of Marriage Markets

The purpose of Illouz's analysis of love and intimacy in late modernity is to shift the emphasis away from Freudian and psychological explanations of the breakdown of marriage and the failure of love, to a set of social and cultural tensions and contradictions which have impacted on the self and identities. The fundamental difference is that Freudians and psychologists more generally operate from a set of normative expectations regarding love and happiness. However Illouz shares with feminists a view of love and marriage where power is the basis of relationships. As Illouz (2012: 4) comments:

> ... [the] claim made by feminists is that a struggle for power lies at the core of love and sexuality and that men have had and continue to have the upper hand in that struggle because there is a convergence between economic and sexual power. Such sexual male power consists in the capacity to define the objects of love and to set up the rules that govern courtship and the expression of romantic sentiments. Ultimately male power resides in the fact that gender identities and hierarchy are played out and reproduced in the expression and experience of romantic sentiments, and that, conversely, sentiments sustain broader economic and political power differentials.

Illouz makes some interesting observations of the relationship between love and patriarchy. She maintains that when patriarchy was powerful, love was less significant in relationships. But with the decline of patriarchy, there has been an increase in "the cultural prominence of love" with a more symmetrical pattern of gender relationships based around egalitarianism. Illouz's point is that because feminism tends to equate love with patriarchal control, they fail to acknowledge the fact that women can draw on love to subvert patriarchy.

The social and cultural dynamics of gender relations are embedded in the institution of marriage that Illouz (2012: 14) maintains "mixes institutional and emotional logics." She analyses a variety of sources for assessing the state of contemporary love and romance as follows:

> My data are varied and include 70 interviews with people living in three large urban centres in Europe, the U.S., and Israel; a wide variety of web-based support groups, nineteenth—century and contemporary novels; a large sample of contemporary guidebooks to romance, dating, marriage and divorce; internet dating sites; and finally, an analysis of *The New York Times* weekly column "Modern Love" for a period of two years.
> (Illouz 2012: 16N32)

Transformation of Love and "Architectures of Choice"

One of the most transformative aspects of love, Illouz claims is the capacity for choice, and she describes this as "architectures of choice": "The architecture of choice consists of a number of cognitive and emotional processes, and more especially it has to do with the ways in which emotional and rational forms of thinking are valued, conceived of and monitored in making a decision" (Illouz 2012: 120).

Relationships characterised by architectures of choice can be compared to the ritualized romantic order of the eighteenth century which Illouz describes as a "regime of performativity" and which lacks authenticity. By contrast modern relationships are characterised by what Illouz (2012: 31) calls "a regime of emotional authenticity." She characterises this as follows: "A regime of emotional authenticity makes people scrutinize their own and another's emotion in order to decide on the importance, intensity, and future significance of the relationship."

The Emergence of Marriage Markets: The Sexualisation of Modern Relationships

Illouz claims that it is conditions within which choices are made which has transformed relationships. She argues that in nineteenth—century English and American culture, romantic choice was characterised by individualism. Illouz shows how the transformation of love and relationships was the result of a number of social and cultural changes. The first of these is what Illouz calls: "the normative deregulation of the mode of evaluation of prospective partners" (Illouz 2012: 41). In other words the removal of choice from the hands of the family and wider social milieux, as had been the case in the eighteenth and nineteenth centuries, and the importance of the media in defining standards of attraction and social worth.

The second factor was a change in the way potential partners are assessed, to include both psychological and sexual dimensions, with the emphasis being on the latter. Thirdly, the increasing potency of "sexual fields", in other words the importance of sexuality in determining relationships, and acting as a significant factor in choices being made in the marriage market. Illouz (2012: 42) highlights both the sexualisation and psychologization of choice:

> The individualization of the criteria of choice of a mate, and its disentanglement from the moral fabric of the group, is illustrated by the emergence and prevalence of two criteria to evaluate a prospective partner: "emotional intimacy and psychological compatibility," on the one hand and "sexiness" on the other. The notion of "emotional intimacy" differs from love based on character because its goal is to make compatible two unique, highly differentiated, and intricate psychological make ups. "Sex appeal," "sexual desirability," or "sexiness" reflects a cultural emphasis

on sexuality and physical attractiveness as such, detached from a moral world of values.

Illouz recognises that the history of romance resonates with examples of the importance of both beauty and erotica in romantic attraction. However, she argues that the pervasiveness and pre-eminence of "sexiness" as "a cultural category" in the evaluation of potential partners and in relationships is a modern phenomenon and as she astutely observes, it is underpinned by an economic and cultural infrastructure dedicated to the commercialisation of romance through sexual attraction. As Illouz (2012: 42) shows:

> "Sexiness" expresses the fact that in modernity men's and especially women's gender identity has been transformed into a sexual identity: that is, into a set of self-consciously manipulated bodily, linguistic, and sartorial codes geared to elicit sexual desire in another. Sexiness in turn has become an autonomous and decisive criterion in the selection of a mate. This transformation emerged as a result of the conjunction of consumerism and of the increasing normative legitimation of sexuality by psychological and feminist cultural worldviews.

For Illouz, the central feature of the modern era is this intersection of consumer culture and desire, which she sees as at the centre of subjectivity. She sees sexuality and desire as interchangeable. The burgeoning of a huge market for consumer products linked to the emergence of the market around beauty and glamour, reinforced the emphasis on sex and desire. Illouz (2012: 43) outlines its historical development drawing on Peiss (1998):

> At the beginning of the twentieth century . . . perfumes, make-up, powders, cosmetics, and creams flooded the emerging markets of consumption, and in trying to promote these goods, advertisers disentangled beauty from character. "Released from the Victorian underworld, painted women now paraded through advertisers' imaginary worlds. Scenes depicted them swimming, sun-bathing, dancing, and motoring—pictures of healthy, athletic, and fun-loving womanhood" (Peiss 1998: 142).

The cosmetics industry and the focus on beauty and youth led to the commodification of the body and this applied to men as well as women. While men's appetite for consumer products was slower than women's, the interest in masculine identity and sexuality was apparent in the nineteenth century: "Indeed, [. . .] an extensive 'bachelor subculture' formed around the network of eating houses, barber-shops, tobacconists, tailors, city bars, theatres and an array of other commercial ventures that thrived on the patronage of affluent young 'men about town'" (Osgerby 2003: 62).

The increasing focus on the body and sex made sexual attraction "*the sine qua non* of romantic partnership." Illouz shows that the implications were much more profound for the moral and normative structures. The emphasis on sex and its disengagement from emotions resulted in a decline in the relevance of moral frameworks for modern relationships. Illouz argues this creates an "open market" in the selection of mates. She maintains that in the eighteenth and nineteenth centuries, romantic choices reflected and reinforced both the stratification system and the attendant class morality, whereas:

> In modernity, the exchange can in principle become asymmetrical: that is, men and women can "exchange" different attributes—beauty or sexiness for, say socio-economic power . . . The trading of assets is thus the result of a historical transformation of the structure of marriage markets.
> (Illouz 2012: 52, 53)

The range of choices available to individuals is not a one dimensional one and can be a mixture of economic, emotional and sexual traits. Illouz (2012: 53) draws on the concept of *habitus* to frame the debate:

> The romantic *habitus* has thus the characteristic of operating at once economically and emotionally. Sometimes this *habitus* makes choices in which economic calculus is harmoniously reconciled with emotions, but sometimes this *habitus* is subject to internal tensions, as when one has to choose between a "socially appropriate" and a "sexy" person. This is why the sexually romantic *habitus* has become a very complicated one, precisely because it contains a variety of dispositions.

Illouz discusses how beauty and sexiness are in fact class-related, and thus can be seen as a new mode of stratification, but she recognises that they are more autonomous and are not tied directly to class. She therefore recognises that the choice of a mate in the open market is not directly connected to class.

Illouz shows how "erotic capital" can be seen as part of women's emotional capital. She recognises that this is not an entirely new phenomenon and that historically women have used erotic capital to gain power and status. However, she shows in postmodern society there are social and cultural elements as well as media culture which encourage "the conversion of erotic capital to social capital" (Illouz 2012: 57).

Illouz draws on Catherine Hakim's (2000) analysis in *Work—Lifestyle Choices in the 21st Century: Preference Theory* to accentuate her critique:

> Catherine Hakim suggests, the girls thought to be most attractive in high-school were more likely than others to marry, to marry young, and perhaps even more surprisingly to have a higher household income (measured fifteen years after initial measurement). Hakim goes as far as to suggest that women can exploit erotic capital for upward social mobility instead of, or as well as, turning to the labour market . . . her

findings are useful in that they imply that marriage markets are analogous to labour-markets in enabling women to gain social status and wealth in modern societies through their sexual personas.

(Illouz 2012: 57).

Conclusion

Feminist theorists have been in the forefront of research on emotions and affect and much of the work has drawn on the pioneering work of Arlie Hochschild. Other major theorists such as Ahmed and Clough have developed the theoretical range into different areas. Perhaps one of the key figures in developing the theoretical issues has been Eva Illouz whose work on relationships and love has enriched the field. Illouz's work is an interesting and dynamic analysis of the changing nature of love and romance from premodern to postmodern society. She shows how social and cultural explanations frame the debates around the emergence of marriage markets in late modernity as well as the "architecture of choice" characterised by an open market in the selection of mates. Illouz shows how the prominence of sex, sexual attractiveness and desire are major factors in the choices being made. She argues that "erotic capital" is an important aspect of women's status and power in relationships and becomes a criterion of stratification in its own right.

Bibliography

Adkins, Lisa. 2002. *Revisions: Gender and Sexuality in Late Modernity*. Buckingham: Open University Press.
Ahmed, Sara. 2000. *Strange Encounters: Embodied Others in Post-Coloniality*. London: Routledge.
Ahmed, Sara. 2004. *The Cultural Politics of Emotion*. Edinburgh: The University of Edinburgh Press.
Alexander, Jeffrey. 2003. *The Meaning of Social Life: A Cultural Sociology*. New York: Oxford University Press.
Berlant, Lauren. 1997. *The Queen of America Goes to Washington City: Essays on Sex and Citizenship*. Durham, NC: Duke University Press.
Brooks, Ann. 2006. *Gendered Work in Asian Cities: The New Economy and Changing Labour Markets*. Aldershot: Ashgate.
Brooks, Ann. 2014. "'The Affective Turn' in the Social Sciences and the Gendered Nature of Emotions: Theorizing Emotions in the Social Sciences from 1800 to the Present." In David Lemmings and Ann Brooks (eds), *Emotions and Social Change: Historical and Sociological Perspectives*. London and New York: Routledge, 43–62.
Brooks, Ann and Theresa Devasayaham. 2011/2013. *Gender Emotions and Labour Markets*. Routledge Studies in Social and Political Thought Series. London and New York: Routledge.
Brooks, Ann and Ruth Simpson. 2012. *Emotions in Transmigration: Transformation, Movement and Identity*. London: Palgrave Macmillan.
Bushnell, Candace. 1996. *Sex and the City*. New York: Atlantic Monthly Press.

Clough, Patricia with Jean Halley (eds). 2007. *The Affective Turn: Theorizing the Social*. Durham, NC: Duke University Press.

Damasio, Antonio. 1994. *Descartes' Error: Emotion, Reason and the Human Brain*. London: Penguin.

Damasio, Antonio. 2003. *Looking for Spinoza: Joy, Sorrow and the Feeling Brain*. Orlando: Harcourt Books.

Deleuze, Giles and Felix Guattari. 1994. *What Is Philosophy?* London: Verso.

Fraser, Nancy with Kate Bedford. 2008. "Social Rights and Gender Justice in the Neoliberal Movement: A Conversation about Welfare and Transnational Politics" *Feminist Theory* 9(2): 225–245.

Gorton, Kristyn. 2007. "Theorizing Emotion and Affect" *Feminist Theory* 8(3): 333–348.

Hakim, Catherine. 2000. *Work-Lifestyle Choices in the 21st Century: Preference Theory*. Oxford: Oxford University Press.

Hochschild, Arlie R. 1983/2003. *The Managed Heart: Commercialization of Human Feeling*. Berkeley: University of California Press.

Hochschild, Arlie R. 1997. *The Time Bind: When Work Becomes Home and Home Becomes Work*. New York: Metropolitan Books.

Hochschild, Arlie R. 2003. *The Commercialization of Intimate Life*. Berkeley: University of California Press.

Hochschild, Arlie R. 2008. "Emotion Work, Feeling Rules and Social Structure." In Monica Greco and Paul Stenner (eds), *Emotions: A Social Science Reader*. London: Routledge, 121–127.

Illouz, Eva. 1997. *Consuming the Romantic Utopia: Love and the Cultural Contradictions of Capitalism*. Berkeley: University of California Press.

Illouz, Eva. 1998/1999. "The Lost Innocence of Love: Love as a Postmodern Condition" *Theory Culture and Society* 12(1): 161–186.

Illouz, Eva. 2010 "Love and Its Discontents: Irony, Reason, Romance" *The Hedgehog Review* 12(1): 18–32.

Illouz, Eva. 2012. *Why Love Hurts: A Sociological Explanation* (Cambridge: Polity).

Kipnis, Laura. 1998. "Adultery" *Critical Inquiry* 24(2): 289–327.

Lash, Scott. 1990. *Sociology of Postmodernism*. London and New York: Routledge.

Leonard, Suzanne. 2010. "'I Hate My Job, I Hate Everybody Here': Adultery, Boredom, and the 'Working Girl' in Twenty-First Century American Cinema." In Diane Negra and Yvonne Tasker (eds), *Interrogating Postfeminisms: Gender and the Politics of Popular Culture*. Durham, NC: Duke University Press, 101–131.

Massumi, Brian. 2002. *Parables of the Virtual: Movement, Affect, Sensation*. Durham, NC: Duke University Press.

Nicholson, Linda. 1999. *The Play of Reason: From the Modern to the Postmodern*. Buckingham: Open University Press.

Ngai, Sianne. 2005. *Ugly Feelings*. Cambridge, MA: Harvard University Press.

Nussbaum, Martha. 2001. *Upheavals of Thought: The Intelligence of Emotions* Cambridge: Cambridge University Press.

Ong, Aihwa. 2006. *Neoliberalism as Exception: Mutations in Citizenship and Sovereignty*. Durham, NC: Duke University Press.

Osgerby, Bill. 2003. "A Pedigree of the Consuming Male: Masculinity, Consumption and the American 'Leisure Class'"In Bethan Benwell (ed.), *Masculinity and Men's Lifestyle*. Oxford: Blackwell, 57–85.

Pedwell, Carolyn. 2012. "Economies of Empathy: Obama, Neoliberalism and Social Justice" *Environment and Planning, D: Society and Space* 30(2): 280–297.

Pedwell, Carolyn and Anne Whitehead. 2012. "Affecting Feminism: Questions of Feeling in Feminist Theory" *Feminist Theory* 13(2): 115–129.

Peiss, Kathy. 1998. *Hope in a Jar: The Making of America's Beauty Culture.* New York: Henry Holt.

Probyn, Elspeth. 2005. *Blush: Faces of Shame.* Minneapolis: University of Minnesota Press.

Smelser, Neil. 1997. *Problematics of Sociology.* Berkeley: University of California Press.

Swan, Elizabeth. 2008. "You Make Me Feel Like a Woman: Therapeutic Cultures and the Contagion of Femininity" *Gender, Work and Organization* 15(1): 88–107.

Turner, Bryan. 1998. "Consuming the Romantic Utopia: Love and the Cultural Contradictions of Capitalism by Eva Illouz" *Body and Society* 4: 115–117.

7 Intimacy, Emotions and the Public Sphere
From Sentimental Ideology to "The Queen of America"—The Public and the Private in the Work of Lauren Berlant

Introduction

Many feminist theorists have made political interventions into theoretical analysis. Lauren Berlant's (1991, 1993, 1998, 2008a and 2008b) work on emotion and affect focuses on the intrusion of the private into the public by showing how intimacy and sexual practices which do not subscribe to a normative framework can be seen as a threat to established values, including traditional family values and heterosexuality. In this chapter I analyse Berlant's contribution to this area and to her work on the relationship between intimacy and therapy. Her work highlights how the concept of therapy has been taken to an extreme in U.S. society and shapes the relationship of emotion and the public sphere. In fact much of Berlant's work is concerned with the history of the relationship of intimacy and its intersection with the public sphere as well as providing a critique of sentimental ideology in a range of literary genres. Berlant (2010: 116), like other feminist theorists is interested in how emotion and affect can lead to transformation and change, although she is aware that changes on the personal level do not directly impact on structural transformation. Berlant's work shows a historical development from a critique of sentimental ideology in literary genre to a more developed theoretical analysis of emotions and affect in contemporary society. I trace the genealogical development of Berlant's treatment of intimacy and emotion in the body of her work.

Berlant (2015) describes her work as follows:

> My work has focused on politics, emotion and intimacy in the U.S. nineteenth and twentieth centuries—now the twenty-first in particular, in relation to citizenship, to informal and normative modes of social belonging, and to affective attachments and fantasies that take shape through ordinary practices. These scenes zone and disturb the relations between public and private, white and non-white, straight and non-straight, and/or citizen and foreigner—along with providing settings for other, inventive kinds of social bond through which people imagine and practice world-making
> (Keynote Address given at the Emotional Geographies Conference, The University of Edinburgh, 10–12 June 2015).

This perspective is reflected across the range of her work including: *Cruel Optimism* (2011), *The Female Complaint: The Unfinished Business of Sentimentality in American Culture* (2009), *Desire/Love* (2013), *Our Monica, Ourselves: Clinton and the Affairs of State* (2001), *Intimacy* (2000), *The Queen of America Goes to Washington City: Essays on Sex and Citizenship* (1997) among others. In this final chapter of the book I consider the contribution of Berlant to debates in the area of emotions, intimacy and affect.

Critique of Sentimental Ideology: Gender and Race Narratives

Berlant's (1988) critique of Alice Walker's *The Colour Purple*, focuses on race, gender and nation in the novel and maintains that the book attempts to represent a national culture that operates according to "'womanist' values rather than patriarchal forms" (1988: 833). Berlant argues that Alice Walker's intent was to overturn the patriarchal concerns of the historical novel. However, Berlant maintains that Walker's novel *Meridian* is in fact her most explicitly and narrowly "political novel" and for Berlant shows the intersection of the private and the public very clearly and draws out a major theme which she develops throughout her work: "It exposes the gap between the official claims of American democracy and the state's exploitative and repressive practices, and views 'personal' relationships as symptoms of the strained political situation" (1988: 835).

Berlant follows this a few years later with a broader analysis of the relationship between gender and the public sphere through a critique of sentimental ideology as captured in the writings of "Fanny Fern" published in *Ruth Hall* (1853/1886) and in an anonymously edited collection of her work *The Life and Beauties of Fanny Fern* (1855) which is a collection of Fern's newspaper columns. Fern was, as Berlant shows, the first American woman to have her own newspaper column and both her essays and books received a great deal of publicity in advance of their publication. Berlant (1991) shows how Fern's work provides a series of insightful commentaries on two areas which contemporary feminists have also focused on, which show how: "Fern's deployment of race and gender stereotypes not only refers to the oft-used women's rights analogy between white heterosexual women and enslaved African Americans, but also to the current problem of women's professional emergence into capitalist culture" (Berlant 1991: 430).

Fern's work highlights in particular what Berlant calls "oppressive practices" directed at women operating in the public sphere which emanate she argues: "in particular from the profession of 'letters': Fern represents newspaper and periodical journalism, as well as book publishing and sales, as another site of gender discipline, where her legitimacy as a journalist always is in question by male culture experts for its non-normativity as feminine labor and also for its vulgar feminine content" (Berlant 1991: 430–431).

Berlant shows how Fern's work was important in providing a bulwark against ideological "sentimentality" which characterised narratives around women's lives across a number of cultures. As Berlant (1991: 431) shows: "In mid-nineteenth-century America, the popular discourse of feminized 'sentimentality' translated the materials of official history and domestic life into the abstract, relatively autonomous realm of 'women's interests', a realm governed by certain immutable 'laws.'"

Drawing on Fern's work, Berlant shows how the onset of capitalism and industrialisation created significant gender distinctions by separating the public and the domestic. As Berlant shows, Fern: "sensed, in a more self-reflexive way than did her sentimental peers, that the meaning, the pacing, and the spaces of everyday domestic life were themselves the effect of a new capitalist ethos of personal instrumentalization, where the woman bore the burden of seeing that there would be no affective, no intellectual, no moral, and of course no economic waste" (Berlant 1991: 431). Within the established sentimental culture so pervasive at the time, Fern's work establishes a wide range of positions, contesting popular discourses on women.

Berlant shows that while "sentimental culture" clearly attracted a broad based audience of women which provided a comfort zone for domestic women, providing reinforcement for their emotional, intellectual and economic practices, many women writers provided a more contested set of discourses within this "sentimental ideology". As Berlant (1991: 434) notes: " . . . many popular women writers, among them Fern, Harriet Beecher Stowe, and Louisa May Alcott developed a counterstrain, which aimed critically to distinguish 'women' in their particularity from 'woman' in her generic purity." As Berlant notes "sentimental activists" established a separate agenda for social change. Fern's work explicitly addresses the contestation operating within these different narratives as shown by Berlant (1991: 436):

> Women's sentimental culture, and the industry of productions addressed specifically to the "subject" of femininity, generated an enormous amount of material dedicated to explicating the relation between what Fern calls "the female woman" as she appeared to be and "woman" as she appeared in her dignified, abstracted dreams of herself. (*Life and Beauties* 80)

Fern satirises women who she regards as "coquettes, wives who adhere to marriage manuals, and rigidly bluestockinged feminists" and Berlant (1991: 439) argues that it is through "this parody of patriarchal practices, the culture of sentimental desire is revealed as an archive of subjugation and distortion." Fern's views are captured in the novella *Fanny Ford* where she paints a picture of women trapped in hopeless marriages. Berlant points out that: "So vulnerable are all women to uninvited male mental and physical abuse that Fern links herself and her 'common' sisters with prostitutes who are simply exaggerated embodiment of the 'woman' who has silently submitted to the sexual economy of patriarchal culture (Ruth Hall 308–309)" (cited in Berlant 1991: 439).

In addition to Fern's attack on patriarchy and its impact on women, is her emphasis on national identity. Her views on national identity and citizenship rights provide a critique of liberal culture and she is critical of British and French society which she argues reflects the gap between women's rights and citizenship or national personhood. Berlant maintains that in "[h]er columns 'Independence' (from *Ruth Hall*) and 'A Little Bunker Hill'(from *Fern Leaves*), for example, that American rights refer only to 'masculine rights', for women cannot be considered 'free' in America, either in the political or the urban public sphere" (Berlant 1991: 442). Fern's view of the relationship between women's rights and the public sphere is captured in the following quotation:

> "FOURTH OF JULY." Well—I don't feel patriotic . . . I'm glad we are all free; but as a woman—I shouldn't know it, didn't some orator tell me. Can I go out of an evening without a hat at my side? Can I go out with one on my head without danger of a station—house? Can I clap my hands at some public speaker when I am nearly bursting with delight? Can I signify the contrary when my hair stands on end with vexation? Can I stand up in the cars "like a gentleman" without being immediately invited "to sit down"? Can I get into an omnibus without having my sixpence taken from my hand and given to the driver? Can I cross Broadway without having a policeman tackled to my helpless elbow? Can I go to see anything *pleasant*, like an execution or a dissection? . . . Can I be a Senator, that I may hurry up that millennial International Copyright law? Can I *even* be President? Bah-you know I can't. "*Free!*" Humph!
>
> (*Ruth Hall* 314–315).

In this context Berlant points out Fern's conception of citizenship is not just an abstract concept but is directly related to the law and the public sphere. Fern focuses on laws that limit women's rights as wives and mothers within marriage and in the labour force. In a surprisingly contemporary analysis she shows the absurdity of the way in which society regulates juridically what women wear and what they say.

It is in this area of American citizenship that "Fern finds her strongest link to the rhetoric of nineteenth century feminism, which derived its first documentary model in the Declaration of Independence" (Berlant 1991: 443). Berlant shows how: "the challenges of American, constitutional, juridicial and ideological gender mystification brought by women's rights activists became, by the 1860s, increasingly central to Fern's thought about what it would take for women to gain dignity in modern America" (Berlant 1991: 443).

Fern's work on the intrusion of the private into the public and: "Fern's intervention into the spaces of the home, the nation and language is more radical than that of many sentimental domestics because she has seen the power of women's culture to deform the women it addresses by enforcing the distance between domestic ideology and everyday experience" (Berlant 1991: 444).

As a backdrop to Fern's writings, her own personal circumstances in relation to the role of her brother add an additional dimension. Fern's brother N.P. Willis, was as Berlant notes, a central figure in "the sentimentalization of national culture" and was also one of first publishers and editors of a national newspaper the *Home Journal* which highlighted conservative male and female ideologies. Her brother refused to publish Fern's writings while she and her children starved in city tenements. Willis regarded Fern's writings as too vulgar for his or for other journals and he said that she lacked talent. In addition Berlant outlines how Willis did not protect Harriet Jacobs (alias Linda Brent) who authored *Incidents in the Life of a Slave Girl* (1861) and he did not support her attempts at freedom. At the same time as Willis was refusing to publish Fern's work, he was also employing Harriet Jacobs, who was a fugitive slave. Despite the efforts of his wife to protect Jacobs, from her Southern owners, Willis made no attempt to support her.

National Identity and Affective Experience

Berlant's (1993) "The Queen of America Goes to Washington City: Harriett Jacobs, Francis Harper, Anita Hill" focuses on three women writers who have all represented in their writings their failure to secure control over their bodies and who challenge America's judicial system. The three writers represent historical and contemporary cases. In this range of case studies Berlant draws attention to the intersection of personal and national life *vis-à-vis* sexuality. She shows how all three women have made: "the nation listen to them, to transform the horizons and terms of authority that mark both personal and national life in America by speaking about sexuality as the fundamental and fundamentally repressed horizon of national identity, legitimacy and affective experience" (Berlant 1993: 552).

She maintains that these cases: "link experiences of violated sexual privacy to the doctrine of abstract national 'personhood', making America accountable for the private sexual transgressions of its privileged men and radically transforming the history of the 'public' and the 'private' in America" (Berlant 1993: 553).

Berlant selects texts by Jacobs, Harper and Hill to provide what she calls a "sensorium of citizenship" (Berlant 1993: 553). They are Harriet Jacob's (Brent) slave narrative *Incidents in the Life of a Slave Girl*, Frances Harper's novel *Iola Leroy*, and Anita Hill's testimony in the Clarence Thomas case. As Berlant (1993: 553) notes: "Even if sexual relations directly forced on these women mark individuals as corrupted by power, the women's narratives refuse to affirm the private horizon of personal entitlement as the cause of their suffering. America becomes explicitly, in this context, accountable for the sexual exploitation it authorizes in the guise of the white male citizen's domestic and erotic privilege."

In Jacob's *Incidents in the Life of a Slave Girl*, Berlant describes her experience as "hybrid" combining intimacy and alienation which Berlant argues is typical of the experience of African American women's of "national sexuality under slavery". There is a wide-ranging literature on the area including: Hazel Carby's (1987) *Reconstructing Womanhood* and Jane Gaines (1988) "White privilege and looking relations: Race and gender in feminist film theory" among others.

Frances Harper's *Iola Leroy* was written around the same time as emancipation in 1892. Harper spoke at suffrage conferences as well as at the National Congress of Negro Women, . . . she argued that: "more than changing institutions we need the development of a national conscience, and the upbuilding of national character" (Berlant 1993: 561). Berlant shows that Jacobs's "solution to the enigma of social life under racism and misogyny—to privatize social relations—was not the only solution to this violent touching of hands." In *Iola Leroy*, Harper takes the concept of citizenship and refocuses it "imagining a liberal public sphere located within the black community" (Berlant 1993: 561).

In the text Jacobs presents a "monarchical fantasy politics" and uses the figure of "the Queen" to "represent the 'state of civilization in the late nineteenth century of the United States'" (Berlant 1993: 566). Jacobs shows this in the following way:

> One woman begged me to get a newspaper and read it over. She said her husband told her that the black people had sent word to the queen of Merica that they were all slaves; that she didn't believe it, and went to Washington city to see the President about it. They quarrelled; she drew her sword upon him, and swore that he should help her to make them all free.
>
> That poor ignorant woman thought that America was governed by a Queen to whom the President was subordinate. I wish the President was subordinate to Queen Justice (45).
>
> (cited in Berlant 1993: 567)

As Berlant shows, Harper thus "interferes with the fantasy norms of democratic abstraction" (Berlant 1993: 567) and offers an alternative American history.

Her final example is the Anita Hill/Clarence Thomas hearings. As Berlant (1993: 552) indicates:

> Anita Hill is the most recent in a tradition of American women who have sought to make the nation listen to them, to transform the horizons and the terms of authority that mark both personal and national life in America by speaking about sexuality as the fundamental and fundamentally repressed horizon of national identity, legitimacy and affective experience.

Berlant understands that the Anita Hill case is not one that can be framed as contesting "the sexual economy of white erotics" but as one of abuse in the workplace. As she notes in this case "two histories of corporeal identity converge" (Berlant 1993: 552). She also notes that the hearings raise the issue of what constitutes "'consent' in the public sphere". As Berlant (1993: 568) comments:

> It was alluded to in the corporeality of Thomas himself: in his alleged exploitation of personal collegiality in federal workspaces; in the racist fantasies that he evoked to account for his victimization by Hill and on the Hill; in the aura of the minority stereotype black authority represents as a "token" on the Supreme Court.

Berlant draws parallels between the personal and the public by comparing the national body politic with Hill's "minoritized body".

> The national body is signified by Hill's own body as well, which displayed all of the decorums of bourgeois national polity while transgressing the veil between official and private behaviour that grounds the erotic power of the state. Finally, the body of the nation was configured in the images of senators sitting in judgment and in the experts they brought in to testify to the law and issues of "character" and "appearance".
> (Berlant 1993: 568)

In conclusion, Berlant sees the three examples, Hill, Harper and Jacobs as providing examples of how the public and the private intersect in the sphere of intimacy, the erotic and political dominance. As Berlant (1993: 554) comments:

> ... it would link experiences of violated sexual privacy to the doctrine of abstract national "personhood", making America accountable for the private sexual transgressions of its privileged men and radically transforming the history of the "public" and the "private" in America; it would show how vital the existence of official sexual underclasses have been to producing national symbolic and political coherence; finally, and more happily, it would provide an archive of tactics that have made it possible to reoccupy both the sexual body and America by turning the constraints of privacy into information about national identity.

Berlant (1998) returns to the intersection of intimacy and the public sphere in "Intimacy: A Special Issue" of *Critical Inquiry*. This collection of essays explores the relationship between the intimate and the public. Berlant (2000: 1) argues that "the inwardness of the intimate is met by a corresponding publicness . . .". As she argues the essays in the collection address: "the contradictory desires" that "mark the intimacy of daily life" (2000: 5) (see also Berlant and Warner 2000). Gorton (2007: 336) maintains that "Berlant's work . . . has been addressed . . . by theorists who find her explication of the way in which the intimate meets the public useful in articulating the relationship between emotion and the public sphere." In the Introduction to this collection, Berlant looks at the relationship of intimacy to the public sphere as viewed by Habermas and calls for a rethinking of intimacy beyond the role of the state. She also focuses on therapy and the intersection of intimacy and therapy particularly in the U.S.

Since the early twentieth century, Berlant maintains there has been a proliferation of forms of therapy: "At present, in the U.S., therapy saturates the scene of intimacy, from psychoanalysis and twelve-step groups to girl talk, talk shows, and other witnessing genres" (Berlant 1998: 282). This has parallels with the discussion of therapy in Giddens (1992) but Berlant adds in a further dimension by including in her analysis sexual harassment as an aspect of the "sexualization of institutional spaces" and highlights the complexity of the public and private contextualisation of intimacy. As she comments: " . . . we see how hard it is to adjudicate the norms of a public world when it is also an intimate one, especially where the mixed—up instrumental and affective relations of collegiality are concerned" (Berlant 1998: 282).

Berlant (1998: 281) argues correctly that intimacy and desire have become inextricably linked to therapy. "These relations between desire and therapy, which have become internal to the modern mass-mediated sense of intimacy, tells us something else about it: intimacy builds worlds; it creates spaces and usurps places meant for other kinds of relation." She raises the issue of how intimacy implicitly presents issues of scale: " . . . that links the instability of individual lives to the trajectories of the collective" (Berlant 1998).

In raising this issue she draws on the work of Jurgen Habermas (1989). Berlant maintains there is: " . . . a history to the advent of intimacy as a public mode of identification and self-development . . . Jurgen Habermas has argued that the bourgeois idea of a public sphere relied on the emergence of a mode of critical public discourse that formulated and represented a public's interests within civil society against the state" (Berlant 1998: 283).

Habermas talks about the notion of a democratic public sphere which: "made collective intimacy a public and social ideal . . . " (Berlant 1998: 283), he recognises that the development of critical publicness is linked to the expansion of "institutions like the salon and the café, circulating print media and industrial capitalism" (Berlant 1998: 283). He also notes: " . . . that liberal society was founded on the migration of intimacy, expectations between the public and the domestic" (Berlant 1998: 284).

However Berlant (1998: 284) counters the Habermasian perspective in arguing that: "the expansion of minority publics that resist or are denied universalist collective intimacy expectations, has much complicated the possibility of . . . a general mass-critical public sphere deemed to be culturally and politically intimate with itself." As she goes on to note: "intimacy refers to more than that which takes place within the purview of institutions, the state and an ideal of publicness" (Berlant 1998: 284). In doing so she draws on Foucault (1997) arguing that Foucault's work in recognising the multiplicity of relations engendered at every moment by sexuality, has been an important dimension in thinking through this position.

Berlant therefore calls for a "rethinking of intimacy" and to look at a "transformative analysis" of intimacy in different directions through history and biography. She argues that when institutional (normative) perspectives are threatened through minority perspectives and subordinated groups, there will be a sense of anxiety. The unease and anxiety leads to a lack of stability within nations and populations, leading to a variety of emotions including hate, bitterness and satire. She shows how: "public institutions use issues of intimate life to normalize particular forms of knowledge and practice and to create compliant subjects" and "how discourses of sexual suffering and trauma have so magnetized crises in a whole set of related fields that stories of the intimate have become inseparable from, for example, stories about citizenship, capitalism . . . political violence, and the writing of history" (Berlant 1998: 288). Thus Berlant sets out how public institutions use intimate life to normalise forms of knowledge and practice.

Berlant (2008a) extends the issue of what she calls "my national sentimentality project" in *The Female Complaint*. This book is part of a trilogy focusing on intimacy and the public sphere, which is flanked on one side by *The Anatomy of National Fantasy*, and on the other by *The Queen of America Goes to Washington*. Berlant (2008a: x) maintains that the three books chart the relationship between intimacy and the public sphere and in particular the U.S. political sphere as an affective space.

Berlant maintains that: "if from a theoretical standpoint an intimate public is a sphere of mediation in which the personal is refracted through the general, what's salient for its consumers is that it is a place of recognition and reflection. In an intimate public sphere emotional contact, of a sort is made" (Berlant 2008a: viii).

In the first of the books in the series, *The Anatomy of National Fantasy*, Berlant focuses on "the development of official and intimate publics in the early U.S. period." She shows how the last chapter of *Anatomy* opens up into *The Female Complaint* which highlights "how Hawthorne's concept of a public was shaped by the sentimental focus on feminine suffering and conventions of reparative compassion" (Berlant 2008a: xii).

The Female Complaint tells a story about the emergence and conventions of the first mass cultural intimate public in the United States. Berlant (2008a: xii) maintains that "starting in the 1830s an intimate public sphere of femininity constituted the first sub-cultural mass-mediated market population of relatively politically disenfranchised people in the United States . . .". As she notes: "This 'women's culture' is distinguished by a view that the people marked by femininity already have something in common and are in need of a conversation that feels intimate, revelatory, and a relief even when it is mediated by commodities . . ." (Berlant 2008a: viii–ix). In *The Female Complaint*, Berlant focuses on the ways in which " 'non-privileged subjects' circulate through intimate publics" to cultivate what is defined as "insider recognition", which act to provide an "experience of social belonging" and which make "the nation itself a site of affective investment and emotional identification" (Berlant 2008a: x–xi).

Berlant does not only address the historical dimensions of so called "women's culture" but also addresses the commodification of intimacy in contemporary culture, as she notes:

> Commodified genres of intimacy, such as Oprahesque chat shows and "chicklit", circulate among strangers, enabling insider self-help talk such as "girltalk" to flourish in an intimate public. These genres claim to reflect a kernel of common experience and provide frames for encountering the impacts of living as a woman in the world.
>
> (Berlant 2008a: x)

The third publication in the series *The Queen of America*, continues this genealogy of public intimacy, and tracks "the development of a dominant public sphere organized around suffering and other intimate topics in the U.S." (Berlant 2008a: xii).

In his article "The Public, the Private and the Intimate: Richard Sennett and Lauren Berlant's Cultural Criticism in Dialogue" Gabriele Link (2011) draws comparisons between Sennett and Berlant's work along a range of issues. Linke maintains that Sennett and Berlant have both been absorbed by the production of citizenship and the shifts in social attachment since the nineteenth century. They both approach the cultural transformations involved in these processes at different points in time and from different perspectives, Sennett from a sociological analysis, based on class, while Berlant focuses on popular culture and literature. In making a comparison between Sennett and Berlant, Linke discusses Sennett's *The Fall of the Public Man* (1977) and Berlant's *Intimacy* (1998) and *The Female Complaint* (2008a).

Linke draws on Sennett's analysis of the decline of the public sphere as he searches for the economic and cultural forces that led to the change. He traces changes in the public sphere in London and Paris from the beginning of the eighteenth century through the nineteenth and into the twentieth century. Sennett follows Jurgen Habermas's argument about the formation of the "bourgeois public" and its subsequent decline since the nineteenth century.

Sennett argues that it was the balance between private and public geography, in the second half of the eighteenth century at the height of the Enlightenment, which allowed public interchange and which led to the expression of feeling. As Linke (2011: 13) comments: "With the turn of the nineteenth century, Sennett finds society and public life in turmoil, arguing that 'the nineteenth century traumas of public life prepared for the twentieth century denial of the public itself'([Sennett 1977] 127)." Sennett is critical of aspects of intimacy which focus on selfhood. As Linke comments: "He sees in the 'tyrannies of intimacy' a 'transposing' of structures of dominance in society into psychological terms ([Sennett 1977]: 337, 338)" (Linke 2011: 13).

Berlant also endorses Habermas's description of the conditions which lead to the production of intimacy, particularly industrial capitalism but she does not follow Sennett's critique of the value of the media and print media. Like

Sennett, Berlant goes back to the nineteenth century for her reference points but rather than embarking on a sociological analysis of European society, Berlant draws on texts, published in the United States, which contain slave narratives (examples *Fanny Fern* and *The Queen of America*). It is in these narratives that Berlant shows how a minority subject can circulate in a majority public sphere. Berlant frames the debate in terms of nineteenth century discourses on citizenship.

Sennett is more consistently critical of what he defines as "the tyranny of intimacy" and the focus on the personal rather than the social. He argues that the focus on the self leads to self-absorption and people are preoccupied with their own life stories and their own emotions. Sennett makes the point that the self-absorption which characterise people's emotions has led to a decline of the public life. He argues that: " 'confusion has arisen between public and intimate life'([Sennett 1977]: 5)" (Linke 2011: 14).

Sennett's work anticipated that of Lynn Jamieson's (1998) critique of Giddens' conceptualisation of intimacy in *Intimacy: Personal Relationships in Society* which focuses on intimacy experienced in primary relationships by family members, friends and couples. As Linke (2011: 14) comments Jamieson "embeds changing notions of intimacy in the economic and social structures of (industrial) capitalism ([Jamieson 1998]: 17–34)." She draws a distinction between "public stories about personal life and the life that is lived" (Linke 2011: 10). Linke comments: "Furthermore she addresses the question of gender inequality arguing that disclosing intimacy has not necessarily resulted in greater equality ([Jamieson 1998]: 165–168)" (Linke 2011: 10).

Linke argues that Jamieson's "interpretation of the situation is concurrent with Sennett's (and Berlant's) in that 'disclosing intimacy' cannot resolve the 'pervasive social divisions' of late capitalism ([Jamieson 1998]: 175) but makes social ties more fragile rather than strengthening them" (Linke 2011: 14). He maintains that holding these positions: "she appears to be part of a wider social discourse on intimacy that took shape in the late 1990s in sociology as well as literary criticism questioning traditional dichotomies and attempting to redefine and revalue intimacy and its relation to the public" (Linke 2011: 14).

Linke (2011: 15) points out that whereas there are parallels between Sennett and Berlant there are also differences:

> Berlant stresses the power of shared knowledge and experience. Sennett's understanding of public geography favours face-to-face interaction, but Berlant takes a more general approach that acknowledges the importance of the media, and historically, especially its print media.

Sennett "detects a potentially oppressive character in two kinds of intimacy: in familial and governmental surveillance" (1997: 337). He distinguishes between intimacy based on market exchange and genuine intimacy. "Berlant bridges the rift between intimate and public through the concept of an 'intimate public'" she sees these "intimate publics as part of the mechanisms of capitalism" (Linke 2011: 16). However as Linke also notes: "Unlike Sennett, she does not envision a kind of positive intimacy detached from the capitalist exchange of commodities, but accepts that intimate publics are a by-product of capitalist consumer culture" (Linke 2011: 16).

Linke maintains that the connection between gender, sexual culture, and intimacy is one point in question. Linke argues that Sennett conducts his social analysis from a masculine perspective on public life, he presupposes a private-public dichotomy of a gendered nature and uses gender differentiated pictures of the nineteenth century public: "suggesting that for nineteenth century men the public was positively connoted as a region of freedom and escape from the pressures of idealized private life, while for women, it was associated with disgrace ([Sennett 1977]: 23)" (Linke 2011: 17).

Linke shows that by contrast: "Berlant questions the assumptions of clear boundaries between private and public and she criticises the public sphere as not free" (Linke 2011: 18). In Berlant's article "The Queen of America", . . . Link argues, Berlant "reads women's public testimonies of sexual abuse as politically functional and not at all destructive of the public sphere" (Linke 2011: 18). In addition Berlant: "locates gender and sex at the center of the shifting configurations of the intimate and the public, especially as she demonstrates and critiques how images of heterosexual normativity and privileged institutions of intimacy are circulated and renegotiated in American women's culture" (Linke 2011: 18).

In assessing her contribution overall, Linke maintains that: "[although] her concept of intimate publics retains some ambiguity, Berlant offers, along with other feminist theoreticians of the public-private relationship, a challenge to include diverse life narratives that may inspire serious thought on social structures, a challenge particularly relevant to powerful mediators in publishing, museums, broadcasting, and new media" (Linke 2011: 22). Linke's comparative analysis of Sennett and Berlant provides a useful and insightful summary of some crucial issues in the significance of the public sphere for both writers.

Further analysis of Berlant's unique critique of contemporary society is offered by de Villiers (2012), who focuses his analysis on Berlant's (2011) *Cruel Optimisim*. He argues that in *Cruel Optimism*, Berlant analyses the way in which people stay attached to a number of fantasies including the quest for "the good life", the search for "upward mobility, job security, political and social equality, durable intimacy . . ." (de Villiers 2012: 195). In other words, de Villiers shows how Americans generally believe in their ability to attain the American Dream.

Drawing on the Pew Research Center's Report (2011) on U.S. lifestyles, de Villiers notes that: "only 36 per cent of Americans polled said that they thought their economic fortunes were determined by forces beyond their control" compared to "70 per cent of Germans who believe their financial fates are beyond their personal control" (de Villiers 2012: 195). Berlant also distances herself from the trauma theory which as de Villiers notes has provided that main way "of periodizing any crisis–shaped historical present (Berlant 2011: 54)" (de Villiers 2012: 196).

One example drawn on by Berlant is the obesity epidemic which she sees rather as "endemic", which is a biopolitical concept that Berlant borrows from Foucault. However, de Villiers points out that each time Berlant gave a talk on this topic, the audience responded in arguing that: "obesity and overweight are forms of resistance to the hegemony of the productive/bourgeois body as well as to white class-aspirational beauty culture" (de Villiers 2012: 197).

Conclusion

Feminist theorists share with social theorists more broadly a focus on ideologicisation of intimacy in the course of the development of the twentieth and twenty-first centuries. What these theorists share is a focus on shifting values away from traditional conceptions of the bourgeois family. These theorists confirm patterns of detraditionalisation in late modernity and also confirm the central theme of this book which is that there is a fundamental incompatibility between intimacy and traditional normative, heterosexual structures of marriage and the family.

Bibliography

Berlant, Lauren. 1988. "Race, Gender and Nation in 'The Color Purple'" *Critical Inquiry* 14(4): 831–859.
Berlant, Lauren. 1991. "The Female Woman: Fanny Fern and the Form of Sentiment" *American Literary History* 3(3): 429–454.
Berlant, Lauren. 1993. "The Queen of America Goes to Washington City: Harriet Jacobs, Frances Harper, Anita Hill" *American Literature* 65(3): 549–574.
Berlant, Lauren. 1997. *The Queen of America Goes to Washington City: Essays on Sex and Citizenship*. Durham, NC: Duke University Press.
Berlant, Lauren. 1998. "Intimacy: A Special Issue" *Critical Inquiry* 24(2): 281–288.
Berlant, Lauren (ed.). 2000. *Intimacy*. Chicago: University of Chicago Press.
Berlant, Lauren. 2001. *Our Monica, Ourselves: Clinton and the Affairs of State*. New York: New York University Press.
Berlant, Lauren. 2008a. *The Female Complaint*. Durham, NC and London: Duke University Press.
Berlant, Lauren. 2008b. "Cruel Optimism: On Marx, Loss and the Senses" *New Formations* 63(1): 33–51.
Berlant, Lauren. 2010. "Cruel Optimism." In Melisssa Gregg and Greg Seigworth (eds), *The Affect Theory Reader*. Durham, NC: Duke University Press, 93–117.
Berlant, Lauren. 2011. *Cruel Optimism*. Durham, NC: Duke University Press.
Berlant, Lauren. 2013. *Love/Desire*. Brooklyn, NY: Punctum Books.
Berlant, Lauren and Mark Warner. 2000. "Sex in Public." In Lauren Berlant (ed.), *Intimacy*. Chicago: University of Chicago Press, 311–330.
Brent, Linda. (Harriet Jacobs). 1861/1987. *Incidents in the Life of a Slave Girl: Written By Herself*. Ed. Jean Fagan Yellin. Cambridge: Harvard University Press.

Carby, Hazel V. 1987. *Reconstructing Womanhood: The Experience of the Afro-American Woman Novelist*. New York: Oxford University Press.

De Villiers, Nicholas. 2012. "'Love in a Hopeless Place' Review of *Cruel Optimism*" *Cultural Critique* 82: 195–202.

Fern, Fanny. 1853/1886. *Ruth Hall and Other Writings* Ed. Joyce W. Warren. New Bruswick: Rutgers University Press.

Fern, Fanny. 1857. *Fresh Leaves*. New York: Mason Brothers.

Foucault, M. 1997. "Friendship as a Way of Life" and "Sex, Power and Politics of Identity." In Paul.Rabinow (ed.), *Ethics, Subjectivity and Truth*. New York: New Press, 163–173.

Gaines, Jane. 1988. "White Privilege and Looking Relations: Race and Gender in Feminist Film Theory" *Screen* 8: 12–27.

Giddens, Anthony. 1992. *The Transformation of Intimacy: Sexuality, Love and Eroticism in Modern Society*. Stanford, CA: Stanford University Press.

Gorton, Kirstyn. 2007. "Theorizing Emotion and Affect" *Feminist Theory* 8(3): 333–348.

Habermas, Jurgen. 1989. *The Structural Transformation of the Public Sphere: An Inquiry into a Category of Bourgeois Society* Trans. Thomas Burger and Frederick Lawrence. Cambridge, MA: Cambridge University Press.

Harper, Francis. 1892/1969. *Iola Leroy* or *Shadows Uplifted*. College Park, MD: McGrath.

Jamieson, Lynn. 1998. *Intimacy, Personal Relationships in Modern Societies*. London: Blackwell.

Linke, Gabrielle. 2011. "The Public, the Private, and the Intimate: Richard Sennett and Lauren Berlant's Cultural Criticism in Dialogue" *Biography* 34(1): 11–24.

Pew Research Center. 2011. Global Attitudes Project, "American Exceptionalism Subsides: The American—Western European Values Gap" 17 November 2011, http://www.pewglobal.org/files/2011/11/Pew-Global-Attitudes-Values-Report-Final-November-17–2011-pdf (accessed 29/07/15)

Seigworth, Greg. 2012. "Reading Lauren Berlant Writing" *Communications and Critical Cultural Studies* 9(4): 346–352.

Sennett, Richard. 1977. *The Fall of the Public Man*. New York: Norton.

Conclusion

In drawing together the theoretical and conceptual debates which have illuminated the chapters of this book, it is clear there is some disagreement around the role of intimacy, love, emotions and desire across different emotional regimes from medieval society to late modernity. A significant contribution to the debate has been the work of Michel Foucault (1978) and in particular his book: *The History of Sexuality, Volume 1: An Introduction*. I have analysed the importance of poststructuralism and discourse in Foucault's work in an earlier book, (Brooks 1997, see also Chapter 2). As Foucault (1972: 55) put it:

> Discourse is not the majestically unfolding manifestation of a thinking, knowing, speaking subject, but, on the contrary, a totality, in which the dispersion of the subject and his discontinuity with himself may be determined.
>
> (cited in Shumway 2003: 4)

Poststructuralism is an important way we can understand that there is no universal application of the concept of love, intimacy and desire. As Shumway (2003: 11) comments:

> "Romantic love" in this sense is best understood as a culturally specific discourse. The point is not that humans elsewhere lack the capacity to experience what we typically call romance or that they never do so. Rather it is that place that passionate love is given in Western culture and the specific form it has taken there are not universal.

In this regard as I explored in Chapter 3, the question of courtly love and whether it existed outside the extensive mythology and literature surrounding it, remains something of a mystery. As Boone (1987: 34) comments: "The extent to which *amour courtois* [courtly love] existed as a real phenomenon beyond literary conventions remain open to speculation."

The relationship between love, intimacy and marriage is also contentious as has been shown through the work of a number of theorists, and even in romance narratives the issues are fairly clear, that love and intimacy have historically existed outside marriage. Shumway (2003: 15) shows that even in traditional romantic tropes the underlying tensions are around marriage:

> ... in most other European romances, the obstacles standing between Tristan and Isolde result from the fact that she is married to someone else. Tristan ... is not a story of love that can never be consummated; it is a tale of an adulterous affair. What is impossible for Tristan and Isolde is not love but marriage.

Intimacy and Individualisation

To what extent romantic love was directly linked to the rise of capitalism and the growth of inidvidualization, as claimed by Giddens (1992) and followed by Shumway is again contentious historically. Shumway argues that it became the dominant discourse among the bourgeoisie along with the "dawning of individualization". However, Shumway does recognise that this was not a relationship that was at ease with itself. As Shumway (2003: 21) notes: "in the nineteenth century, romance became grafted onto marriage but it was never entirely at ease with the union. This combination produced a tension with the discourse because its essential characteristics derive from adulterous love." Despite the optimism of Giddens that democratic relationships can be found within marriage, Shumway and others show that in fact the late nineteenth and early twentieth centuries show the catastrophic breakdown of marriage and the rise of divorce (see Chapter 1).

It has been argued that love and intimacy can be conceptually distinguished and again following Giddens, Shumway (2003: 133) argues that intimacy has replaced love as the major relationship discourse. It is of course this paradigm which Giddens (1992) maintains is captured in his concept of "the transformation of intimacy." Giddens (1992: 58) sees this shift in the nature of relationships in what he calls the "pure relationship":

> The term "relationship" meaning a close and continuing emotional tie to another, has only come into general usage relatively recently. To be clear what is at stake here, we can introduce the term *pure relationship* to refer to this phenomenon ... It refers to a situation where a social relation is entered into for its own sake, for what can be derived by each person from a sustained association with another; and which is contained only in so far as it is thought by both parties to deliver enough satisfactions for each individual to stay within it. Love used to be tied to sexuality for most of the sexually "normal" population, through marriage; but now the two are connected more and more via the pure relationship. Marriage—for many, but by no means all groups in the population—has veered increasingly towards the form of a pure relationship, with many ensuing consequences.

Gross and Simmons (2002: 552N1) maintain that in making his case Giddens draws on a wide range of historical sources as well as other theorists including Cancian (1987), Illouz (1997), Seidman (1991) and Stone (1982) among others. They note that:

> Many of the arguments Giddens advances are in agreement with the work of these scholars, but others—especially his claims about the causes of the shift from romantic to pure love—are very much at odds with them.

Gross and Simmons (2002: 536) also draw out what they regard as the key distinctions between romantic love and the "pure relationship" in Giddens (1992):

> Whereas romantic love relationships revolved around idealized visions of manly strength and womanly virtue, the pure relationship is an effort to achieve, through constant communication, an intimate knowledge of the other's unique and authentic self. Whereas romantic love entailed a lifelong commitment, a defining feature of pure love is that intimacy is sought as a means of self-development, so that a condition for entry into such relationships is the implicit agreement that if the values, interests and identities of the partners begin to diverge in non-complementary ways, the relationship loses its reason for being and becomes subject to dissolution . . . Finally, whereas romantic love relationships were normatively heterosexual, "confluent love, while not necessarily androgynous . . . presumes a model of the pure relationship in which . . . a person's sexuality is [but] one factor that has to be negotiated as part of a relationship".
> (Giddens 1992: 63)

Giddens' work has been the subject of considerable critique from sociologists such as Jamieson (1998) and even Shumway states that Giddens "overstates his case", as marriage is of course a product of normative expectations and patterns, and characterised by patterns of gender inequality as well as economic inequalities. Marriage also acts to contain relationships of domestic violence directed at both women and children. Giddens is also really unable to distinguish the impact of changes emerging from intimacy discourses and those independently emerging from feminist interventions. I develop these points in Chapters 5, 6 and 7.

Sex, Power and Colonial Cultures

Laura Ann Stoler has transformed the analysis of colonial cultures by focusing on intimacy and sex in such cultures and she sees sex as foundational to the colonial project. There are two main elements to the kind of transformation Stoler has made to thinking and writing in this area. Firstly she has challenged the dominance of this field by male social and cultural theorists and the kind of emphasis they give to this area. Secondly, she has drawn on the analysis of power put forward by Michel Foucault to understand both micro and macro dimensions of power.

There has been a tradition of critiques of power and exploitation based on gender and ethnicity in colonial cultures by male cultural theorists (Bhabha 1990; Fanon 1959, 1965, 1986; Said 1979). While Said focused on the nature of "orientalism" he defined sexual exploitation in terms of what Hyam (1986) calls "the export of male sexual energy". Said defines "Orientalism" in terms of a "male power fantasy," as shown by McClintock (1995: 14): "For Said, Orientalism takes peverse shape as a 'male power fantasy' that sexualizes a feminized Orient for Western power and possession." However as McClintock (1995: 14) notes with regret:

> But seeing sexuality only as a metaphor runs the risk of eliding *gender* as a constitutive dynamic of imperial and anti-imperial power. I make this point not to diminish the enormous importance and influence of Said's work on male imperial relations but rather to regret that he does not systematically explore the dynamics of gender as a critical aspect of the imperial project.

Stoler's intervention provides a systematic analysis of gender relations of power based on sex in different colonial cultures. In doing so she draws on Michel Foucault's concept of "biopolitics". As I indicated in Chapter 1, Stoler approaches sex and intimacy in colonial cultures from a different perspective. Stoler sees sexual relations not as "a metaphor for colonial inequities" but as foundational to the way in which Empire developed. In drawing on Foucault's concept of "biopolitics" she is able assess why the "microsites" of intimate spaces intersect with the macropolitics of imperial power. Stoler's work highlights the intersection of gender, class and race in colonial cultures and she documents "the racial politics of colonial rule" in French Indochina and the Dutch East Indies. Stoler is of course not the only feminist analyst to have investigated colonial cultures, looking at the intersection of gender and ethnicity. The work of Levine (2004, 2004a), Wilson (2004) and Bush (1990) also offer important contributions to this debate which I consider in Chapter 4. As Wilson (2004: 20) shows:

> In garrisons, forts, and factories, plantation societies and urban centres, the utilization of enslaved indigenous, subaltern, and "respectable" women's bodies, the regulation of sexuality and lineage, and the demarcation of masculinity's and femininity's roles and privileges constitutes in no small part the substance of imperial power and domination.

However one of the innovative characteristics of Stoler's analysis is her engagement with Foucault's work. As I show in Chapter 4, while Stoler (2002) draws on Foucault's range of conceptual frameworks, in her chapter entitled

"Colonial Reading of Foucault" she is critical of Foucault's absence of race as central in his analysis as she points out:

> In rerouting the history of sexuality through the history of empire, modern racism appears less "anchored" in European technologies of sex than Foucault claimed. Both racial and sexual classifications appear as ordering mechanisms that *shared* their emergence with the bourgeois order of the early nineteenth century.

Stoler does share with Foucault a critique of the distribution and education of desire within the bourgeois family as described by Foucault in that "tiny sexually saturated familial space" (Foucault 1978: 47). Stoler also agrees with Foucault in his rejection of explanations for desire as having a biological foundation or one which emphasises repression. Foucault's model of power facilitates an analysis of the "microsites" of familial and intimate space and how they intersect. Stoler thus locates the micropolitics of imperial rule in the intersection of intimacy and power and her analysis provides an important contribution to the value of "affective politics".

Romance and Consumption

One of the key feminist contributors to the debates around the relationship between capitalism, late modernity and romance is Eva Illouz. Illouz's (1997, 2012, 2014) work is concerned with how intimacy is structured by its relationship to late capitalism, in particular the relationship between romance and consumption. Skeggs (2010: 34) argues that for Illouz (1997): "as capital enters more domains, feelings and emotions become value statements about one's capacity and are crucial to the exploitation and display of the morality of the person on television." Illouz shows how the growth of popular magazines had an impact on women's expectations of men, marriage and of themselves and along with this came different expectations of intimacy and love (see Chapter 5).

These inevitably led to pressures and the turn to psychological discourses and thereby to finding explanations for marital and relational problems As Illouz shows the emphasis was on the search for happiness in partnerships and marriage and a linking of happiness with mental health. Love in other words became a prerequisite of happiness. She also shows how psychological and pseudo-scientific explanations became part of an emotions discourse introduced into an understanding of relationships and marriage. This provided an opening for therapeutic discourses to be introduced which put emotions and relationships centre-stage as the significance of marriage and the family occupied a less central role as a socio-economic infrastructure.

Thus Illouz (1997, 1998) can be seen to offer a very different model of intimacy and relationships in late modernity to Giddens (1992). Whereas Giddens sees intimacy and marriage as interlinked in the "pure relationship," Illouz does not. She does not share Giddens' optimism about the emotional stamina of marriage or of intimacy in marriage in late modernity. She argues that this is particularly the case for women and for conceptions of intimacy. As shown above the problem with Giddens' concept of the "transformation of intimacy" is that it assumes far too close a relationship between intimacy and marriage which as Illouz shows is problematic at a moment when the skills involved in traditional marriage have been rendered obsolete.

Illouz's (2012) work shows the romantic self has changed in late modernity. As I indicated in Chapter 5, Illouz differs from the theorists of "reflexive modernization" by recognising the gender politics inherent in marriage in late modernity, rendering any conceptualization of intimacy as reflected "the pure relationship" within marriage a naïve one and fundamentally problematic for women. Illouz (2012: 9) captures the issue in the following comment on love: "the profoundly split and dual aspects of love—both as a source of existential transcendence and as a deeply contested site for the performance of gender identity—that characterizes contemporary romantic culture."

Perhaps one of the most interesting dimensions of the role of love and intimacy in late modernity as identified by Illouz (2012), is the relationship of love and social mobility and how relationships and partnerships are defined by the intersection of "emotional and economic aspirations" (2012: 10). This is an area completely absent from the work of Giddens (1992) as well as Beck *et al.* (1996).

Feminist and cultural theorists have made significant interventions into theorising emotions and intimacy, which is captured to some extent in the concept of the "turn to affect". The theoretical debates extend beyond the issue of intimacy and love. The breadth of theoretical engagement from feminists regarding emotions and affect is part of what is described as the "emotionalisation of society" and the intensification of interest in emotions and affect as the subject of scholarly research. The shift is part of an emphasis on the emotional and subjective. I consider the contribution of a wide range of feminist theorists of affect and emotion in Chapter 6 which also focuses on the transnational and cross-cultural application of such theorising. This is reflected in much of my own work and with others: Brooks 2006; Brooks and Devasayaham 2011/2013; Brooks and Simpson 2012.

Illouz has also focused on love in contemporary relationships and makes comparisons between modern love and contemporary relationships, she describes the process of change as a process of "disenchantment". She also claims that contemporary relationships are partially emerging from internet technology and what Illouz identifies as "technologies of choice". Illouz maintains that the characteristics of "postmodern love" is a shift in the way people select partners and the way in which individuals identify the kind of partners they want.

The availability of the internet, the influence of psychology and the influence of market philosophy are all important factors within capitalism. Illouz contextualises the impact of technology on relationships by indicating it is an aspect of a rationalisation process which characterises late modernity. Illouz sees these processes as leading to a "commodification of romance". Illouz's analysis has been criticised for failing to present a more complete picture of contemporary love and by failing to address the issue of adultery within contemporary marriage. However, her view of "affairs" as a contemporary relational phenomenon, tends to counteract this point.

Regardless of this, Illouz (1998) does recognise that the narrative of life-long romance within marriage has largely disappeared and that much more emphasis is now placed on "the affair". As Illouz shows this is related to the role of sex and pleasure in relationships and historically it is the antithesis of "waiting" (particularly for women) in the Victorian period. Relationships are now characterised by selection and choice for many but not all. So the pattern of relationships as understood by Illouz is "sporadic romantic intensity" typical of a postmodern fragmented era. A key characteristic of affairs is sexual pleasure experienced by women and men and not restricted to men as had been the case in the past. She points out that the "affair" is not about transgression but more about choice, which Illouz calls "Architectures of choice" which is related to a redefinition of identity and to a change in normative structures and expectations.

Thus for Illouz, the key emphasis of her analysis of love and intimacy is to shift the focus away from Freudian and psychological explanations of marriage and relationship breakdown to social and cultural explanations of changes in relationship patterns generated by the contradictions of late modernity. She does, however, agree with the "reflexive modernization" theorists in how individuals reflect on the nature of relationships and assess their viability for the future.

This continual assessment and reassessment of relationships has to do with the broader range of criteria, including psychological and sexual dimensions involved in the selection of partners. Illouz argues that the "sexualization" of relationships is related to the commercialization of romance and the role of sexiness in the process. She sees the media as instrumental in translating "erotic capital" to emotional and social capital particularly for women. This is not to argue that "erotic capital" has not been a feature of relationships historically but the conversion of "erotic" to social capital has been supported in late modernity by a range of social and cultural dimensions. She argues that "erotic capital" undercuts traditional marriage and is an aspect of an insecure society. Illouz highlights how sexual relationships in late modernity are, both emotionally and existentially insecure because of the choices available to individuals in the selection of partners. Her work has highlighted the precarity of relationships in late modernity.

In the final chapter (Chapter 7), I focus on the contribution of Lauren Berlant. Berlant's work provides a fascinating analysis of intersecting discourses around intimacy, politics and emotion. In a recent keynote address entitled "On Being in Life without Wanting the World: Living in Ellipsis" at the Emotional Geographies Conference at The University of Edinburgh in June 2015, Berlant outlines some of her concepts around emotion and affect. She seeks to define a range of new affective states for addressing sex, democracy and belonging. Drawing on one of the classical social theorists Georg Simmel's work on *Metropolis and Mental Life*, Berlant explores the concept of disassociation.

Her work shows how the political operates in the private and public spheres of intimacy to reinforce normative structures. As Berlant (2000: 6) comments: "To rethink intimacy is to appraise how we have been and how we live and how we might imagine lives that make more sense than the ones so many are living." While the range of Berlant's analysis has been wide, the focus has remained the same, the intersection of the private and the public and in particular the focus on the public sphere. The significance of the public sphere in the theoretical history of intimacy is traced back by Berlant to Habermas and the importance of his perspective to Berlant's work is developed in Chapter 7 as is her critique of his work.

Berlant deftly interweaves her analysis of citizenship, patriarchy, nationhood with a critique of discourses of sentimentality, sexual harassment and slavery as reflected in a wide range of literary texts including Alice Walker's (1982) *The Colour Purple*, Fanny Fern's (1853, 1857) *Ruth Hall* and *Fresh Leaves*, Harriet Jacobs' (1861) *Incidents in the Life of a Slave Girl*, and Frances Harper's (1892) *Iola Leroy*, among others.

Throughout this book, I have drawn on social, cultural and feminist theorists to examine how intimacy has acted as a driver of emotions and historical change. As I complete this book I have just returned from the American Sociological Association Conference 2015 in Chicago where the theme was "Sexualities in the Social World", set against the backdrop of the *Ashley Madison* scandal, which highlighted the extensive nature of adultery in this internet age of love and romance. Plenary sessions at the ASA Conference included: Modern Romance: Dating, Mating and Marriage; The Rise of Nonmarital Births; Internet Dating; Cohabitation; and Abortion in America.

A packed Saturday evening Plenary Panel entitled "Romance Matters" included Eric Klinenberg (New York University), Aziz Ansari (Comedian, Author and TV Presenter), Helen Fisher (Rutgers University, Psychotherapist and consultant to Match.com), Christian Rudder (OK Cupid) and Eli Finkel (Northwestern University). A hugely interested audience was enthralled by serious and more amusing presentations. This was followed by the signing of the new book by Ansari (with Eric Klinenberg) (2015) entitled *Modern Romance*.

At the outset of *Modern Romance* a summary is provided of what the book encapsulates as follows:

> Just a few years ago, in 2010, 10 per cent of single Americans said they met their significant other online. Three years later, in 2013, that number was up to 35 per cent ... But the transformation of our romantic lives can't be explained by technology alone. In a short period of time, the whole culture of finding love has changed dramatically. A few decades ago people would find a decent person who lived in the neighbourhood. Their families would meet and after deciding neither party seemed like a murderer,

they would get married and soon have a kid—all by the time they were twenty-four. Today, people marry later than ever and spend years of their lives on a quest to find the perfect person, a soul mate.

So we can expect a series of sociological oriented books in the area of love, romance, intimacy and the internet. For now my work is done for this book and I close drawing on Shumway (2003: 133) who shows that:

> The discourse of intimacy ... represents itself as the truth about love and relationships, ... I believe that this discourse has come to be for many today the most important paradigm for understanding love, courtship, marriage, and other relationships, not so much by displacing romance as by coexisting with it and, to a great extent, incorporating it.

Bibliography

Ansari, Azis (with Klinenberg, Eric). 2015. *Modern Romance.* New York: Penguin Press.
Beck, Ulrich and Elizabeth Beck-Gernsheim. 1996. *The Normal Chaos of Love.* Cambridge: Polity.
Berlant, Lauren (ed.). 2000. *Intimacy.* Chicago: University of Chicago Press.
Bhabha, Homi. 1990. *Nation and Narration.* New York: Routledge.
Boone, Joseph Allen. 1987. *Tradition Counter Tradition: Love and the Forms of Fiction.* Chicago: University of Chicago Press.
Brent, Linda. 1861/1987. *Incidents in the Life of a Slave Girl: Written by Herself.* Eds. Harriet A Jacobs, Lydia Maria Child and Jean Fagan Yellin. Cambridge: Harvard University Press.
Brooks, Ann. 1997. *Postfeminism: Feminism, Cultural Theory and Cultural Forms.* London and New York: Routledge.
Brooks, Ann. 2006. *Gendered Work in Asian Cities: The New Economy and Changing Labour Markets* London: Ashgate Publishers.
Brooks, Ann and Theresa Devasayaham. 2011/2013. *Gender, Emotions and Labour Markets* Routledge Studies in Social and Political Thought Series. London and New York: Routledge.
Brooks, Ann and Ruth Simpson. 2012. *Emotions in Transmigration: Transformation, Movement and Identity.* London: Palgrave Macmillan.
Bush, Barbara. 1990. *Slave Women in Caribbean Society 1650–1838.* Bloomington: Indiana University Press.
Cancian, Frances. M. 1987. *Love in America: Gender and Self-Development* (Cambridge: Cambridge University Press).
Fanon, Franz. 1965. "Algeria Unveiled." In *A Dying Colonialism* Trans. Haakon Chevalier. New York: Grove Press, 35–67.
Fanon, Franz. 1986. *Black Skin, White Masks.* Trans. Charles Markman. London: Pluto Press.
Fern, Fanny. 1853/1886. *Ruth Hall and Other Writings.* Ed. Joyce W. Warren. New Bruswick: Rutgers University Press.
Fern, Fanny. 1857. *Fresh Leaves.* New York: Mason Brothers.

Foucault, Michel. 1972. *The Archeology of Knowledge*. Trans. A.M. Sheridan Smith. New York: Pantheon.

Foucault, Michel. 1978. *The History of Sexuality, Volume 1: An Introduction*. New York: Vintage.

Giddens, Anthony. 1992. *The Transformation of Intimacy: Sexuality, Love and Eroticism in Modern Societies*. Stanford, CA: Stanford University Press.

Gross, Neil and Solon Simmons. 2002. "Intimacy as a Double-Edged Phenomenon? An Empirical Test of Giddens" *Social Forces* 81(2): 5311–5555.

Harper, Francis. 1892/1969. *Iola Leroy* or *Shadows Uplifted*. College Park, MD: McGrath.

Hyam, Ronald. 1986. "Concubines and the Colonial Service: The Crew Circular. . . . " *Journal of Imperial and Commonwealth History* 14(3): 170–186.

Illouz, Eva. 1997. *Consuming the Romantic Utopia: Love and the Cultural Contradictions of Capitalism*. Berkeley: University of California Press.

Illouz, Eva. 1998/1999. "The Lost Innocence of Love: Love as a Postmodern Condition." In M. Featherstone (ed.). *Love and Eroticism*. London: Sage, 161–186.

Illouz, Eva. 2012. *Why Love Hurts: A Sociological Explanation*. Cambridge: Polity.

Illouz, Eva. 2014. *Hard Core Romance*. Chicago and London: The University of Chicago Press.

Jamieson, Lynn. 1998. *Intimacy, Personal Relationships in Modern Society*. Cambridge: Polity.

Levine, Philippa (ed.). 2004a. *Gender and Empire*. Oxford and New York: Oxford University Press.

Levine, Philippa. 2004b. "Introduction: Why Gender and Empire?" In *Gender and Empire*. Oxford and New York: Oxford University Press, 1–13.

McClintock, Anne. 1995. *Imperial Leather: Race, Gender and Sexuality in the Colonial Contest*. New York and London: Routledge.

Said, Edward. 1979. *Orientalism*. New York: Vintage.

Seidman, Steven. 1991. *Romantic Longings: Love in America, 1830–1980*. New York: Routledge.

Shumway, David R. 2003. *Modern Love: Romance, Intimacy and the Marriage Crisis*. New York and London: New York University Press.

Skeggs, Beverley. 2010. "The Value of Relationships: Affective Scenes and Emotional Performances" *Feminist Legal Studies* 18: 29–51.

Stoler, Laura Ann. 2002. *Carnal Knowledge and Imperial Power: Race and the Intimate in Colonial Rule*. Berkeley: University of California Press.

Stone, Lawrence. 1982. *The Family, Sex, and Marriage in England 1500–1800*. London: Pelican.

Walker, Alice. 1982. *The Colour Purple*. San Diego: Harcourt Brace Publishers.

Wilson, Kathleen. 2004. "Empire, Gender and Modernity in the Eighteenth Century." In Philippa Levine, ed. *Gender and Empire*. Oxford and New York: Oxford University Press, 14–45.

Author Biography

Ann Brooks is Professor of Sociology and Head of Research and Professional Practice in the Faculty of Health and Social Sciences at Bournemouth University. She is author of *Academic Women* (Open University Press, 1997); *Postfeminisms: Feminism, Cultural Theory and Cultural Forums* (Routledge, 1997); *Gender and the Restructured University* (Open University Press, 2001); *Gendered Work in Asian Cities: The New Economy and Changing Labour Markets* (Ashgate, 2006); *Social Theory in Contemporary Asia* (Routledge, 2010); *Gender, Emotions and Labour Markets: Asian and Western Perspectives* (Routledge, 2011); and *Emotions in Transmigration: Transformation, Movement and Identity* (Palgrave, 2012). Recent books include *Popular Culture, Global Intercultural Perspectives* (Palgrave, 2014); *Consumption, Rights and States—Comparing Global Cities in Asia and the US* (Anthem Press, 2014) (with Lionel Wee); and *Emotions and Social Change: Historical and Sociological Perspectives* (Routledge, 2014) (co-edited with David Lemmings). Forthcoming books include *Love and Intimacy in Contemporary Society* (in progress) and *The Emotional City* (with Lionel Wee).

Index

Adkins, Lisa 11, 12, 104, 114
adultery 3, 107, 108–10, 137, 138
advertising: commodification of romance and beauty via 107, 112
Ahmed, Sara 7, 12, 102–4, 114
Alcoff, Linda 33, 43
Alexander, Jeffrey 28, 88, 106
Amato, Paul R. 24, 29
American Sociological Association Conference, "Sexualities in the Social World" 138–9
The Anatomy of National Fantasy (Berlant) 125
Ansari, Azis 138–9
Ansari, *Modern Romance* 138–9
Anthias, Floyd 82, 87
Archer, Margaret S. 27, 29, 89, 100
'architectures of choice' 110–11, 137
Austen, Jane: *Emma* by 51, 53; *Persuasion* by 54; *Pride and Prejudice* by 51, 52; romantic and courtly love critique by 51, 52–5

Baudelaire, Charles 55, 56, 57–60, 63–4
Bauman, Zygmunt 48, 64, 88, 90–1, 100
beauty: eroticism, sexuality, and 62–3, 112–14; romantic and courtly love perspective on 55, 62–3, 112
Beck, Ulrich 4–5, 7, 10, 12, 24, 26–7, 30, 88–90, 96–9, 100, 136, 139
Beck-Gernsheim, Elizabeth 4–5, 7, 10, 12, 24, 26–7, 30, 88–90, 96–8, 100, 136
Bedford, Kate 104, 115
Benichou, Paul 57, 64
Benjamin, Walter 58, 64
Berlant, Lauren 3, 5, 8, 12, 102, 114, 117–29, 130, 137–8, 139; *The Anatomy of National Fantasy* by 125; *Critical Inquiry* by 123–4; *Cruel Optimism* by 118, 128; *The Female Complaint* by 125–6; intimate public sphere analysis of 102, 117–29, 137–8; *The Queen of America Goes to Washington* by 118, 121, 125, 126
Bhabha, Homi 31, 82, 85, 134, 139
Bickers, Robert 81, 85
'biopower' concept 6, 20, 35, 36, 41, 42, 72, 76, 77
Bizet, Georges: *Carmen* 56
Bloch, R. Howard 18, 30
bohemian love 55–62
Boone, Joseph Allen 131, 139
Booth, Alan 24, 29
Brennan, Teresa 12
Brent, Linda 121, 129, 138, 139
Brooks, Ann 35, 43, 96, 100, 104, 114, 131, 136, 139
Brown, Kathleen 79, 85
Burns, E. Jane 9, 12, 18, 30
Bush, Barbara 68, 70, 81–2, 85, 86, 134, 139
Bushnell, Candace 105, 114

Cancian, Frances M. 3, 12, 28, 30, 93–4, 100, 133, 139
Capellanus, Andreus 2, 13
capitalism: 'erotic capital' in 113–14, 137; intelligence of emotions in relation to 10–11, 104–10, 112–14; intimate public sphere impacted by 118–19, 124–6, 128; late modernity love and intimacy in relation to 7, 10, 24, 25, 27, 28, 93–4, 97–9, 100, 107, 135–9; romantic love and social class in relation to 7, 49, 107, 112, 135–9
Carby, Hazel V. 122, 130
Carmen (Bizet) 56

Castells, Manual 90, 100
Chatterjee, Indrani 71, 86
Clough, Patricia 12, 13, 103, 114, 115
Collins, Patricia Hill 29, 30
colonial culture intimacy and sex: chattel slavery in 69–70; children from 21, 22, 69, 70, 71, 75, 81; concubinage in 21–2, 66–7, 73–8, 83–4; context for sex and sexuality in 66–72; emotional regime changes and 19–24; European women in 22–3, 43, 71–2, 74–5, 78, 80–2; Foucault's genealogy of sexuality comparison to 20, 23–4, 32, 41–3, 72, 76–8, 134–5; gender roles in 20–1, 43, 66–72, 78, 80–5, 134–5; imperial power and 6, 10, 19–20, 23–4, 42–3, 72, 76–8, 133–5; intelligence of emotions and 8, 10, 103–4; marriage in 43, 67, 69, 71–2, 73, 78, 79–80, 81, 83–4; nationalism and 7, 43, 68, 80–1, 82–3; Orientalism in 20–1, 71, 73, 78, 79, 81, 82, 134; overview of 9–10, 66, 85; politics of intimacy in 78–80; prostitution in 20, 21, 67, 68, 73, 84; psychoanalytic perspective on 84–5; race and 6, 10, 20, 22–4, 41–3, 66, 67, 68–9, 70, 72–3, 74–5, 76, 77–85, 134–5; same-sex relationships in 22, 24; sensibility concept in 51, 54, 68–9; sexual threat and assault allegations in 22–3, 75, 81; social class and status in 19–24, 43, 66–85, 134–5
The Colour Purple (Walker) 118
Comaroff, Jean 41, 43
concubinage 20–2, 66–7, 71, 73–8, 83–4
'confluent love' 91–3, 133
Coontz, Stephanie 93, 100
Cosi fan Tutti (Mozart) 51, 63n1
courtly love *see* romantic and courtly love
Critical Inquiry (Berlant) 123–4
Cruel Optimism (Berlant) 118, 128
Cvetkovich, Ann 11, 13

Damasio, Antonio 102, 115
Davin, Anna 84, 86
Deleuze, Giles 103, 115
de Rougemont, Denis 2, 13, 46, 64
desire, genealogy of *see* genealogies of emotions, intimacies and desires

de Troyes, Chretien, *Lancelot ou le chevalier de la charrette* 9, 18
Deutscher, Penelope 40, 42, 43
Devasayaham, Theresa 104, 114, 136, 139
de Villiers, Nicholas 128–9, 130
Dirks, Nicholas B. 41, 43
Don Giovanni (Mozart) 3, 63n1
Donovan, Catherine 92, 101
Duby, George 1, 13, 18, 30
Du Gay, Paul 10, 13, 24, 30
Dunne, Gillian 92, 100

Elias, Norbert 20, 30, 44, 49, 64
Emma (Austen) 51, 53
emotional regime changes: colonial culture intimacy and sex and 19–24; Foucault's genealogy of sexuality and 9, 15–18, 20, 23–4; gender dynamics in 16–17, 20–1, 25–6, 28; intimacy as driver of 3, 5, 6, 8, 15, 16, 72; late modernity love and intimacy and 3, 24–9; marriage separation from intimacy and eroticism in 17, 18–19; overview of 3–4, 8, 15, 29; race and ethnicity with 20, 22–4, 29; romantic and courtly love and 6, 17, 18–19, 28–9; sex and sexuality driving 15–18, 19–24, 25–6, 28; social class and status with 16–17, 18–24
emotions: emotion-affect distinction 102–3; emotional authenticity 55, 111; emotional labour 11, 104; emotional regime changes 3–4, 8, 9, 15–29; feeling rules on 11, 104; genealogy of (*see* genealogies of emotions, intimacies and desires); intelligence of 8, 10–11, 102–14, 136–7; intimate public sphere and 8, 11, 12, 102, 117–29, 137–8; 'turn to affect' and 8, 10–11, 12, 102–3, 136
Evans, Mary 45–6, 50–2, 63, 64

Falzon, Christopher 32, 43, 44
families, late modern structure of 90, 92–3; *see also* parents and parenthood
Fanny Ford (Fern) 119
Fanon, Franz 82–3, 85, 86, 134, 139, 140
Featherstone, Mike 45–9, 55–6, 61–2, 64, 100, 101
feeling rules 11, 104
The Female Complaint (Berlant) 125–6

feminisation of love 28, 50, 55, 58, 92, 94, 110
feminist theories: on colonial culture intimacy and sex 6, 8, 10, 66, 72–3, 84–5, 134, 136, 138; on Foucault's genealogy of sexuality 8, 32, 35; genealogies of emotions, intimacies and desires reflecting 3–4, 5, 8, 72, 117; on intelligence of emotions 8, 10–11, 102–14, 136–7; on intimate public sphere 8, 12, 102, 117–29, 137–8; on late modernity love and intimacy 7, 8, 10, 11, 90, 91–2, 96
Fern, Fanny 118–21, 127, 129, 130, 138, 140; *Fanny Ford* by 119; journalism and gender narratives of 118–21; *The Life and Beauties of Fanny Fern* on 118; personal circumstances of 121; *Ruth Hall* writings of 118, 120
films: adultery depicted in 109–10; commodification of romance via 107; *see also* theatre and opera
Flaubert, Gustave: *Madame Bovary* 50–1, 109–10
Foucault, Michel 2–6, 8–9, 13, 15–18, 20, 23, 29, 30, 32–43, 44, 66, 72, 76–7, 86, 89, 91, 100, 124, 129, 130, 131, 134–5, 140
Foucault's genealogy of sexuality: anti-psychology, anti-Freudianism in 36, 38, 39–40; 'biopower' concept in 6, 20, 35, 36, 41, 42, 72, 76, 77; colonial culture intimacy and sex comparison to 6, 9–10, 20, 23–4, 32, 41–3, 72, 76–8, 134–5; concept of genealogy for 3–4, 9, 15–16, 34–9; emotional regime changes and 15–18, 20, 23–4; Enlightenment Thinking critique in 9, 16, 32–4; epistemological framework of 4–5, 15; on genealogy as 'anti-science' 4, 9, 15–16, 34; Greek and Roman pleasures studied in 16–17, 37–8; *The History of Sexuality* on ix–xxi, 2, 4, 9, 15, 16, 23, 32, 33, 34, 35–9, 41, 42–3, 46, 76–8, 131, 135; intimate public sphere analysis reference to 124; marriage separation from intimacy and eroticism in 3–5, 17, 38–9; overview of 2, 9, 15–16, 32, 43; power and sex relationship in 5–6, 20, 23–4, 33, 35–6, 41–3, 76–8, 124, 134–5; racial discourse in 6, 20, 23–4, 32, 41–3, 66, 72, 76, 77–8; same-sex relationships in 2, 17, 33–4, 38; social class and status in 16–17, 38, 40, 72; social control in 17, 39
Fraser, Nancy 35–6, 44, 104, 115

Gaines, Jane 122, 130
Gautier, Theophile 55, 57, 64; *Mademoiselle de Maupin* 57
gay and lesbian relationships *see* same-sex marriage and relationships
gender: colonial culture views of 6, 10, 19–21, 23, 43, 66–72, 75, 78, 80–5, 134–5; emotional regime changes in relation to 16–17, 20–1, 25–6, 28; equality and democratisation of 25–6, 90–1, 92–3, 97, 98–9, 127–8, 133; feminisation of love 28, 50, 55, 58, 94; feminist theories on (*see* feminist theories); idealisation of women 1, 133; intelligence of emotions and dynamics of 8, 10, 102–14; intimate public sphere for narratives of 102, 118–23, 124, 128, 138; late modernity love and intimacy in relation to 25–6, 28, 88, 90–4, 97, 98–9; national identity and citizenship in relation to 120, 121–9; parenting and 2, 71, 92–3; patriarchy and 4, 5, 69, 90, 109, 110, 118, 119–20; romantic and courtly love in relation to 6, 46–7, 50, 51, 55–9; sex and sexuality in relation to 16–17, 20–1, 25–6, 28, 38, 43; social class and status tied to 16–17, 38, 43
genealogies of emotions, intimacies and desires: aims and objectives of excavating 4–6, 16; colonial culture intimacy and sex 6, 7, 9–10, 19–24, 32, 41–3, 66–85, 103, 133–5; emotional regime changes 3–4, 8–9, 15–29; Foucault's genealogy of sexuality ix–xxi, 2, 4, 5–6, 9, 15–18, 20, 23–4, 32–43, 72, 76–8, 124, 131, 134–5; intelligence of emotions 8, 10–11, 23, 102–14, 136–7; intimate public sphere 12, 102, 117–29, 137–8; late modernity love and intimacy 7, 10, 15, 17, 24–9, 59, 88–99, 107, 132–3, 135–9; overview of 1–12, 15–16, 23, 29, 32–3, 34–5, 131–9; romantic and courtly love 1–3, 4, 5, 6–7, 9, 17, 18–19, 28–9,

45–63, 89, 99, 105–7, 112, 131–3, 135–9
Giddens, Anthony 2–5, 7, 10, 13, 24–8, 30, 47, 64, 88–93, 96–9, 100, 124, 127, 130, 132–3, 136, 140
globalisation 10, 24–6, 27–8, 88–9
Gonzalez-Lopez, Gloria 29, 30
Gordon, Linda 79–80, 86
Gorton, Kirstyn 102, 115, 123, 130
Grace, Wendy 39–40, 44
Greco, Monica 11, 13, 115
Gregg, Melissa 12, 13, 129
Gross, Neil 6, 9, 13, 18, 27–9, 30, 88–90, 100, 133, 140
Gross, Otto 61, 62
Guattari, Felix 103, 115
Gutierrez, Ramon 79, 86

Habermas, Jurgen 124, 126, 130
Hakim, Catherine 113, 115
Halley, Jean 12, 13, 115
Harper, Frances 121–3, 130, 138, 140; *Iola Leroy* 121, 122, 123, 138
Heaphy, Brian 92, 101
Hill, Anita: judicial testimony of 121, 122–3
The History of Sexuality (Foucault) ix–xxi, 2, 4, 9, 15, 16, 23, 32, 33, 34, 35–9, 41, 42–3, 46, 76–8, 131, 135
Hochschild, Arlie R. 5, 7, 10–11, 13, 24, 27, 30, 88, 90, 100, 104, 114, 115
homosexual relationships *see* same-sex marriage and relationships
Howell, Philip 68, 86
Hyam, Ronald 20, 30, 78, 86, 134, 140

idealisation: of love 1, 6–7, 17, 18–19, 28, 38, 48–9, 56; of women 1, 53, 56, 59, 133
Illouz, Eva 3–5, 7–8, 10–11, 13, 24, 27, 30, 47, 50–1, 53–5, 62–3, 64, 88, 90, 93–9, 100, 104–14, 115, 133, 135–7, 140
Incidents in the Life of a Slave Girl (Jacobs aka Brent) 121–2, 138
Indiana (Sand) 60
individualism: late modernity love and intimacy and 7, 10, 17, 24–8, 88, 89, 98, 99, 132–3, 136–7; romantic and courtly love reflecting 19, 49, 99
intelligence of emotions: adultery and 107, 108–10, 132, 137–8; 'architectures of choice' and 104–110, 110–11, 137; capitalism and commercialisation of intimate life in 10–11, 104–10, 112–14; colonial culture intimacy and sex and 8, 10, 103–4; emotion-affect distinction in 102–4; emotional authenticity in 53, 55, 111; emotional labour in 11, 104; feeling rules in 11, 104; gender relations dynamics and 110; intimate public sphere and 8, 102, 125; love affairs in 107–8, 109, 132, 137; marriage market emergence and 104–110, 111–14; mate selection and 105–6, 108, 111–14, 136–7; overview of 8, 10–11, 102–4, 114, 135–6, 137–8; power and 8–11, 102–4, 110–11, 133–5; refashioning of love in 105–6; sex and sexuality impacting 8–12, 102, 104, 108–10, 111–14; 'turn to affect' and 8, 10–11, 12, 102–14, 136
Internet: mate selection and online dating via 106, 110, 136–7
intimacy: capitalism and commercialisation of 3, 5, 7, 10–11, 24–5, 27, 28, 93–4, 98–9, 107, 119, 126, 128, 135–9; colonial culture intimacy and sex 6, 7, 9–10, 15, 19–24, 29, 32, 41–3, 66–85, 103, 133–5; emotional regime changes driven by 3–4, 8, 15, 16, 131; genealogy of (*see* genealogies of emotions, intimacies and desires); intimate public sphere 12, 99, 102, 117–29, 137–8; late modernity love and intimacy 7, 10, 24–9, 59, 88–99, 107, 132–3, 135–9; marriage separation from 1–3, 4, 5, 6, 17, 18–19, 38–9, 48, 56, 78, 132
intimate public sphere: capitalism effects on 118–19, 124–5, 126–8; critique of literary sentimental ideology and 117, 118–21, 127; gender and race narratives in 118–23, 128; intelligence of emotions and 11–12, 102; national identity and citizenship in 11, 120, 121–9; overview of 12, 102, 117–18, 129, 137–8; patriarchy in 118, 119–20; sex and sexuality in 12, 102, 117–18, 121–3, 124–5, 128; therapy-intimacy intersection in

12, 117, 124; 'turn to affect' and 10, 12, 102
Iola Leroy (Harper) 121, 122, 138

Jacobs, Harriet (aka Linda Brent): *Incidents in the Life of a Slave Girl* 121–2, 129, 138, 139
Jamieson, Lynn 7, 26, 30, 88, 90–3, 100, 101, 127, 130, 133, 140

Kennedy, Raymond 22, 30
Kern, Stephen 88, 101
Kipnis, Laura 10, 13, 24, 30, 90, 101, 109, 115

La Boheme (Puccini) 56
Laclos, Pierre Choderlos de, *Les Liaisons Dangereuses* 3
Lancelot ou le chevalier de la charrette (de Troyes) 9, 18
Lash, Scott 88, 100, 108, 115
Laslett, Peter 10, 13, 24, 30
late modernity love and intimacy: capitalism and commercialisation of intimacy in 7, 10, 19, 24, 25, 27, 28, 93–4, 97–9, 100, 107, 135–9; 'confluent love' in 91–3; detraditionalisation of 4, 7, 10–11, 24–9, 88–9, 129; emotional regime changes and 3, 8, 15–29, 131; equality and democratisation of gender in 25–6, 90–1, 92–3, 97, 98–9; family structure and 90, 92–3; feminisation of love in 28, 90, 92, 94, 107, 110; gender influences and dynamics in 17, 19, 23, 25–6, 28, 88, 90–4, 97, 98–9, 110; globalisation and 10, 24–6, 28, 88–90; individualism and 7, 10, 16–17, 19–20, 21, 22, 24–5, 26–7, 28–9, 88, 89, 91, 95, 98, 99, 132–3; literature on 19, 28, 91, 93, 94; marriage in 15, 16–19, 21, 24–5, 28–9, 88–9, 93, 94, 97–8, 99, 132–3, 135–7; overview of 7, 10, 15, 29, 88–91, 99, 136; parenting and 24, 92–3, 94; plastic sexuality in 25–6, 91–3; psychology and *psy*-disciplines impacting 89, 93, 94–6, 97; 'pure relationships' in 25–7, 89, 90–1, 92–3, 96, 132–3, 136; reflexive modernization theory on 7, 25–6, 27–9, 88, 96–7, 99, 136,

137; religion and religious conflict impacting 90; romantic and courtly love comparison to 28–9, 59, 89, 99, 132–3, 135–9; same-sex marriage and relationships in 24, 25–6, 28, 92; scientific perspectives on 94–6; sex and sexuality in relation to 15–24, 25–6, 28, 91–3, 98–9, 137; social class and status in relation to 16–17, 19, 22–3, 29, 96, 98–9, 136; therapeutic discourse on 91, 93, 96, 97–8
Lelia (Sand) 60
Leonard, Suzanne 107, 109–10, 115
lesbian and gay relationships *see* same-sex marriage and relationships
Les Liaisons Dangereuses (Laclos) 3
Levine, Philippa 66–8, 86, 87, 134, 140
The Life and Beauties of Fanny Fern 118
Linke, Gabrielle 126–8, 130
literature: Austen's 51, 52–5; Baudelaire's 56, 57–60; bohemian 55–62; 'chick-lit' genre 105–6, 126; colonial era 81; critique of sentimental ideology in 117, 118–21, 122, 126; 'femme fatale' character in 56; gender and race narratives in 56, 79, 118–23; late modernity love and intimacy in 19, 28, 91, 93, 94, 98; poetry as 9, 18, 46–7, 48–9, 55, 57–60; popular and literary fiction as 3, 7, 19, 45, 49, 50–1, 59–61; romantic and courtly love depicted in 3, 7, 9, 18, 19, 45–63; Sand's 56, 59–61
love: adulterous 3, 107, 108–10, 132, 137–8; bohemian 55–62, 88; confluent 91–3, 133; feminisation of 4–5, 10, 28, 77, 92, 94, 102, 110, 120; genealogy of (*see* genealogies of emotions, intimacies and desires); idealisation and sacrilisation of 1, 6, 18, 28, 38, 49, 59; late modernity love and intimacy 7, 10, 24–9, 59, 88–99, 107, 132–3, 135–9; love affairs 107–8, 137; 'love at first sight' in 49, 52, 53, 105; marriage separation from 1–3, 4, 5, 6, 17, 18–19, 48, 56, 132; romantic and courtly love 1–3, 4, 5, 6–7, 9, 17, 18–19, 28–9, 45–63, 89, 99, 105–7, 112, 131–3, 135–9; social class and 2–4, 7, 18–19, 46–8, 49–50, 55; traditional meaning of 1
Lucrezia Floriani (Sand) 60–1

148 Index

Luhmann, Niklas 1–3, 13, 47–8, 64, 90, 101
Lynch, Richard 35–6, 39, 44

McClintock, Anne 3, 5, 7–10, 13, 14, 31, 44, 66–85, 86, 87, 134, 140; on colonial culture intimacy and sex 7, 10, 66, 80–5, 134
McNeil, Maureen 35, 44
Madame Bovary (Flaubert) 50–1, 109–10
Mademoiselle de Maupin (Gautier) 57
marriage: adultery outside 3, 107, 108–10, 138; colonial culture on 43, 67, 69, 71–2, 73, 78, 79–80, 81, 83–4; Foucault's genealogy of sexuality on 17–18, 38–9; inter-racial 67, 83–4; late modernity views of 88–9, 93, 94, 97–8, 99, 132–3, 135–7; marriage markets for 110, 111–14; mate selection for 105–6, 108, 111–14, 136–7; patriarchy in 119–20; romantic and courtly love separation from 1–3, 4, 5, 6, 17, 18–19, 48, 56, 132; same-sex (*see* same-sex marriage and relationships); sex separation from 108
Massumi, Brian 102, 115
The Master Pipers (Sand) 60–1
Melman, B. 81, 86
Meridian (Walker) 118
Midgely, Clare 68, 86
Ming, Hanneke 21, 30
Modern Romance (Ansari with Klinenberg) 138–9
Moers, Ellen 59, 64
Morgan, Jennifer L. 79, 86
Mozart, Amadeus: *Cosi fan Tutti* by 51, 63n1; *Don Giovanni* by 3, 63n1
Musick, Kelley 24, 30

nationalism and national identity: colonial culture intimacy and sex in relation to 7, 43, 68, 80–1, 82–3; in intimate public sphere 120, 121–9
Neale, Barry 92, 101
Ngai, Sianne 102, 115
Nicholson, Linda 102, 115
Nussbaum, Martha C. 28, 30, 102, 115

O'Leary, Timothy 32, 43, 44
Ong, Aihwa 41, 44, 104, 115
Orientalism 20–1, 71, 73, 78, 79, 81, 82, 134
Osgerby, Bill 112, 115

parents and parenthood: colonial culture views of 21, 22, 69, 70, 71, 75, 81; late modernity views of 92–3; *see also* procreation and reproduction
patriarchy 4, 5, 69, 90, 109, 110, 118, 119–20
Paz, Octavia 45–7, 64
Pedwell, Carolyn 102–4, 116
Peiss, Kathy 112, 116
Persuasion (Austen) 54
plastic sexuality 25–6, 91–3
Pollman, Tessa 21, 31
Poster, Mark 48, 65
power: 'biopower' concept 6, 20, 35, 36, 41, 42, 72, 76, 77; imperial 6, 10, 19–20, 23–4, 42–3, 72, 76–8, 133–5; intelligence of emotions and 103, 110–11; knowledge relationship to 33, 35–6; sex relationship to 5–6, 10, 19–20, 23–4, 33, 35–6, 41–3, 72, 76–8, 110, 133–5
Pride and Prejudice (Austen) 51, 52
Probyn, Elspeth 102, 116
procreation and reproduction 23, 24, 28, 40, 46, 70, 73, 81, 88; *see also* parents and parenthood
prostitutes and prostitution: bohemian *vs.* romantic love involving 55, 56, 58–9, 60; colonial culture intimacy and sex with 20, 21, 67, 68, 73, 84; patriarchy and 109, 119–20
psychoanalytic and Freudian perspectives: colonial culture intimacy and sex in 84–5; Foucault's genealogy of sexuality *vs.* 36, 39–40; intelligence of emotions in 110; late modernity love and intimacy in 94–5, 97; romantic and courtly love *vs.* 61–2
psychology and *psy*-disciplines: late modernity love and intimacy impacted by 89, 93, 94–6, 97; psychoanalytic and Freudian 36, 39–40, 61–2, 84–5, 94–5, 97, 110; *see also* therapy
public sphere *see* intimate public sphere
Puccini, Giacomo: *La Boheme* 56
'pure relationships' 25–7, 89, 90–1, 92–3, 96, 132–3, 136

The Queen of America Goes to Washington (Berlant) 121, 125, 126

race and ethnicity: 'biopower' concept in relation to 6, 20, 29, 35, 36, 41, 42, 72, 76, 77; colonial culture intimacy and sex in relation to 6, 10, 20, 22–4,

41–3, 66, 67, 68–9, 70, 72–3, 74–5, 76, 77–85, 134–5; emotional regime changes and 20, 22–4, 29; Foucault's genealogy of sexuality on 6, 20, 23–4, 41–3, 76, 77–8; intimate public sphere for narratives of 118, 120, 121–3; national identity and citizenship in relation to 120, 121–9
Ralston, Caroline 78, 86
rational choice and behaviour 52
Reddy, William 4, 13
reflexive modernization 7, 25–6, 27–9, 88, 96–7, 99, 136, 137
religion 46, 48; late modernity love and intimacy impacted by 90; quasi-religious aspect of enchanted love 105; sacrilisation of love 6, 18, 28
reproduction *see* procreation and reproduction
romantic and courtly love: Austen's critique of 51, 52–5; Baudelaire and the *flaneur* depicting 56, 57–60; beauty and 55, 62–3, 112; bohemian love as 55–62; capitalism and commodification of romance 7, 49, 107, 112, 135–9; character and 18, 49, 53; contested narratives of 52; courtly love, specifically in 2, 6, 9, 18–19, 48–9, 131; courtship, calling and 53–5; Eastern *vs.* Western 45–6, 131; emotional regime changes and 17, 18–19, 28–9; eroticism and 62–3, 112; 'femme fatale' character in 56; gender in relation to 46–7, 50, 51, 55–9; German bohemian tradition of 56, 61–2; historical and contemporary narratives of 6–7, 9, 18–19, 28–9, 45–8; idealisation and sacrilisation of 6, 18, 28; individualism reflected in 19, 89, 99, 111; intelligence of emotions and 105–7; late modernity love and intimacy comparison to 28–9, 59, 89, 99, 132–3, 135–9; literature depicting 3, 7, 9, 18, 19, 45–63; 'love at first sight' in 49, 52, 53, 105; marriage separation from 1–3, 4, 5, 6, 17, 18–19, 48, 56, 132; men in love and heroes in 51; overview of 6–7, 9, 45–8, 63; in poetry 9, 18, 46–7, 48–9, 55, 57–60; in popular and literary fiction 3, 7, 19, 45, 49, 50–1, 59–61; rational choice and behaviour *vs.* 52; same-sex relationships with 46, 55, 56–9; Sand's depiction of 56, 59–61; social class and status in relation to 2–3, 7, 18–19, 46–8, 49–50, 55; theatre and opera depicting 3, 56, 57; women's emancipation and 51, 99
Ruth Hall, Fern writings in 118, 120, 138

sacrilisation of love 6, 18, 28
Said, Edward W. 20–1, 31, 73, 78, 82, 86, 134, 140
same-sex marriage and relationships: colonial culture on 22; Foucault's genealogy of sexuality on 17, 33–4, 38; Greek pleasures including 17, 38; late modernity love and intimacy in 25–6, 28, 92; marriage and sexuality in 2; romantic and courtly love in 46, 55, 56–9
Sand, George 56, 59–61, 64, 65; *Indiana* by 60; *Lelia* by 60; *Lucrezia Floriani* by 60, 61; *The Master Pipers* by 60–1; romantic and courtly love portrayal by 56, 59–61
Sawicki, Jane 43, 44
Seidman, Steven 16–17, 24, 31, 32–5, 37–9, 44, 88, 101, 133, 140
Seigworth, Greg 12, 13, 129, 130
Sennett, Richard 126–8, 130
sensibility concept 51, 54, 68–9
sentimental ideology 117, 118–21
sex and sexuality: adulterous 3, 107, 108–10, 138; beauty and 62–3, 112–14; colonial culture intimacy and sex 6, 7, 9–10, 19–24, 32, 41–3, 66–85, 103, 133–5; emotional regime changes driven by 15–18, 19–24, 25–6, 28; eroticism, sexiness, and 62–3, 112–14, 137; Foucault's genealogy of sexuality ix–xxi, 2, 4, 5–6, 9, 15–18, 20, 23–4, 32–43, 72, 76–8, 124, 131, 134–5; gender in relation to 16–17, 20–1, 25–6, 28, 38, 43; intelligence of emotions impacted by 108, 111–14; intimate public sphere including 117, 121–3, 124, 128; late modernity love and intimacy in relation to 25–6, 28, 91–3, 137; marriage separation from 108; plastic 25–6, 91–3; power relationship to 5–6, 10, 19–20, 23–4, 33, 35–6, 41–3, 72, 76–8, 110, 133–5; for procreation and reproduction 23, 24, 28, 40, 46, 70, 73, 81, 88; psychoanalytic and Freudian views of 36, 39–40, 61–2, 84–5; race intersection with 66, 67, 68, 72–3;

sexualisation of modern relationships 111–14, 137; social class and status in relation to 16–17, 19–24, 38, 40, 113
Shorter, Ella 24, 31
Shumway, David R. 1–3, 13, 131–3, 139. 140
Simmel, George 58, 65, 138
Simmons, Solon 133, 140
Simpson, Ruth 104, 114, 136, 139
Skeggs, Beverley 135, 140
Smart, Carol 92, 101
Smelser, Neil 106, 116
Smith, Dennis 36–8, 44
social class and status: bourgeois 2–4, 7, 18–19, 40, 49–50, 135; colonial culture intimacy and sex in relation to 19–24, 43, 66–85, 134–5; emotional regime changes and 16–17, 18–24; late modernity love and intimacy in relation to 98–9, 136; romantic and courtly love in relation to 2–3, 7, 18–19, 46–8, 49–50, 55; sex and sexuality in relation to 16–17, 19–24, 38, 40, 113
Somers, Margaret 3–4, 9, 14
Stenner, Paul 11, 13, 115
Stoler, Laura Ann 3–6, 8–10, 12, 14, 15, 19–24, 31, 32, 41–3, 44, 66–85, 87, 133–5, 140; on colonial culture intimacy and sex 6, 8, 9–10, 19–24, 32, 41–3, 66, 72–9, 83–4, 85, 133–5
Stone, Lawrence 2–3, 14, 50, 65, 133, 140
Strobel, Margaret 23, 31, 78, 86
Sussman, Charlotte 68, 87

Swan, Elizabeth 11, 14, 104, 116
Swidler, Anne 5, 7, 14, 18–19, 28, 31, 48–9, 65

Taylor, Geltman, J. 79, 87
Teltscher, Kate 71, 87
theatre and opera: romantic and courtly love depicted in 3, 51, 56; *see also* films
therapy: therapeutic discourse on late modernity love and intimacy 91, 93, 96, 97–8; therapy-intimacy intersection in intimate public sphere 117, 124; *see also* psychology and *psy*-disciplines
Turner, Bryan 107, 116
'turn to affect' 8, 10–11, 12, 136
twentieth century colonial intimacy and sex *see* colonial culture intimacy and sex

Unfaithful (film) 109

Walker, Alice 138; *The Colour Purple* by 118, 138, 140; *Meridian* by 118
Weber, Max 61, 62, 65
Weeks, Jeffrey 92, 101
Whitehead, Anne 102–4, 116
Willis, N. P. 121
Wilson, Elizabeth 45, 55–8, 61, 65, 88, 101
Wilson, Kathleen 66, 68–72, 87, 134, 140
Wolff, Janet 58–60, 65

Yuval-Davis, Nira 82, 87